THE
ULTIMATE
GUIDE TO
KIDS'
ACTIVITIES

1,001 GREAT IDEAS FOR KIDS OF ALL AGES

D1446581

TERESA SELLS

BARBOUR BOOKS
An Imprint of Barbour Publishing, Inc.

ACKNOWLEDGMENTS

A number of people contributed to this project. Thanks are due to Linda Alves, Rhonda Amore, Steve Anderson, Trudi Anderson, Daniel Baker, Carole A. Barber, Michele Crowley, Jim Davis, Judy Davis, Ann Ecker, Virginia Edwards, Amy Hanson, Shirley Heibert, Marylin Keller, Melisa Keller, Melody Kirchner, Gail McKenney, Beverly Merritt, Dr. David Miller, Kathy Ohlson, Kirsten O'Sullivan, Jeanie Parsons, Mary Lou Phipps, Jan Roberts, Jason Sells, Juliana Sells, Patrick Sells, Dena Sharp, Michelle Stirton, Dorothy Wong, Laurel Worth, and Marquita Wright. A list of the specific contributions of each can be found in the back of this book.

© 2000 by Teresa Sells

ISBN 1-57748-823-7

Scripture quotations, unless otherwise noted, are taken from the King James Version of the Bible.

Scripture quotations marked NASB are taken from the New American Standard Bible, © 1960, 1962, 1963, 1968, 1971, 1972, 1973, 1975, 1977 by The Lockman Foundation. Used by permission.

Scripture quotations marked NIV are taken from the HOLY BIBLE, NEW INTERNATIONAL VERSION®. NIV®. Copyright © 1973, 1978, 1984 by International Bible Society. Used by permission of Zondervan Publishing House. All rights reserved.

Published by Barbour Books, an imprint of Barbour Publishing, Inc., P.O. Box 719, Uhrichsville, Ohio 44683, www.barbourbooks.com

 Member of the Evangelical Christian Publishers Association

Printed in the United States of America.
5 4 3

TABLE OF CONTENTS

DEDICATION

To my husband, Pat,
and children, Juliana and Jason,
for their help with this project.

INTRODUCTION

"It's a rainy day in the summertime. How can I keep my kids occupied?"

"I teach Sunday school. I need activity ideas to go with the children's lesson."

"These kids don't need television as a babysitter. There must be something more productive to do."

If you've ever found yourself making comments like these, you need *The Ultimate Guide to Kids' Activities.* Here, in one book, are 1,001 activities for kids of all ages—fun, educational, and faith-building activities that will keep children busy. . .and adults happy.

In *The Ultimate Guide to Kids' Activities,* you'll find hundreds of projects organized into loose categories. The main breakdown is by the child's age:

- Younger Children (preschool through first grade)

- Middler Children (second through fourth grades)

- Older Children (fifth grade and up)

While we have created this structure to help parents choose appropriate activities for their children, please note that the ranges are only approximations; your children may enjoy activities in categories above or below their particular age ranges. The choice is up to you—and your children.

Under each of these age headings, projects are organized into the following categories:

- Paper Projects (those that primarily use paper, scissors, glue, crayons, and markers)

- Paint Projects (those in which paint is the primary element)

- Craft Projects (those in which something is created from other readily available items)

- Games (to be played alone or with others)

- Educational Projects (those which teach something: whether geography, science, or the Bible)

- Food Projects (those which have an edible result)

- Holiday Projects (those which relate to the major holidays of the year)

- Miscellaneous (a grab bag of additional activities)

Each activity is accompanied by a code which explains the approximate cost, the amount of time involved, and the level of adult involvement required. The three-part codes are read as follows:

The first element (C or $) stands for the approximate cost of a project:

$$C = \$0-.99$$
$$\$ = \$1.00-\$3.99$$
$$\$\$ = \$4.00-\$9.99$$
$$\$\$\$ = \$10.00+$$

The second element (time) is the approximate amount of time to finish a project.

The third element (1–5) stands for the approximate amount of parental help, with 1 being the least amount of parental assistance, and 5 being the greatest.

You'll find that many of the activities have a specific tie to a Bible story or some character-building concept. Others are simply good, clean fun. All will give you, as an adult, great ideas to help the children in your care pass their time constructively.

ACTIVITIES FOR YOUNGER CHILDREN
PAPER PROJECTS

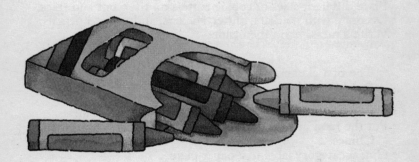

1. KISS-OF-LOVE CARD
C 15 MIN. 1

- Fold a 9"x 12" sheet of white paper in half.
- Decorate the card by putting lipstick on your lips and kissing or "printing" the front of the card.
- Print several kisses.
- Write a message on the inside.

2. SQUIGGLE ART
C 30 MIN. 1

- Draw large, spontaneous squiggles on a 9" x 12" sheet of white construction paper.
- Turn the squiggles into shapes like trees, flowers, a baseball field, etc.

3. HOMEMADE COOKIE CUTTER CARDS
C 30 MIN. 1

- Fold a 9" x 12" sheet of construction paper in half.
- Place different sizes of cookie cutters on the front and trace.
- Decorate with markers, glitter, stickers, and colored pencils.
- Write a message on the inside.

4. PAPER PLATE DINNER
C 30 MIN. 1

- Cut out food pictures from old catalogs and magazines.
- Put the food in categories like Mexican, Italian, Vegetarian, or Chinese.
- Glue a category label to a paper plate.
- See how many different dinner plates you can "cook."

5. NAPKIN HOLDER
C 30 MIN. 2

- Fold the bottom of a 9" paper plate 2½" toward the center.
- Turn the plate and fold the other edge up 2½".
- Stand up the plate like a napkin holder.
- Decorate the front of the holder with tempera paint, glitter, construction paper shapes, and sequins.

6. TULIP GARDEN
C 30 MIN. 3

God has created many beautiful flowers for us to enjoy.
Now you can bring a flower garden inside!

• Paint a 9" x 12" sheet of white construction or watercolor
 paper with blue watercolor paint to create a sky.
• Cut a 2" x 12" strip of green construction paper.
• Make small cuts in the green to create fringe or grass. Leave
 about ¼"–½" of paper at the bottom of the green.
• Cut different colors of 2" x 2" construction paper for the
 flowers.
• Fold corner to corner to create a triangle, then fold the bottom
 corners up.
• Glue the grass to the blue background paper. Do not glue
 down the grass fringe.
• Glue the flowers on the blue sky, each at a different
 distance from the grass.
• With a green crayon or marker draw flower stems ending in
 the grass.
• Cut leaves from construction paper and glue them to the stems.

7. GIANT HAMBURGER
C 30 MIN. 3

Children enjoy making larger-than-life projects.
Here's one they can almost taste!

• Cut a hamburger bun from 2 sheets of 9" x 12" construction paper.
• Add other food to your hamburger by cutting construction
 paper into various shapes. For example, a pickle from
 green paper, hamburger from brown, and an onion from
 white paper.
• Construct the hamburger by gluing each food item on top of
 the bottom bun.
• Finish the hamburger with the top part of the bun.
• Make a drip of ketchup or mustard from construction paper;
 glue so it's dripping down the side.

8. THUMBPRINT ANIMALS
C 30 MIN. 1

- Press your thumb onto an ink pad then onto a sheet of white paper.
- Make a lot of prints.
- Add pencil details to the thumbprints to create animals. For example, add a mane, eyes, nose, mouth, and whiskers for a lion head. Add dots and lines for a ladybug.
- Use your imagination!

9. CIRCLE DRAWING
C 30 MIN. 1

- On a piece of white paper see how many objects you can draw using circles.
- Try to draw a whole scene without lifting the pencil from the paper.
- After practicing, draw a scene using circles.

10. CROWN ME
$ 30 MIN. 1

Crowns can be used for practically any occasion—a birthday, a special accomplishment at school or in sports, or for good behavior that needs to be reinforced.

- Cut a piece of colored poster board 12" wide and long enough to fit around your head, making sure to add ½" to overlap the ends.
- Cut the top of the strip like a crown.
- Decorate the crown with yarn, markers, construction paper, or small plastic jewels.
- Overlap the ends and glue or staple together.

11. GOOD FOOD POSTER
C 30 MIN. 1

In Daniel 1, King Nebuchadnezzar ordered
the captives from Israel to eat certain foods.
But Daniel requested to eat only vegetables and drink water.

• Read Daniel 1 and list the king's food and Daniel's food.
• Cut out pictures from catalogs and old magazines of the different foods.
• Draw a line down the center of a 9" x 12" sheet of white paper.
• Write "The King's Food" on one side of the line and "Daniel's Food" on the other side.
• Glue the pictures on the correct side.
• Write "Daniel 1" at the bottom.

12. CLOWN FACE
C 45 MIN. 2

• Draw an oval face on a 9" x 12" sheet of flesh-colored construction paper.
• Cut out the face.
• Cut out construction paper facial features, like big ears, a smile, eyes, etc.
• Cut out a tie, a hat with flowers, stripes, and dots.
• Glue to the face.

13. SHOE DRAWING
C 45 MIN. 1

• Pick out your favorite shoe.
• Draw the shoe on a 9" x 12" piece of white paper.
• Draw it as big as possible.
• Watercolor or color the shoe.
• Cut out the shoe.
• On the back, write the verse, "1 John 1:7," "Ephesians 5:1–2," or "Romans 6:4."

14. SNOWMAN PAPER PUPPET
C 45 MIN. 2

- Cut 3 circles from white paper, one small, medium, and large. The smallest circle should be big enough to cover the bottom of a brown paper lunch bag when laid flat.
- Glue the smallest circle to the bottom of the bag.
- Glue the medium circle to the bag. The circle should go under the flap of the bag that forms the bottom when the bag is folded flat.
- Glue the large circle to the bag, overlapping the medium circle a little bit.
- Make a black construction paper hat and glue it to the top white circle.
- Decorate your little snowman by adding construction-paper buttons, eyes, and scarf. The mouth can be drawn.

15. THANKFUL PICTURE
C 45 MIN. 1

- Gather art supplies such as paper, glue, watercolors, and crayons.
- Create a picture of something you are thankful for.

16. CREATURE CREATION
C 45 MIN. 1

- Draw a new creature by combining different animals. For example, the legs of a zebra, the ears of an elephant, and the body of a camel.
- For references, use pictures of animals and drawing books from the library.
- Color your new creature with colored pencils.

17. SUNBURSTS
C 45 MIN. 1

- Draw a few large dots spaced around a 9" x 12" white sheet of construction paper.
- With one color, draw a set of lines radiating from the dot, making a sunburst pattern.
- Change to another color and make another set of lines extending from the first set.
- Continue until you have 3 or more sets of lines.
- Make sunbursts around each dot.
- Mount by gluing to a sheet of black construction paper.

18. BAKER'S HAT
$ 45 MIN. 3

- Cut a piece of construction paper 5" wide and long enough to fit around your head. Two sheets of construction paper may have to be glued together to get the right length.
- Glue the ends of the strip together.
- Glue the edges of large sheets of white tissue paper to the inside of the headband to form a chef's hat.
- The sheets should overlap.
- Fold over any free edges.
- Wear the hat while helping fix a family meal.

19. POSTER BOARD MASK
C 45 MIN. 3

- Cut a piece of white poster board about 9" long and 12" wide.
- Cut a small hole on each 9" side.
- Mark the eyes and mouth.
- Cut out the eyes and mouth.
- Decorate the mask as a man or a woman from Bible times.
- Cut two 6" lengths of yarn.
- Tie one end of each piece of yarn around the holes.
- Bend the poster board to form around your face.
- Wear the mask by tying the yarn in a bow at the back of the head.
- Use the mask in acting out a Bible story.

20. HAPPINESS COLLAGE
C 45 MIN. 1

How do people act when they are happy?
Do they jump up and down, clap their hands, smile?

- Read Job 5:17, Psalm 1, Proverbs 3:13, Proverbs 29:18, and
  Matthew 5:1–12 to see what makes a person truly happy.
- Cut out pictures from catalogs and magazines of people show-
  ing the emotion of happiness.
- Glue the pictures to a sheet of construction paper so they
  overlap in a collage design.
- Write a verse around the edge.

21. RATTLER
C 45 MIN. 1

- Draw and color a snake on the back of a paper plate.
- Curl the snake's body around and around in a coil, following
  the edge of the plate.
- Color the snake.
- Place the snake plate on top of another plate and staple
  around the edge leaving an opening.
- Pour rice or beans through the opening.
- Staple closed.
- Rattle the snake!

22. COMPASS DRAWING
C 45 MIN. 3

- Place a white sheet of paper on top of a piece of cardboard.
  This will create a grip for the compass point.
- Use a compass to create a design of circles.
- Color in each section with crayons or markers.
- Mount on a piece of black construction paper a little bigger
  than the design.

23. ANIMAL CARDS
C 45 MIN. 2

• Decide what type of animal you want to use for your card.
• Fold a 9" x 12" sheet of construction paper in half.
• Draw a simple animal shape on the front, making sure the
    animal's back starts and ends on the top fold.
• Cut out the shape.
• Add details, like stripes, spots, eyes, and whiskers, with con-
    struction paper.
• Glue the details to the card.
• On the inside left of the card, write a poem about the animal,
    or find a poem in a book from the library.
• Write a message on the inside right of the card.
• Give to a friend or relative.

24. ISAIAH SNOW SCENE
C 1 HOUR 2

• Lay horizontally a 12" x 18" sheet of blue construction paper.
• Write the words of Isaiah 1:18 on the left side of the paper.
• Trace over the verse and reference with a brush and white
    paint.
• On the right side of the paper draw a snow scene. For exam-
    ple, snow-covered mountains and pine trees.
• Cut some very small pieces of white yarn for snow.
• Dot the scene with glue and place the yarn pieces in the glue.
• Certain areas, like the mountain tops, can be spread with glue
    and yarn pieces for snow.

25. BIRTHDAY GIFT-WRAP
$ 1 HOUR 2

• Partially unroll a tube of white or brown butcher paper and
    weigh down the corners.
• Cut a potato in half and draw a triangle or another basic
    shape on the cut side with a pencil.
• Cut away the potato on the outside of the line.
• Place a small amount of tempera or acrylic paint on a paper
    plate.

- Dip the potato stamp into the paint, being careful not to get too much paint. Practice stamping on a piece of newspaper.
- Press the potato stamp on the paper.
- Reload the stamp with paint and stamp until the paper is covered.
- Let dry, then unroll paper to the next section and continue stamping until the whole roll of paper has been stamped.
- Wrap the gift.

26. "WHITER THAN SNOW" SCENE
C 1 HOUR 2

The hymn "Whiter Than Snow" reminds us of
Christ's power to cleanse our hearts and our lives.

- Draw a winter scene on a 9" x 12" sheet of white paper.
- With an old paintbrush, cover the areas that are to be white with rubber cement.
- Wash out the brush.
- Let the rubber cement dry.
- Paint the rest of the scene with watercolor.
- Let dry.
- Rub off the rubber cement.
- Write along the top or bottom, "Wash me, and I shall be whiter than snow. Psalm 51:7."

27. MY HOUSE
C 1 HOUR 1

- Draw the outline of a roof and one side of a house on a 9" x 12" sheet of construction paper.
- Divide the house into rooms.
- Cut out pictures from old magazines and newspapers of ways to serve the Lord. For example, a person singing, distributing food, helping a sick or elderly person. . .
- Glue the pictures to the rooms of the house.
- On the roof, write, "As for me and my house, we will serve the LORD. Joshua 24:15."

28. FINISH THE DRAWING
C 1 HOUR 2

- Cut a picture of an animal in half.
- Glue half of the animal to a piece of white paper.
- Draw the other half of the animal on the paper.
- Color with colored pencil.

29. EYE DRAWING
C 1 HOUR 1

We are very special to God.
So special that He says in Psalm 17:8
that we are the apple of his eye.

- Draw a large eye on a 9" x 12" sheet of white paper.
- Cut out the pupil or center of the eye.
- Color the eye with crayons or colored pencil.
- Tape a picture of yourself to the back of the paper so your smiling face shows through the front of the drawing.
- Along the side or bottom, write, "I'm the center, or the apple, of His eye!"

30. INSECT BOOK
C 1 HOUR 1

- Collect pictures of insects.
- Fold several sheets of 9" x 12" construction paper in half.
- Stack folded sheets with the fold on the left, and staple down the left side.
- Decorate the front cover with several pictures and the title "My Insect Book."
- Glue the pictures in the book.
- Label each picture with the name of the insect.

31. JUMBO CRAYON
C 1 HOUR 2

- On a large sheet of butcher paper draw a crayon. (It's helpful to have an actual crayon in front of you to copy.)
- Paint the crayon with tempera paint.
- Let dry.
- Paint the word "crayon" and the color name in black.
- Outline the crayon and draw lines like a real crayon.
- Hang on the wall or from the ceiling. If hanging from the ceiling, paint both sides of the crayon.

32. CHILDREN-OF-THE-WORLD PUPPETS
C 1 HOUR 2

- Cut, from old magazines, pictures of children who illustrate each color (red, yellow, black, and white) in the song, "Jesus Loves the Little Children."
- Glue the pictures to lightweight cardboard.
- Cut out the pictures.
- For a handle, glue a Popsicle stick or ruler to the back of each puppet.
- Use the stick puppets when singing the song, or make up your own song or play.

33. WALLPAPER QUILT SQUARE
C 1 HOUR 4

- Ask for old wallpaper sample books at a wallpaper store.
- Look at books about quilt making to find a simple pattern that you like.
- Trace the pattern onto white paper.
- Trace the pattern on different wallpaper designs and cut out.
- Cut a piece of lightweight cardboard that fits your pattern exactly.
- Glue the wallpaper pieces to the cardboard.

34. PAPER BAG ANIMAL VEST
C 1 HOUR 2

- Lay a paper bag flat and cut up the center from the top of the bag.
- Cut off the bottom of the bag.
- Near the top of the vest, cut a V at the neck.
- Cut 2 arm holes on the sides.
- Decorate the bag with stripes or spots depending on the animal.
- Color with markers and crayons, or paint with tempera paint.
- Add any details, like glued-on buttons or fringe.

35. SPRING TREE
C 1 HOUR 1

- Dip a sponge in blue tempera paint and print on a 12" x 18" sheet of blue construction paper.
- Cover the whole paper.
- Let dry.
- Draw a tree branch, starting with a thick branch at the left, 12" side of the paper and getting thinner toward the right.
- Add smaller branches.
- Glue on green leaves cut from construction paper.
- Glue on popped popcorn for blossoms.
- Around the edge or on one side, write the phrase from Psalm 1:3, "Like a tree planted by the rivers of water."

36. SHAPES PICTURE
C 1 HOUR 1

- Cut several different shapes from construction paper.
- Arrange the shapes on a 12" x 18" sheet of construction paper to illustrate a particular Bible story. For example, David and Goliath. Use circles for the heads; rectangles for the body, arms, and legs; and triangles for the mountains; etc.
- Glue the shapes down.
- Write a title at the top.

37. EAR COLLAGE
C 1 HOUR 1

- Cut out pictures of ears and mouths from old magazines. Trim close to each picture.
- Cut 2 strips of 1" x 9" construction paper.
- Cut 2 strips of 1" x 12" construction paper.
- Glue the strips 1" from the edges of a 9" x 12" sheet of construction paper. The strips will overlap near the corners.
- Arrange the ears and mouths on top of the strips around the edge.
- Glue the pictures down.
- In the center of the paper, write or cut the words from an old magazine, "Everyone must be quick to hear, slow to speak and slow to anger. (James 1:19 NASB)"

38. BIG LETTERS AND NUMBERS
C 1 HOUR 2

Children love making their rooms special and personal.
By spelling out their name or age in big letters or numbers
and displaying it in the room,
children can help identify the room as their own.

- Draw a "fat" letter or number on a large piece of thin cardboard.
- Decorate it with colored pencil, marker, crayon, or tempera paint.
- Outline the letter or number in black to help it stand out.
- Cut out the number or letter and hang it on a wall, prop it on a shelf, or simply place it on a dresser.
- Make the letters of your initials, or spell out your name.

39. PAPER PICKUP TRUCK
C 1 HOUR 2

- Fold a piece of 8" x 11" construction paper in half.
- Draw a pickup truck on the folded paper. Make sure the roof of the truck is on the fold.
- Cut out the truck, leaving the fold of the roof.
- Cut out window.
- Cut out pictures from a magazine or use old photographs, for example, a driver behind the wheel and things you haul in a truck.
- Open the folded truck and glue in the picture of a driver.
- Glue the pictures in the back of the pickup.
- Draw 4 circles on a piece of black construction paper.
- Cut out circles and glue the 2 "wheels" on each side of the pickup.
- Cut 4 slightly smaller circles from a piece of aluminum foil.
- Glue these smaller circles in the center of the larger wheels.

40. SAMSON BOX MASK
$ 1½ HOURS 4

Samson was a Nazirite dedicated to the Lord.
Read about him in Judges 13–16.

- Find a box that will fit over your head.
- Paint the sides and front of the box with flesh-colored tempera paint.
- Cut out eye holes.
- Paint or glue facial features cut from construction paper to the front of the box.
- Cut ears from lightweight cardboard. Draw a tab on the side of each ear where it will be attached to the box.
- Paint with flesh-colored paint.
- Cut small slits in each side of the box and fit the ear tabs through the slits.
- Tape down the tabs on the inside of the box.
- Cut long lengths of brown and black yarn for hair, and glue

them to the box, alternating the colors.
• Put on the mask and act out a part of the story of Samson.

41. MOSAIC PICTURE
$ 2 HOURS 2

• Tear out an uncolored picture from a coloring book (a picture
  with large details works best), or draw a picture, such as a
  flower.
• Glue the picture to a piece of cardboard.
• Spread glue on a small section of the picture. Then lay beans,
  seeds, rice, and popcorn kernels in the glue.
• Continue to spread the glue over the entire picture, adding
  beans, seeds, and kernels as you go along.
• Small pieces of cut or torn construction paper could also be
  used to fill in the picture.

ACTIVITIES FOR
YOUNGER CHILDREN
PAINT PROJECTS

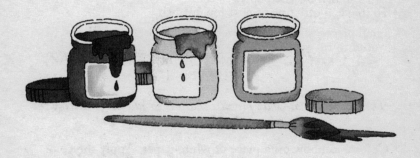

42. PULLED STRING DESIGN
C 15 MIN. 1

- Fold a 9" x 12" sheet of white paper in half.
- Open and drop a few dots of tempera or acrylic paint onto one side.
- Lay a string in the paint.
- Fold the other side of the paper onto the paint and string.
- Hold the paper down with one hand and pull the string out.
- Open the paper and let dry.
- Examine your string design to see if you can add a few lines to make an animal or other subjects.

43. FISH PRINT
$$ 30 MIN. 3

- Buy a whole small fish.
- With watercolor, paint an entire piece of white construction paper blue and let dry.
- Draw seaweed.
- Watercolor seaweed green and brown, then let dry.
- With a brush, paint the fish on one side with tempera or acrylic paint.
- Lay the fish, paint side down, on the watercolor picture.
- Press on the fish to release the color, being careful not to move it.
- Lift the fish off the paper.
- To make another print, just repaint fish.

44. CRAYON/WATERCOLOR RAINBOW ART
C 30 MIN. 1

The rainbow was God's promise that He would never destroy the earth with another flood (Genesis 9:8–17).

- Color a rainbow on a piece of white paper. Apply the color heavily.
- Paint the entire surface of the paper with watercolor. The watercolor will be absorbed by the paper but not by the areas covered with heavy crayon.

45. ROCK PAINTING
C 30 MIN. 1

- Paint flat rocks with acrylic paint.
- Use your imagination to decide what to paint on each rock. For example, a point could be a nose. Or paint an ocean, a beach scene, butterflies, or a rainbow.
- Use the painted rocks as paperweights or in the flower garden.

46. JOSEPH'S COAT
C 30 MIN. 3

- Find an old men's shirt.
- Trim the sleeves if they are too long.
- Button the shirt and lay flat on top of a layer of newspapers.
- Cut a large piece of cardboard and slip inside the body of the shirt.
- Cut long cardboard rectangles to fit inside the sleeves.
- Paint stripes on the front of the shirt and sleeves with tempera paint.
- Let dry.
- Turn the shirt and cardboard over and paint the back.
- Let dry.
- Use a belt or piece of rope as your sash.

47. WATERCOLOR PAINTING
C 45 MIN. 1

*This simple project is a great way to
practice using watercolor paints.*

- Choose a picture from a coloring book.
- Paint the picture with watercolor paints. The less water used, the brighter and darker the color will be.

48. SQUIRT PAINTING
$ 45 MIN. 3

*This is a fun project to do outside.
Wear old clothes and cover any area that
you don't want paint on.*

- Hang a rope between 2 trees.
- Clothespin a large tarp or shower liner to the rope.
- Pin a large piece of white or brown butcher paper to the tarp.
- Fill empty, clean plastic dish detergent and mustard bottles with tempera paint.
- Stand back from the paper and squirt paint onto it.

- Try to balance the use of color.
- Thin the paint with water if needed.
- Use the painting as a backdrop for a puppet play or a skit.

49. DOORSTOP
C 45 MIN. 1

- Find a large rock that has an interesting shape.
- Paint the rock with acrylic paints using the shape of the rock in your design. For example, a point for a nose or a bump for eyebrows.
- Seal with clear spray sealer.

50. WATERCOLOR ANIMALS
C 45 MIN. 1

- Wet a piece of watercolor paper.
- Load a brush with watercolor and touch the paper lightly. The color will spread out.
- Try several different colors.
- Let the paper dry.
- See if you can see an animal in the design. For example, a fish, bear, or bird.
- Outline the animal with black watercolor.
- Add details like eyes, a beak, or claws.

51. STUFF KEEPER
C 1 HOUR 3

*This box is a great organizer for things like
Barbies or Matchbox cars.*

- Paint a large box and lid with acrylic paint.
- Let dry.
- Put the lid on the box and trace around the bottom of the lid onto the box.
- Mix 1 cup flour, 1 cup salt, and 1 cup water.

• Divide into several bowls.
• Add food coloring to each bowl to mix different colors.
• Fill cleaned-out glue, mustard, or ketchup bottles with the
    colorized mixture, one color per bottle.
• Turn the box so the side to be decorated is facing up.
• Decorate below the line on the sides with the paint.
• Let dry.
• Decorate each side and the box lid.
• Let dry.
• Spray with a clear sealer.

52. FOIL BUTTERFLIES
$ 1 HOUR 3

• Draw several different sizes of butterflies on a large piece of
    foil.
• Cut out the butterflies.
• Paint a pattern on the wings of the butterflies with tempera
    paint. Do not cover all the foil.
• Make the body of the butterfly by rolling foil into a coil.
• Glue a body to the center of each butterfly.
• Make antennas by rolling foil into a thin coil.
• Glue the butterflies to a black sheet of construction paper.
    They can be glued flat or bend the wings so they stand up
    off the paper.
• Glue the antennas to the paper at the top of each butterfly
    body.
• Glue a small ball of foil on the end of each antenna.

53. GIANT GUMMY WORMS
C 1 HOUR 1

• Stick a toothpick into a Styrofoam worm.
• Holding on to the toothpick, paint the worm with acrylic
    paint.
• Paint several worms different colors with the acrylic paint.
• Display the worms in a large glass jar.

54. SWINGING ART
$ 1 HOUR 5

- Tie string around the top of a small funnel and hang it from a light fixture or from a low tree branch or bush.
- Make sure that the funnel can swing freely.
- Cover the table or ground with newspaper.
- Place a large piece of paper on the newspaper.
- Cover yourself with an old shirt or apron.
- Cut off the end of a paper cup cone, or make a cone with a circle of paper taped into a cone shape. Do not cut off too much of the tip.
- Put the cone in the funnel.
- Put your finger over the tip and pour some tempera paint into the cone.
- Take your finger away and gently swing the funnel. Do not swing it so hard that it goes past the edge of the newspaper.
- To drip another color, remove the cone, clean the funnel, and put in a new cone and color. If the paint does not drip freely, thin with a little water or make the hole bigger.
- Let dry.
- Experiment swinging the funnel in different ways.

55. FOOTPRINT POSTER
C 1 HOUR 5

- Place several layers of newspaper in a large square on the floor.
- Place a large cookie sheet at one end of the newspaper.
- Place a 12" x 18" sheet of construction paper in the middle of the newspaper.
- Place a tub filled with water and an old towel or rag at the other end of the newspaper.
- Spread a layer of tempera paint in the cookie sheet.
- Step barefooted into the paint, then step onto the newspaper. Place the right foot on the right side of the construction paper and the left foot on the left side.
- Step off the paper into the water and clean up.
- Let the footprints dry.
- Between the footprints, write or cut the words from magazines and newspapers to the hymn "Footsteps of Jesus."

56. MENU POSTER
$ 1 HOUR 4

This is a fun project for a special meal like Thanksgiving.

- Cut a piece of poster board in half.
- Cut a mushroom, an orange, a pineapple, and an apple in half.
- Spread different colors of tempera or acrylic paint on a paper plate. A cookie sheet will work for larger items like the pineapple.
- Lay the pineapple in the paint, then print on a layer of newspaper to remove the excess paint.
- Set up the poster board vertically.
- Print the pineapple in the bottom middle of the poster board.
- Print the other fruit and vegetables around the edges of the poster.
- Leave the center space to write the menu.
- Write the menu in the center lightly in pencil.
- Trace the words with a marker.
- Hang in the dining room.
- Or print the foods mentioned in the Bible in the center and hang in the Sunday school room.

57. GIGANTIC TEAPOT
$ 1 HOUR 3

- Using a pencil, draw a teapot on a sheet of poster board.
- Cut out the teapot.
- Draw a design on the pot. For example, a stripe with dots inside, checks, flowers, or cherries.
- Place on a layer of newspaper and paint with tempera paint.
- Hang.

58. SHADE AND TINT COLLAGE
C 1 HOUR 3

A "shade" is a color with black added to it,
and a "tint" is a color with white added to it.

- Pick 2 favorite colors.
- Place about a quarter-sized drop of each color in separate bowls.
- Paint a 3"-wide strip of color across a heavy piece of paper, like watercolor paper.
- Add a tiny drop of black to each color and mix.
- Paint a second strip of color.
- Keep adding a drop of black to each color and see how many shades you can come up with.
- In clean bowls, place a quarter-sized drop of paint, and this time add white. See how many tints you can come up with.
- Let dry.
- Cut shapes and strips of color from the different tints and shades and arrange them on a sheet of black construction paper. The pieces can overlap.
- Glue the shapes down.

ACTIVITIES FOR YOUNGER CHILDREN
CRAFT PROJECTS

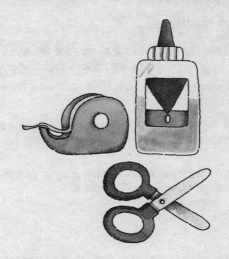

59. HORSESHOE PARTY FAVOR
$ 15 MIN. 1

- Decorate a horseshoe by gluing on wrapped candy.
- Add horse stickers.

60. PAPERWEIGHT
C 15 MIN. 1

- Fill a small clear glass jar with layers of some of your favorite things, like pretty buttons, marbles, hair ribbons, coins, or Lego pieces.
- Use on your desk as a paperweight.

61. PORCUPINE
$ 15 MIN. 1

- Form self-hardening clay or Play-Doh into a medium-sized ball.
- Slightly flatten the ball.
- Pull out a nose.
- Poke a clove into the nose and 2 cloves for the eyes.
- Poke a lot of large toothpicks into the dough for porcupine quills.

62. POPSICLE STICK BOOKMARK
C 15 MIN. 1

- Paint designs on a Popsicle stick with acrylic paints. Designs could include dots, stripes, X's, and O's.
- Lay it on wax paper to dry.
- Spray with clear sealer.

63. WHIMSICAL FLOWER ARRANGEMENT
C 15 MIN. 1

This makes a fun centerpiece or decoration for each table setting.

- Fill a clear glass flower vase, a large glass, or a bowl with plastic toys, Barbie accessories, or marbles.
- Add water and flowers.
- Place on a table.

64. DECORATOR SWITCH PLATE
$ 15 MIN. 2

- Cut a rectangle of wallpaper a little bigger than the light switch plate.
- Glue the wallpaper to the front of the plate.
- Fold over the edges and glue down.
- Cut out a hole for the switch.

65. STICKER SOAP
C 15 MIN. 1

Make this project really fun by picking out soap and stickers that coordinate, like animal-shaped soap and stickers.

- Cover the top of a bar of soap with a coat of clear nail polish.
- Arrange stickers on the polish.
- Let dry.
- Coat with another layer of nail polish.
- Let dry.
- Give as a gift or use as your own special bar of soap.

66. BIRD TREAT
C 15 MIN. 1

- Tie a string on a fat pretzel for a hanger.
- Cover the pretzel with peanut butter.
- Sprinkle bird seed onto the peanut butter.
- Hang in a tree for the birds to enjoy.

67. POTATO MAN
C 30 MIN. 4

- Lay a potato on a work area in several positions to see which way it lies best.
- Carve out a hole in the top of the potato.
- Dampen a cotton ball and place in the hole.

- Glue on moveable eyes.
- Poke the ends of a short piece of pipe cleaner into the potato under the eyes for a mouth.
- Sprinkle grass seeds onto the cotton ball.
- Put the potato on a window sill.
- Keep the cotton ball damp.
- Soon the potato man will have green hair!

68. FLOWER BASKET
$$ 30 MIN. 3

- Line a basket with plastic bags.
- Fill it with potting soil.
- Plant flowers and plants in the soil.
- Pack more soil around the plants.
- Water.
- Set on the front porch, or, if a small basket has been used, place on a table. Make sure the bottom is not wet.
- Or place plastic cups in the basket and plant the flowers in the cups.
- Fill in around the cups with moss.

69. CEREAL STEGOSAURUS
C 30 MIN. 1

- Draw an outline of a dinosaur.
- Paint the dinosaur with watercolor or tempera paint.
- Cut out the dinosaur.
- Glue different types of cereal on the dinosaur. For example, corn flakes for the back and tail; Cheerios for the eyes and toes.

70. BARRETTE
$ 30 MIN. 1

• Glue objects to a blank barrette.
• Objects could include sequins, miniature figures, and plastic jewels.

71. HEART PICTURE MAGNET
C 30 MIN. 2

• Cut 2 small hearts out of red construction paper.
• Fold one heart in half.
• Cut a heart from the folded heart, starting and ending on the fold.
• Cut a picture of yourself and glue it to the solid heart.
• Glue the heart frame on top of the picture.
• Glue a small magnet on the back.
• Give to a parent or grandparent.

72. BIRDIE SMORGASBORD
$ 30 MIN. 2

• Purchase several types of birdseed.
• Cut off the top of a Styrofoam egg carton.
• Fill the egg carton cups with the different types of bird seed.
• Label the lip of the carton with the types of seed.
• Cut a length of string at least 24" long.
• Tie the string to each end of the carton.
• Hang the smorgasbord outside.

73. SHAMPOO BOTTLE DOLL
C 30 MIN. 3

• Cut a piece of construction paper wide enough to wrap around an empty shampoo bottle and tape it at the back.
• Cut a flesh-colored piece of paper to fit around the spout and tape it at the back. This will be the face.

- Draw on the face and add hair to the head and clothes to the body.
- The doll can be decorated as a soldier, cowboy, cowgirl, or Bible character. Use your imagination!

74. FIRST-DAY-OF-SCHOOL BOX
$$ 45 MIN. 2

- Cover a small box with wrapping paper or construction paper.
- Cover the lid.
- Fill the box with items for your teacher. For example, gum, small packages of Kleenex, tea, chocolate, and cough drops.
- Give to your teacher on the first day of school.

75. SEASHELL FRAME
$ 45 MIN. 2

- Cover a picture frame with seashells by gluing on the large shells first, then filling in with small shells. A flat frame works best.
- Slip in a picture and display.

76. SUNSHINE TAMBOURINE
C 45 MIN. 1

Children love music—
now they can play along with their favorite songs!

- Decorate the backs of 2 paper plates with a sun.
- Color the rims with sunny colors like reds, yellows, and oranges.
- Place one paper plate, decorated side down, on a table.
- Cut long strips of red, yellow, and orange tissue paper.
- Glue the strips around the edge of the plate so they hang from the rim.
- Put some rice or small beans on the plate.
- Place the second paper plate on top with the design facing up.

• Staple the plates together. The staples should be close enough
  that the rice or beans do not escape.

77. BALLOON ANIMAL
C 45 MIN. 2

• Decide on an animal.
• Draw 2 paws or hooves on an 8" x 8" piece of lightweight
  cardboard so the backs or heels are touching.
• Cut out the feet in one piece.
• Cut a small slit from the middle back about 3" long.
• Cut a smaller slit horizontally across the top of the first slit.
• Blow up and tie a balloon. Pick a color that goes with your
  animal. For example, orange for a tiger.
• Decorate the balloon with markers to look like the animal.
• Slip the knotted end of the balloon into the slits of the paw.

78. MINIATURE FOOD
$$ 45 MIN. 5

Even Barbies and toy soldiers need to eat!

• Form different colors of Fimo clay into tiny food. Make fruit,
  vegetables, pizza, bread, fried eggs, etc.
• Bake according to the instructions on the package.
• Invite your Barbies or soldiers to sit down to a meal that's just
  their size!

79. HOMEMADE PLAY-DOH
$ 45 MIN. 4

• In a large pot, mix together 2 cups flour, 1 cup salt, 4 teaspoons cream of tartar, 2 cups water, 3 teaspoons oil, and 2
  teaspoons vanilla.
• Cook and stir over medium heat for about 5 minutes, until it
  forms a ball. (It won't look right until you knead it!)
• Let cool slightly.

- Knead about 6 minutes.
- Divide into balls and store in Ziploc-style bags.
- For color, add a few drops of food coloring and knead it into the dough. If you don't want your hands to stain, wear rubber gloves while kneading.
- Have fun with the dough and use your imagination as you build things!

80. CLOTHESPIN DOLLS
$ 45 MIN. 1

- Paint a face on the top of a clothespin with acrylic paint.
- Glue on yarn for hair.
- Dress the doll by glueing on scraps of fabric.
- Paint on shoes.

81. DANCE STREAMERS
$ 45 MIN. 1

- Paint a long dowel with acrylic paint.
- Cut very long pieces of different colors of crepe paper.
- Glue one end of each streamer to the top of the stick.
- Decorate a few of the streamers with glue and glitter.
- Dance with the streamer in a large space, like the backyard or park.

82. FOIL-COVERED GIFT BOX
C 45 MIN. 1

- Cut out stars from thin cardboard.
- Glue the stars to the lid of a jewelry box or any other small box.
- Cover the box and lid with foil.
- Trace gently around the stars with a cotton swab.
- Use the box for a special gift.

83. MEMORY KEEPER
C 45 MIN. 1

Children tend to keep lots of special odds and ends,
especially when traveling.
Here's a fun way to display all those special treasures.

• Collect treasures—rocks, seashells, sand flowers, ticket stubs,
   pictures, etc.
• Arrange the treasures in a clear plastic take-out box.
• The background of the pictures can be trimmed so only the
   person, animal, or main subject is left.
• Glue treasures so they are secure in the box.
• Close the lid and display.

84. FISH BOOKMARK
$ 45 MIN. 3

Find your page quickly!
With this bookmark,
you no longer have to "fish around" for it!

• Draw a simple fish outline on a 2" x 3" piece of felt or fabric.
• Cut out.
• Trace and cut out a second fish.
• Cut a 5" length of ribbon.
• Place a strip of glue on the front and center of one fish.
• Lay the end of the ribbon in the glue.
• Lay the other fish on top and secure with straight pins.
• Sew around the edge, leaving a small opening to stuff the fish.
• Stuff the fish with small pieces of cotton or panty hose.
• Sew the opening shut.
• Put the bookmark in your Bible or in a book that you are
   reading.

85. HAPPY/SAD DOLL
$ 1 HOUR 2

- Mark a line to show the middle of a paper towel roll.
- Decorate one end of the paper towel roll with a happy face and a blouse. The blouse should stop at the center line.
- Decorate the opposite end with a sad face and a blouse. End the blouse at the center line.
- Cut a piece of fabric for the skirt. It should be long enough to cover half the paper towel roll and wrap around the tube.
- Glue the top edge of the fabric to the center line on the tube.
- The doll can be flipped so one face shows and the skirt covers the other face.
- Use this doll when studying Saul, the wise man and the foolish man, or Psalm 1. Or use it as a part of a right vs. wrong lesson—when discussing right, show the happy doll, and wrong, the sad doll.

86. PIPE CLEANER NUMBER COLLAGE
$ 1 HOUR 2

- Cut a 9" x 12" piece of lightweight cardboard.
- Glue a 9" x 12" sheet of construction paper to the cardboard.
- Bend different colors of pipe cleaners into numbers.
- Cut the pipe cleaners into different lengths to make different sizes of numbers.
- Arrange the numbers on the cardboard upside down, right side up, and at different angles.
- Glue the numbers to the cardboard.
- Hold the pipe cleaners down until the glue dries.

87. TRENCHER
$ 1 HOUR 5

*Wooden trenchers were used in early colonial days as plates. People usually ate with their fingers or wooden spoons.
Try this version of a trencher at the dinner table tonight.*

- Mix together 2 cups flour and 1 cup salt. Stir in 1 cup water.

- Knead for about 7 minutes. The dough should not be sticky; if it is, add a little more flour.
- Shape the dough into a rectangle.
- Scoop out some dough from the center of the rectangle. This will be where the food is placed. Leave about a 1" border around the edge.
- Smooth the scooped out area.
- Bake at 325° for 30–40 minutes, depending on the thickness. Cover with foil any areas that seem to be baking faster. Prick any bubbles.
- Let cool.

88. SALT DOUGH SPOON
$ 1 HOUR 5

This recipe will make several spoons.
Use with a trencher like the one in Project #87.

- Mix together 2 cups flour and 1 cup salt. Stir in 1 cup water.
- Knead for about 7 minutes. The dough should not be sticky; if it is, add a little more flour.
- Divide the dough.
- Shape the dough into a spoon.
- Scoop out some dough from the bowl area of the spoon.
- Bake at 325° for 30–40 minutes, depending on the thickness. Cover with foil any areas that seem to be baking faster. Prick any bubbles.
- Let cool.

89. SAND SCULPTURE
$ 1 HOUR 1

- Do this project outside.
- Fill a large plastic storage container with sand.
- Add enough water to make the sand moldable.
- Plan your design. Illustrate the wind and waves and clouds from Luke 8:22–25, or create Noah's ark and animals.
- Draw the design in the sand with your fingers or a stick.
- Carve away sand around the design to give it depth.

90. SNOWMAN
$ 1 HOUR 3

• Purchase 3 different sizes of Styrofoam balls.
• Cut off the bottom of the largest ball so that it will stand.
• Poke a few toothpicks into the medium-sized ball.
• Squirt glue around the toothpicks.
• Press the medium ball down onto the largest ball so the toothpicks go into the ball.
• Repeat with the small ball.
• Cover the snowman by gluing on cotton balls.
• Add details like sticks for arms, a scarf, small paper mittens, buttons, eyes, and a construction-paper hat.

91. METHUSELAH DOLL
$ 1 HOUR 4

Genesis 5:27 tells us that Methuselah was the oldest man to ever live—969 years!

• Crack a walnut in half.
• Take out the meat.
• Fold a long pipe cleaner in half.
• Leaving a loop at the top, twist the pipe cleaner together for a body, leaving some at the end for legs.
• Bend up the ends for feet.
• Twist another pipe cleaner around the upper body for arms.
• Bend the ends up for hands.
• Glue the loop into one walnut shell half.
• Glue the other half on top.
• With a marker, mark the eyes, nose, and mouth on the walnut shell. The grooves in the shell will give the doll an aged look.
• Glue on cotton or yarn for hair.
• Glue on a scrap of fabric for a tunic.
• Use a strip of fabric for a sash.

92. FEED-THE-BIRDS PARTY
$ 1 HOUR 5

*To celebrate the holidays or overcome rainy day blues,
have a "Feed the Birds" celebration!*

- Cover the work area with newspaper.
- Pour birdseed into a deep pan or cookie sheet.
- Cover split bagels and pinecones with peanut butter.
- Roll in the birdseed.
- Tie a length of yarn to the bagel or pinecone.
- String popcorn and cranberries.
- Hang the bird treats on a tree.
- If you have a large group, consider a bonfire and hot chocolate to finish off a fun evening.
- Watch the birds come and have a feast!

93. FINGER PUPPET
$ 1 HOUR 4

- Cut a piece of felt big enough to wrap around your largest finger. The piece should not be as wide at the top as the bottom.
- Overlap the sides and glue. Use paper clips to hold the sides together until the glue dries.
- Cut 2 arms, 2 hands, and 2 heads from felt.
- Glue the hands to the arms.
- Glue the ends of the arms to the back of the tube body.
- Break a Popsicle stick in half.
- Place a dot of glue on one head and lay the broken end of the stick in it.
- Glue the other head on top.
- Insert the head into the top of the body and glue in place.
- Glue on details, like yarn hair, moveable eyes, trim, feathers, sequins, and a smaller piece of felt over the body for a blouse or shirt.
- Facial features could be added with markers.
- Make several puppets to act out a story from the Bible. For example, Joseph, Pharaoh, a sheaf of grain, a sun, moon, and stars from Joseph's dreams in Genesis 37.

94. PASTA WREATH
$ 1 HOUR 2

- Draw a circle on a 5" x 5" piece of lightweight cardboard.
- Cut out the circle.
- Draw another circle in the middle and cut it out to create a wreath.
- Glue different pasta shapes to the cardboard. The pasta can be layered.
- Let dry.
- Place the pasta-covered wreath on a sheet of newspaper.
- Paint with green tempera or acrylic paint.
- Paint a bow pasta shape with red paint.
- Glue the bow to the top of the wreath.
- Let dry.
- Hang with a ribbon or yarn.

95. MY BACKYARD BOX
$ 1 HOUR 2

- Collect small pieces of grasses, flowers, feathers, leaves, seeds from the fruit of a fruit tree, etc. from the backyard.
- Press between paper towels placed between the pages of a book.
- Top with heavy books.
- Cut circles and rectangles from heavy paper like watercolor paper.
- Glue one pressed specimen to each paper shape and label.
- Sponge-paint a wooden or papier mâché box with acrylic paint. Make sure it is large enough to hold the largest specimen.
- Place the specimens in the box.

96. YARN SCENE
$ 1 HOUR 2

- Cut a 6" x 9" piece of lightweight cardboard.
- Draw a scene on the cardboard using simple shapes. For example, a summer scene of the Fourth of July.

- Cover an area of the cardboard with glue.
- Cut different colors of yarn to size and place in the glue. For example, use white yarn for clouds or blue for the sky.
- Cover the entire cardboard with yarn.

97. SPICE PICTURE
$ 1 HOUR 1

Spices were used in the tabernacle (see Exodus 35:28), and to preserve the body of Jesus (see John 19:40). Here's a way to create an aromatic scene with lots of texture.

- Choose a picture from a Bible coloring book.
- Cut a piece of construction paper a little bigger than the picture.
- Glue the picture to the paper with rubber cement.
- Decide which parts of the picture you want to cover with which spices.
- Color the areas the will not be covered with spices.
- Spread a little glue on a colored section and sprinkle spices, such as cinnamon, oregano, pepper flakes, and dried parsley, onto the glue.
- Gently press down the spices with your finger.
- Let the glue dry.
- Knock off any excess spice.

98. PAINTED FLOWER POT
$ 1 HOUR 2

- Clean and dry a flower pot.
- Paint the pot with several coats of acrylic paint.
- Decorate the pot with stripes, dots, flowers, stars, or moons.
- Let dry.
- Cover with a coat of clear sealer.
- Fill with potting soil and a plant or flower!

99. FOUND OBJECTS SCULPTURE
C 2 HOURS 2

- On a plywood base, glue together "junk" objects, like pieces of wood, spools, plastic cups, Tinkertoys, straws, marbles, and clothespins.
- Glue the objects into a standing sculpture.

100. MOSS AND PINECONE BIRDHOUSE
$ 2 HOURS 4

- Draw a circle on the front of a half-gallon milk carton about 4" from the bottom.
- Cut out the circle.
- Poke holes in the 2 sides, thread twine through, and tie the ends for a hanger.
- Tape the top of the carton closed.
- Poke a small hole through the carton under the circle cutout. This will be the hole for the perch.
- Cover the entire carton with moss by spreading a thick layer of glue on a small section of the milk carton and pressing moss into the glue. Do not cover the small hole for the perch.
- Glue moss over the edge of the circle cutout.
- Take the petals off a pinecone.
- Glue the pinecone petals to the top of the moss-covered milk carton, overlapping each petal like shingles.
- Poke a stick or small dowel through the hole for a perch.
- Hang the birdhouse.

101. RUBBER BAND PAPERWEIGHT
C ONGOING 1

- Wad a small piece of foil into a ball.
- Wrap rubber bands around the ball.
- Keep adding rubber bands.
- Keep a tally of how many bands are used.
- This makes a great paperweight and conversation piece.

102. DRIED GOURD PEOPLE
$ ONGOING 3

- Make several small holes in the bottom of the gourd with a hammer and nail.
- Place the gourd on a newspaper, in a warm area, to dry.
- Every day, wipe off any condensation that has formed on the gourd and turn it over.
- The gourd will take a long time to dry, up to 4 months, depending on the size and thickness.
- When dry, paint a face on the gourd with acrylic paint.
- Make the gourd into a Bible character like Elijah from 1 Kings 17–2 Kings 2.

ACTIVITIES FOR
YOUNGER CHILDREN
GAMES

103. INSIDE OBSTACLE COURSE
C 15 MIN. 1

*This is a great activity for a rainy day, or,
move it outdoors on a nice day!*

• Set up an obstacle course in one room or throughout the
  house. Use chairs, boxes, etc.

- At certain stations, tape a piece of paper with instructions to recite a verse, sing a song, or do jumping jacks.
- Time the obstacle runners to see who can run through the obstacle course the fastest.

104. FRUIT RELAY
C 15 MIN. 1

- Cut flat slices of an apple, an orange, a kiwi, and a banana.
- Divide into teams.
- Give each team 2 slices of each fruit on a paper plate and an empty paper plate.
- Place the plate of fruit at one end and the empty plate at the other end of each line.
- Have each team stand side by side in a line.
- At the start signal, the first person on each team must pick up a slice of fruit and place it in the palm of his hand.
- Then pass it to the palm of the next person in line.
- Keep passing the fruit palm to palm until it reaches the last person who palms it onto the paper plate.
- Only when the fruit is on the paper plate may the first person pick up the next piece of fruit and pass it.
- The first team to palm-pass all their fruit to the opposite end of their line wins.

105. WATER BRIGADE
C 15 MIN. 1

- Divide into 2 teams.
- Mark a starting line.
- Place, at a distance, a bucket of water, an empty bucket, and a cup for each team.
- At the start signal, a player from each team runs to the bucket and fills the cup with water and dumps it into the empty bucket.
- The player then returns to his team and the next player runs to the buckets.
- When every player on each team has had a turn, the team with the most water in the bucket wins.

49

106. COUNTING GAME
C 15 MIN. 1

*This is a great game to play while waiting
in the grocery line, traffic, or at the doctor's office.*

- Count by 1's, 5's, 10's, 20's, 50's, 100's, etc.
- Time each other to see who can count to a certain number the fastest.

107. MARBLE ROLL
C 15 MIN. 1

- Draw a large circle on the cement with a piece of chalk.
- Draw a smaller circle inside the large one and another smaller circle in the middle.
- Divide each circle into sections.
- Mark a point value inside each section with the outside sections given the lowest point value.
- Give the center section the highest point value.
- Give each player 5 marbles of the same size. Each player should have one color of marbles.
- To play, each player rolls one marble at a time into the circles, trying to land on the highest point value.
- Keep track of the points.
- If a player hits an opponent's marble and moves it out of a section, the opponent must subtract that section's point value from his score.
- After each player has rolled 5 marbles, the winner is the player with the most points.

108. STATIC BALLOONS
$ 15 MIN. 1

This activity is very simple and lots of fun!

- Blow up and tie the necks of a bunch of balloons.
- Rub the balloons on your hair, on the carpet, or on your clothes to create static electricity.

- See how many balloons will stick to your hair, clothes, the wall, etc.
- For a fun game, divide into teams and see which team can cover one player with the most balloons.

109. HOT AND COLD
C 15 MIN. 1

This game can be played inside or outside.

- One player, *It*, hides an object like a small ball or a coin.
- The other players try to find the object.
- *It* tells the players they're hot when they are coming close to the object, and that they're cold when they move away from the hidden object.
- The player who finds the object becomes the next player to be *It*.

110. MUSICAL CHAIRS
C 15 MIN. 1

- Chose a favorite tape or CD.
- Place one less chair than the number of players. Arrange the chairs back to back in a row or in a circle.
- Have the players stand by the chairs.
- Start the music.
- The players walk or march around the chairs.
- When the music stops the players find a seat.
- The player left standing is out.
- Remove a chair.
- Start the music.
- The last player in the chair is the winner.

111. HOT POTATO
C 15 MIN. 1

- Choose a favorite tape or CD.
- Players stand or sit in a circle.
- Give one player a potato.
- When the music starts, the potato is quickly passed from one player to the next around the circle.
- The player holding the potato when the music stops is out.
- The player who lasts longest is the winner.

112. ESTIMATING JAR
$ 15 MIN. 1

- Place items like jellybeans, popped corn, nails, etc., in a jar with a lid.
- Have each person write down his or her guess of the number of objects in the jar.
- Pour out the jar and count the items.
- The person who guesses the closest gets to make a new estimating jar!

113. POP-THE-BALLOON GAME
$ 15 MIN. 2

- Blow up a balloon for each child.
- Tie a string to the end of the balloon and then to an ankle.
- At the start signal, each player tries to break the other players' balloons by stepping on them.
- The last person with an unbroken balloon wins.

114. ROOT BEER RELAY
$ 15 MIN. 2

- Divide into teams.
- On a table, pour one small paper cup of root beer per player.
- Form the cups into one line for each team.

- Pass out a straw to each player.
- At the sound of the whistle, the first person on each team runs to the table and sips the root beer from his cup, then runs back to his line.
- The team that empties its cups first wins!

115. FRUIT GUESSING GAME
C 15 MIN. 2

- Guess how many seeds are in an apple.
- Cut open the apple and count the seeds.
- Eat the apple.

116. TIC-TAC-TOE GAME
C 30 MIN. 2

- Cut a 9" x 9" piece of poster board.
- Draw 2 vertical lines and 2 horizontal lines to divide the board.
- Draw block style X's and O's on 2 different colors of poster board.
- Make the letters small enough to fit in the squares of the game board.
- Cut out the X's and O's.
- Play the game with a friend.
- To store, place in a Ziploc-style plastic bag.

117. HOMEMADE TENTS
C 30 MIN. 1

- Make tents in the house by placing sheets and blankets over chairs and tables.

118. GUESSING GAME
C 30 MIN. 2

- Gather different objects like a marble, paper clip, diaper pin, Band Aid, toothpick, safety pin, lipstick, candy, key, and comb.
- Place each object in an envelope.
- Mark each envelope with a number and keep a list of what is in each one.
- Let each child try to guess what is in each envelope by feeling.
- Write down each number and the guess.
- Give a prize to the child who guesses the most correct answers.

119. ROLL-A-BUG GAME
C 30 MIN. 1

- Take turns rolling one die. The first one to draw a bug wins.
- Roll 1 for each eye.
- Roll 2 for a tail.
- Roll 3 for the head.
- Roll 4 for each leg.
- Roll 5 for each antenna.
- Roll 6 for the body.

120. SQUIRT GUN GAME
$ 30 MIN. 1

- Partially fill liter bottles with water and place on the patio.
- Put a Ping-Pong ball on top of each bottle.
- Mark a line to stand behind. The distance from the bottles will depend on the shooting distance of the squirt gun.
- Use a squirt gun to shoot off the Ping-Pong balls.

121. HIDE AND SEEK
C 30 MIN. 1

- One player is chosen to be *It*.
- *It* closes his eyes and counts to 50 or 100.
- Where *It* is standing is called base.
- The other players scatter and hide.
- *It* tries to find the players.
- If a player touches base, he is safe.
- If a player is tagged by *It*, that person becomes *It*.

122. FREEZE TAG
C 30 MIN. 1

- Pick one player to be *It*.
- *It* tries to tag the other players.
- If a player is tagged he is frozen.
- A frozen player can be unfrozen by being tagged by another player.
- If a player has been frozen three times, he becomes *It*.

123. SHADOW TAG
C 30 MIN. 1

Play this game on a sunny day.

- Choose one player to be *It*.
- *It* tries to tag the other players while they run from one shadow to another.
- If *It* tags a player while he is not standing in a shadow, that player becomes *It*.

124. RED LIGHT, GREEN LIGHT
C 30 MIN. 1

- Choose one player to be *It*.
- The other players stand across the yard from *It*.

- *It* starts the game by facing away from the players and yelling, "Green light!"
- The players then move closer to *It*.
- *It* then suddenly yells "Red light!" and turns around.
- If *It* catches anyone moving, that player is out.
- If a player is able to pass the spot where *It* is standing, he becomes *It*.

125. RED ROVER, RED ROVER
C 30 MIN. 1

- Divide into 2 teams.
- Each team lines up side by side, as far apart as possible, but still holding hands and facing the other team.
- To start the game, one team decides who on the opposite team is to come over. Use the name of a player on the team.
- This team starts by yelling, "Red Rover, Red Rover, send Mark on over!"
- The person (Mark) from the opposite team runs toward the other team line and tries to break through the hand-held line.
- If he breaks through, he takes someone with him back to his team line.
- If he is unable to break through, he joins that team.
- Play continues until all the members of one team end up on the opposite team or time is called, in which case the team with the most players wins.

126. RING TOSS
C 30 MIN. 2

- Stand up paper towel and toilet paper rolls and attach them to a thick piece of cardboard with glue and masking tape.
- Cut out the center of several plastic lids to make rings.
- Mark a line to stand behind.
- Try to toss the rings onto a paper roll.

127. BOTTLE MUSIC
C 30 MIN. 1

• Fill glass bottles with different levels of water.
• Tap each bottle to get a different sound.
• Tap out a song.

128. BUBBLE PLAY
C 30 MIN. 1

• Make a mixture of dish soap and water.
• Put the mixture in a large bowl or tray.
• Cut out the center of a plastic lid.
• Dip the lid in the mixture.
• Create bubbles by waving your arm around.
• Other bubble wands can be made from pipe cleaners bent into
  different shapes.

129. FLASHLIGHT TAG
C 45 MIN. 3

• Choose someone to be *It*.
• The person who is *It* tries to tag other players by shining the
  light on them and freezing them.
• Other players can unfreeze a person by touching him.
• If a player is frozen 3 times, he becomes *It*.

130. BALL BOUNCE
C 45 MIN. 1

• Set up several boxes and buckets in a row on a sidewalk or
  driveway.
• Mark a line to stand behind.
• Assign each box and bucket a point value. For example, the
  container farthest from the line would have the greatest
  point value.

- Each person has the same number of tries to bounce a ball into one of the containers.
- The person with the most points wins.

131. CHALK HOUSE
C 45 MIN. 1

- With chalk, draw a large house with different rooms on the patio, driveway, or sidewalk.
- "Move" items into your chalk house, like a chair for the living room and cooking utensils for the kitchen.
- Have fun playing house!

132. PING-PONG TOSS
$ 45 MIN. 2

- Draw different sizes of circles on a piece of poster board, leaving enough room under each circle for a paper or Styrofoam cup.
- The smallest circle should be slightly larger than a Ping-Pong ball.
- Cut out the circles.
- Tape, staple, or glue a cup under each circle.
- Beside each circle write a point value. The smallest circle should have the most value.
- Prop up the board with chairs or books.
- Stand back away from the board and try to throw a Ping-Pong ball in the cup or through a circle.
- If the ball goes in the cup, double the point value.
- Give each player 5 throws.
- The player with the most points wins.

133. EXPLORATION
C 1 HOUR 5

- Explore a big hotel. This is especially fun at Christmastime.
- Ride the elevator to the top floor to the observation deck.
- Ride the escalator.
- Check out the fountains and decorations.

134. BABY ANIMAL EGG
C ONGOING 1

A baby needs constant care.
See if you can take care of this one all day!

- Decide what baby animal you'd like to take care of for a whole day.
- Use markers to decorate a chicken egg to resemble a baby animal.
- Name the baby.
- Put the baby in a small box with a small scrap of fabric or paper towels for a blanket.
- Take care of the baby for a day or longer. Feed it, take it outside, let it nap, and play with it.
- Take it everywhere you go.

ACTIVITIES FOR YOUNGER CHILDREN

EDUCATIONAL PROJECTS

135. POTATO GROWTH
C 15 MIN. 1

- Wedge a potato into a jar that is filled with water. The water should touch the bottom third of the potato.
- If the potato is too small and will fall through into the jar,

poke a few toothpicks into the potato to hold it up.
- Keep a record of the growth of roots and any other changes you see in the potato.
- Try this with an onion and sweet potato.

136. BASIC SHAPES PICTURES
C 30 MIN. 1

- Cut 3" squares from different colors of construction paper.
- Cut some of the squares on the diagonal to form a triangle.
- Arrange the squares and triangles on a 12" x 18" sheet of black construction paper to form various shapes like fish, buildings, or dinosaurs. Use your imagination and see what you can create.

137. MAP PLACE MATS
$$ 30 MIN. 2

These mats make great conversation pieces around the dinner table.
Pick a map of a vacation spot or an area of the world you want to learn more about.

- Cut a 12" x17" piece of newspaper to use as a pattern.
- Lay the pattern on a map and trace around it with black marker.
- Cut out the place mat.
- Make enough for your family and a few guests.
- On the back, near an edge, write the area of the map, for example, Virginia.
- Cover with clear contact paper.

138. TEXTURE PRINTING
C 45 MIN. 3

- Place a piece of white paper over a rough texture, such as concrete, stone, bark, or wood.

- Rub the paper with a crayon in one direction.
- Make several rubbings of different textures.
- At the bottom of each rubbing, write the name of the texture (for example, "concrete") in block letters.
- Make 7 rubbings.
- On each rubbing, write a letter from the word "TEXTURE."
- Cut out the letters and arrange on a 12" x 18" piece of construction paper. The letters can overlap.
- Trace each letter with a black crayon or marker.
- On each letter, write the name of the texture.

139. CANNED GOODS
C 1 HOUR 3

- Cut 5" x 8" sheets of white paper.
- Cut 2" x 5" strips of gray construction paper.
- Round off the corners of the white paper to form a canning jar shape.
- Round off the corners of the gray paper for the canning jar lid.
- Make the sides of the lid 3 different levels or tiers.
- Trace the edge of the lid with black crayon.
- Draw 2 black lines down the center of the length of the lid.
- Cut fruits or vegetables from colored construction paper—for example, green rectangles for green beans—and glue to the jar to "fill" it.
- Place the jar of fruit or vegetables face down on a sheet of plastic wrap. Turn the wrap over the edges of the jar and glue down.
- Glue the lid on the front and top of the jar.
- Write the name of the fruit or vegetable on a small piece of paper and glue to the front center of the canning jar.
- Make enough different jars to create a whole shelf of canned goods.

140. SAFETY RULES POSTER
$ 1 HOUR 1

- Make a list of things you can do to be safe. For example, look both ways before crossing the street, or don't talk to strangers.

- Cut a sheet of poster board in half.
- Write the list of rules in large print near the bottom of the board.
- Draw and color, or paint with tempera paints, a scene illustrating one of the rules. For example, draw a child standing on a street corner, a street, and a car.
- Add details like houses and trees, and maybe a ball in the middle of the street.

141. TEXTURE LIST
C 1 HOUR 1

- Examine objects in your house and make a list of the different textures you find. For example, the glass screen of the TV is smooth, the wall is bumpy, and the countertop is hard.
- See how many different textures you can list.

142. COLOR OF THE DAY
$ 1 HOUR 3

- Pick a color for the day and do things that involve that color. For example, select the color orange.
- For meals, eat things that are the color orange, such as macaroni and cheese, oranges, and carrots.
- Go to the library to get books about color. They could be books on fruits and vegetables, or about animals, such as an orange tiger.
- Draw pictures of things that are orange using colored pencils, watercolors, or crayons. Then, use this artwork as a place mat.
- Make a small book from lined or construction paper by folding the papers in half and stapling on the folded edge.
- Record in your "journal" what fun you had with your "Color of the Day."

143. ALPHABET HUNT
C 1 HOUR 1

- Collect different types of magazines.
- Cut out a picture for each letter of the alphabet. For example, apples for "A," a baby for "B."
- Glue your pictures onto construction paper.
- Print the letter and name of the object under each picture.

144. FIRE SAFETY GLUE PAINT POSTER
C 1 HOUR 2

- Divide a 9" x 12" sheet of white construction paper into 4 equal parts.
- In the upper left corner of each section, write one number, 1–4, in block style.
- Mix 6 teaspoons of glue and 2 teaspoons of black paint, and pour the mixture into a clean glue bottle.
- Trace each number with the black glue.
- Write the following rules by each number: 1) Stop, drop, and roll. 2) Get below the smoke. 3) If a door is hot, don't open it. 4) Know two ways out.
- Illustrate the four rules with your own pictures and symbols, or cut pictures from magazines.
- Paint inside the glue lines of each number with watercolors.
- Hang in your room or on the refrigerator as a good reminder of fire safety.

ACTIVITIES FOR
YOUNGER CHILDREN
FOOD PROJECTS

145. ORANGE SHERBET CUPS
$ 15 MIN. 3

- Cut an orange in half.
- Scoop out the fruit.
- Fill with orange or rainbow sherbet, then freeze.
- Serve as dessert on a hot summer day.

146. FUN-SHAPED SANDWICHES
C 15 MIN. 3

- Use cookie cutters to cut shapes from sandwich bread.
- Make sandwiches with peanut butter and jelly, tuna salad, or your favorite lunch meat.
- Serve the sandwich with fruit and carrot sticks.

147. FANCY ICE CUBES
C 15 MIN. 2

- Fill an ice cube tray half full of water. Drop a few raspberries and a mint leaf in each section of the ice cube tray. Freeze.
- Fill the tray to the top with water. Freeze.
- Serve ice cubes in a cool drink.

148. HAMBURGER COOKIES
$ 15 MIN. 2

- Squeeze a drop of frosting on the bottom of 2 wafer cookies. Gently press a chocolate cookie between the two to form a "hamburger and bun."
- Squeeze squiggly lines of red and yellow frosting along the edge where the buns meet the burger to resemble ketchup and mustard.
- Optional: Before pressing on the top bun, squeeze extra frosting on top of the chocolate cookie around the perimeter and press on some coconut for "lettuce."

149. SOUP BOWL
$ 15 MIN. 2

- Cut off the top of a small round loaf of bread. Be careful to preserve the top.
- Scoop out the bread to create a bowl. Leave about 1" thickness in the bottom and on the sides.
- Fill with soup.
- Cover with the bread lid and serve.

150. FOOTBALL SANDWICHES
C 15 MIN. 1

- Trim 2 pieces of bread into a football shape.
- Place a filling such as peanut butter and jelly or ham and cheese on one slice of bread.
- Top with the second piece of bread.
- Enjoy the sandwich while watching a football game.

151. MINI PIZZA
$$ 15 MIN. 4

This is a great activity for family night or a birthday party.

- Make a batch of pizza dough.
- Divide the dough into 4 equal parts.
- Roll out the dough on a floured surface and place on a greased cookie sheet.
- Form an edge around the dough.
- Top with your favorite ingredients.
- Bake and enjoy.

152. BAGEL PIZZAS
$$ 15 MIN. 4

- Cut mini bagels in half.
- Top each half with pizza sauce, pepperoni, cooked crumbled sausage, olives, shredded cheese, or any other favorite topping.
- Bake at 350° until the cheese melts and the pizza is heated through.
- Enjoy!

153. TRAIL MIX
$$ 15 MIN. 1

- In a bowl, mix a can of nuts, raisins, M & M's, dried fruit, sunflower seeds, and Cheerios.
- Divide into Ziploc-style bags and freeze.
- When going on a hike or a day trip, grab a couple of trail mix bags from the freezer to take along!

154. ANTS ON A LOG
$ 15 MIN. 2

- Wash and cut celery into sticks.
- Soak raisins in water for one-half hour.
- Spread peanut butter in the celery.
- Arrange some raisins on top of the peanut butter.
- Cut into bite-size pieces.
- Enjoy this nutritious snack!

155. SPECIAL PANCAKES
$ 30 MIN. 5

- Make a batch of pancakes.
- For St. Patrick's Day add green food coloring.
- Make special shapes by pouring the batter into greased cookie cutters.

156. FOOD ANIMALS
$ 30 MIN. 2

- Gather different types of food, such as canned fruit, raisins, marshmallows, etc.
- Use your imagination to make an animal or insect with the food by arranging it on a plate. For example, raisins for eyes or dots, half a pear for a body, and a cherry for a nose.
- Eat right away or cover in plastic and serve with dinner or dessert.

157. FROSTED FRUIT
$ 30 MIN. 2

- Brush fruit, such as grapes, oranges, apples, and pears, with egg whites.
- Dip into sugar, covering the whole fruit.
- Arrange on a platter, in a clear crystal bowl, or on a cake stand.

158. HOMEMADE POPSICLES
$ 30 MIN. 2

- Mix a package of your favorite juice or Kool-Aid.
- Pour the liquid into small plastic cups, filling the cups approximately ¾ full.
- Put a piece of masking tape across the top of the cup. Cut a small slit in the middle of the tape to hold a Popsicle stick.
- Insert the stick through the tape and into the liquid, then put the cup in the freezer.
- To remove the homemade Popsicle from the cup, run warm water over the cup.
- Eat and enjoy!

159. COOKIE CUTTER JELL-O
$ 30 MIN. 3

- Make a batch of Jell-O according to the package instructions.
- Clear off a shelf in the refrigerator.
- Place an edged cookie sheet on the shelf.
- Pour the Jell-O carefully onto the cookie sheet.
- Let set.
- Cut the Jell-O into different shapes with cookie cutters.
- Lift the shape off the cookie sheet with a wide spatula, placing a shape on each person's plate.

160. CARAMEL APPLES
$ 45 MIN. 4

- Melt a 14-oz. bag of caramels with 2 tablespoons water.
- Insert a Popsicle stick into each of 4 to 6 apples.
- Finely chop walnuts or almonds and spread out on a cookie sheet.
- Dip each apple in the caramel or spoon it over the apple.
- Roll the apples in the nuts.
- Place on wax paper to cool.

161. DECORATED COOKIES
$ 1 HOUR 4

- Make a batch of sugar cookie dough.
- Roll out the dough.
- Use cookie cutters to cut out shapes.
- Bake the cookies.
- Decorate with frosting, M & M's, and sprinkles.

162. COOKIE ON A STICK
$ 1 HOUR 5

- Make a batch of your favorite cookie dough.
- Place a spoonful of dough on a cookie sheet.
- Stick a Popsicle stick into the dough.
- Bake according to the recipe.
- Dip the top of the cookie into melted chocolate.
- Set on wax paper to cool and harden.
- Enjoy, or give as a gift!

163. INITIAL COOKIE
$ 1 HOUR 5

This is a fun activity to do at a party.

• Make a batch of sugar cookie dough.
• Roll out the dough.
• Let each child draw the first letter of his first name in the dough.
• Cut off any excess dough.
• Bake.
• Let cool.
• Frost and decorate the cookie with sprinkles, M & M's, etc.
• Take the cookie home as a party favor.

164. "FRUIT OF THE SPIRIT" SALAD
$ 1 HOUR 3

• Gather nine different types of fruit.
• Wash and peel as needed.
• Cut in small chunks.
• Mix into a large bowl to create a fruit salad.
• Look up Galatians 5:22–23, for a listing of the "Fruit of the Spirit."
• Assign each fruit one of the characteristics from Galatians 5:22–23. For example, "Peace Peach."
• Look up each characteristic in a concordance or in the back of your Bible, and find another verse that relates to it.
• Write the names and verses on a card, and set the card near the bowl as you serve and enjoy the salad!

165. GRAHAM CRACKER BUILDING
$ 1 HOUR 2

• Make up several batches of frosting, adding food coloring to make different colors.
• Make skyscrapers, buildings, cars, and trains by gluing the graham crackers together with the frosting.
• Add details with raisins, nuts, hard candy, and lifesavers.
• Place the 3-D objects on a plate, heavy cardboard covered with foil, or a cookie sheet for display.

ACTIVITIES FOR YOUNGER CHILDREN
HOLIDAY PROJECTS

VALENTINE'S DAY

166. VALENTINE MAILBOX
C 1 HOUR 1

- Tape the spout of a half-gallon milk carton shut.
- Cut a slit wide enough in the top side of the carton to "mail" valentines.
- Cover the carton with pink or red construction paper.

• Decorate the mailbox with hearts, lace, beads, poems, and Scripture verses about love. Verses could include John 3:16 and Proverbs 17:17.

167. LACE AND MACARONI HEART
$ 1 HOUR 1

Show God's love by giving this Valentine to a very special person in your life.

• Fold a sheet of red paper in half.
• Draw half a heart and cut it out. Make sure to start and end on the fold.
• Glue the heart to a lace paper doily. Trim the heart if it is too big. The lace should be a border around the heart.
• Glue macaroni shapes around the edge of the heart.
• Write a love message in the center of the heart.

MOTHER'S DAY, FATHER'S DAY

168. M & M JAR
$ 15 MIN. 1

• Fill a small clear jar with M & M's.
• Make a list of the colors.
• Beside each color write something you would do for your Mom or Dad. For example, Red—give a hug, Brown—set the table, Blue—take the dog for a walk, etc.
• Give to your parent on Mother's or Father's Day or on his or her birthday.
• When your parent picks an M & M, complete the task, then eat the candy!

169. FATHER'S DAY OR MOTHER'S DAY CARD
C 45 MIN. 1

- Fold a piece of construction paper in half.
- Cut out pictures of family members and pets from photographs.
- Arrange the cutouts on the front of the card and glue down.
- Add any details with markers to make a camping scene, shopping at the mall, or something the special person loves to do.
- Write a message inside.
- Pictures can also be glued on the inside!

170. PARENT'S DAY FLOWERPOT
$ 45 MIN. 1

- Write on a Styrofoam cup, "To Mom:" or "To Dad:", "I love you!"
- Write their favorite verse around the bottom of the cup.
- Decorate the cup with markers.
- Fill the cup half full with potting soil.
- Purchase a flower like a marigold or petunia and place it in the cup.
- Fill in around the flower with more potting soil.
- Water.
- Give to your parent.

171. MOTHER'S DAY VASE
$ 1 HOUR 2

*Surprise your mother with this pretty vase
and fresh flowers!*

- Cover a small section of a vase or glass bottle with glue.
- Place different shapes of macaroni in the glue.
- Let dry.
- Continue gluing on macaroni until the whole vase or bottle is covered.
- Cover with gold spray paint or acrylic paint.

- Let dry.
- Fill with water and add a few fresh flowers.

172. FATHER'S DAY PLACE MAT
C 1 HOUR 1

- Cut a 13" x 17" piece of lightweight cardboard, or a size that would fit on a serving tray.
- Glue photographs of the family, pets, and subjects of special interest on the cardboard.
- Use on the dining table or a tray if serving breakfast in bed.
- This place mat could also be made for Mother's Day or a birthday.

4TH OF JULY

173. FOURTH-OF-JULY SUNDAES
$ 15 MIN. 2

- Cut up bananas and strawberries and place them in a serving bowl.
- Add blueberries.
- Place scoops of vanilla and strawberry ice cream in red or blue bowls.
- Top with the fruit, strawberry topping, and whipped cream.

THANKSGIVING

174. THANKSGIVING CENTERPIECE
C 15 MIN. 3

- Cut off the bottom of an apple or pumpkin so it will sit upright.
- Carve a small hole in the top center.
- Arrange several fall leaves in the apple or pumpkin.

175. MINT AND NUT CUPS
C 30 MIN. 1

- Draw a small turkey on a sheet of tan paper.
- Color the turkey.
- Glue the turkey to the front of a paper muffin cup.
- Place a cup at each seat around the Thanksgiving table.
- Fill the cup with mixed nuts and mints.

176. THANKSGIVING TURKEY
$ 30 MIN. 4

- Cut 3 half circles of different sizes from orange, yellow, and red construction paper.
- Glue them together starting with the largest and ending with the smallest.
- Glue-gun to the large end of a pinecone for feathers.
- Cut a red knobby chenille stem into a 2"–3" piece.
- Curve the stem to form the neck and head.
- Glue-gun into place on the small end of the pinecone.

177. PAPER BAG PUMPKIN
C 45 MIN. 2

- Stuff a brown lunch bag ¾ full with crumpled newspaper.
- Dip a sponge in orange tempera paint and sponge the bag.
- Let dry.
- Tie the top of the bag with green yarn.
- Fray the yarn for hair.
- Fold a 2" x 5" strip of brown paper the long way.
- Stick the brown strip in the top of the bag for a stem.
- Cut 2 medium black triangles and glue to the bag for eyes.
- Cut 2 small yellow circles and glue on top of the triangles.
- Cut a mouth from black construction paper.
- Trace the black mouth onto yellow construction paper and cut out.
- Glue the black mouth to the bag and the yellow mouth on top of the black mouth. Place the yellow mouth so parts of the black mouth show.
- Think of a name for the pumpkin. Write it on a piece of orange construction paper.
- Punch a hole in the name tag and tie it to the pumpkin with yarn.

178. YARN TURKEY
C 1 HOUR 2

- Draw a simple turkey on a piece of medium-weight cardboard.
- Lay a strip of glue along the lines of the drawing.
- Place black yarn in the glue that forms the outline of the turkey and its feathers.
- Spread glue on the turkey and fill with yarn following the shape you are filling in.
- Make each feather a different color of yarn. Brown yarn could be used for the body, black for the legs and feet.
- Spread glue on the cardboard outside the turkey and fill in with blue yarn for the sky and green yarn for the grass.

CHRISTMAS

179. CHRISTMAS BOOKMARK
C 30 MIN. 1

• Cut a 2" x 7" strip of red or green construction paper.
• Trim the edges with either pinking shears or edging scissors.
• Cut a 2" x 6" strip of white paper.
• Write a Christmas phrase on the white paper—something like "Noel," "Joy," or "He Is the Reason for the Season."
• Trace over the writing with a marker or crayon.
• Decorate with small Christmas drawings or pictures cut from old Christmas cards.
•Glue the white strip to the red or green strip.

180. PICTURE ORNAMENT
C 30 MIN. 2

Do you ever wonder what to do with
those very small school pictures?
Make this gift for friends and relatives.

• Cut a small piece of thin cardboard to fit inside a small muffin paper cup holder.
• Cover with foil.
• Trim a picture of yourself to fit on the foil-covered cardboard.
• Glue the picture to the foil.
• Glue to the inside bottom of the paper cup.
• Cut a short length of yarn or ribbon.
• Tape or glue both ends to the back of the paper cup for a hanger.
• Write the year on the back.

181. STAR WISE MEN
C 30 MIN. 1

• Draw a 5-point star on a 9" square of white paper.
• Cut out the star.

- Color the 2 bottom points a flesh color for hands.
- Color the top point as a hat or crown.
- Add a face and clothes.
- Fold the star wise men at the elbows, knees, or feet to show movement.

182. POMANDER BALL
$ 45 MIN. 3

These aromatic balls make attractive
and inexpensive Christmas gifts.

- Take an orange and cover it with whole cloves by inserting them into the skin of the orange. (If it's too hard to push in the cloves with your hand, make holes with a pin or nail, then insert cloves.)
- Attach a ribbon with cloves or glue to make a secure loop for hanging.
- For a spicier smell, put the orange in a Ziploc-style bag with cinnamon, shake, then attach ribbon.

183. POPCORN CHRISTMAS TREES
$ 45 MIN. 4

- Make a batch of caramel corn (recipe in Project 652).
- Let cool slightly.
- Form into the shape of a Christmas tree.
- Push M & M's into the tree for ornaments.
- If you're not going to eat them, sprinkle with glitter.

184. HARD CANDY GARLAND
$$ 45 MIN. 2

- Tie plastic-wrapped hard candy to a green pine garland with curling ribbon.
- Tie the candy close together in bunches or spaced out along the garland.
- Hang the garland around a doorway, mantel, or the Christmas tree.

185. CHRISTMAS CARD HOLDER
$ 1 HOUR 3

- Cover work area with newspaper.
- Paint the inside and outside of a shoe box with white, silver, or gold paint.
- Lay out different macaroni shapes on a sheet of wax paper on top of the newspaper-covered work area.
- Spray paint macaroni with a Christmas color.
- Let dry.
- Turn over macaroni and paint this side and let dry.
- Glue macaroni to the outside of the shoe box.
- Fill with Christmas cards.

186. GIANT HOLIDAY COOKIES
$ 1 HOUR 4

- Draw and cut out a paper pattern of a cross, manger, or present.
- Make a batch of gingerbread cookie dough.
- Roll out the dough.
- Lay the pattern on the cookie dough.
- Cut around the pattern and remove excess dough.
- Transfer the cookie to a cookie sheet.
- Bake the cookies.
- Decorate with different colors of icing.
- Eat or give as a gift.
- To hang as an ornament, cut a hole near the top of the cookie with the end of a straw, then bake. Thread with a ribbon after decorating.

187. PINECONE GARLAND
$ 1 HOUR 2

- Attach miniature pinecones to a long Christmas colored ribbon, string, or cord with thin wire or sewing thread.
- Hang on the Christmas tree, mantel, or doorway.

188. CHRISTMAS ALPHABET
C 1 HOUR 1

- On a 12" x 18" sheet of paper, write half the letters of the alphabet down the left side, spacing the letters evenly. Use block or bubble lettering.
- Write the second half of the alphabet down the center of the paper. There will be 2 columns of letters.
- Beside each letter write a Christmas word. For example, angel, baby, Christ, donkey, etc.
- Draw or cut out pictures from old Christmas cards and glue them beside each word.
- Mount on a 14" x 20" sheet of poster board.

189. COOKIE GARLAND
$ 1 HOUR 4

- Make a batch of sugar cookie dough.
- Roll out the dough and cut cookies with holiday cookie cutters.
- Near the top of each cookie, make 2 holes with a drinking straw.
- Bake cookies according to the recipe.
- Decorate the cookies with frosting.
- String cookies on gold or silver thread.
- Hang on the Christmas tree, mantel, or doorway.

190. KUMQUAT, CRANBERRY, AND NUT GARLAND
$$ 1 HOUR 5

- Using a ⅛" drill, put a hole in each nut.
- String kumquats, cranberries, and nuts in a pattern on a heavy thread.
- Hang on the Christmas tree, mantel, or doorway.

191. NUTTY CHRISTMAS TREE
$$ 1 HOUR 5

• Glue unshelled walnuts, hazelnuts, almonds, Brazil nuts, filberts, and pecans to a Styrofoam cone with a low temperature glue gun.
• The nuts can be glued in a pattern or randomly.
• Start at the bottom and work toward the top of the cone.
• Fill in any gaps with small nuts or ball ornaments.
• Coat with a clear spray sealer.

192. GINGERBREAD HOUSE
$$ 2 HOURS 3

• Cut 4 sides, 2 triangle end roof pieces and 2 roof pieces from cork board.
• Glue together with a glue gun.
• Paint the roof white for snow.
• Paint the house brown.
• Decorate by gluing on different types of hard candy, licorice, rice, etc.
• Save after the Christmas season to use next year.

ACTIVITIES FOR YOUNGER CHILDREN

MISCELLANEOUS PROJECTS

193. INVISIBLE PET
$ 15 MIN. 1

Children have vivid imaginations;
you might be surprised what they can create with this project.

- Cut a 36" length of ribbon.
- Wrap the end of the ribbon around a bouncy ball and secure with tape.
- Name the pet and take him for a walk.

194. KITCHEN MUSIC
C 30 MIN. 1

- Gather things from the kitchen that can be used to make musical sounds. For example, a pot and wooden spoon for a drum, tablespoons, keys, funnels, or a jug to blow across the top.
- Try to play a hymn or a chorus.
- Play for an audience and have them guess the song.
- Have the audience sing along!

195. CRAZY PUTTY
$ 30 MIN. 3

- Mix together equal parts cornstarch and white glue.
- Knead to the consistency you like.
- Sculpt, roll, and pull into fun shapes, or press onto colored comic strips to lift the picture off the page.

196. TERRARIUM
$ 30 MIN. 3

- Place a layer of pebbles in the bottom of a large, clear glass jar, such as a mayonnaise jar.
- Pour in potting soil.
- Dig holes in the soil and plant flowers and plants.
- Gently pack more soil around the plants with a long-handled spoon.
- Water.
- Place the lid on the jar.
- Place in a well-lit area.
- If condensation forms on the glass remove the lid for a while.

197. MUD BRICKS
C 30 MIN. 2

*When the children of Israel were in bondage in Egypt
they had to make mud bricks.
Try this project to help you understand how hard
they worked to make thousands of bricks.*

- In a bucket, mix dirt, water, and straw or dried grass. Don't use too much water.
- Line a shoe box with a plastic bag, taping the bag on the outside of the box.
- Pour the dirt mixture into the shoe box.
- Let the mud-filled box dry in the sun.
- Remove the brick from the box.

198. MULTICOLORED CRAYONS
C 45 MIN. 5

- Peel used crayons and place them in an old, ovenproof pan.
- Heat in a 350° oven for 10–20 minutes.
- Let cool.
- Break into pieces.
- Color with the multicolored crayons.

199. ADOPT A ROADSIDE OR FIELD
C 45 MIN. 5

*This project will keep your community beautiful,
and you'll feel good about helping out.*

- Pick a roadside or field in your neighborhood that you pass by frequently.
- Once or twice a month, pick up any trash in that area.
- Wear gloves to protect your hands.

200. TRAFFIC JAM
C 1 HOUR 1

• Draw roads and signs with chalk on the sidewalk or driveway.
• Drive Matchbox cars or Lego vehicles around your "city."

201. SINK OR SWIM
C 1 HOUR 4

• Fill a sink, bathtub, or small pool with water.
• Gather all kinds of objects that would be okay to get wet. For example, a feather, a bar of soap, toys, and a ball.
• On a piece of paper make 2 columns, and at the top of the columns write, "Sink" and "Swim."
• Test which objects will sink or swim.
• After an object has been tested, write it in the correct column.

202. PSALM 104 NATURE OBSERVATIONS
C 1 HOUR 5

• Read Psalm 104 and make a list of the things God created. For example, verse 2—light and heaven, or verse 18—mountains and animals.
• Take the list and a pencil on a hike, to the ocean, a park, or around your neighborhood.
• Check off the things on the list you see. Write a sentence about each thing you check off.

203. MAGNIFYING GLASS "I SPY"
C 1 HOUR 1

• Walk around your house and yard examining everything you see with a magnifying glass.
• Write down any discoveries. For example, the fabric weave of the couch, the tiny holes in the concrete, or the number of legs on a bug.

204. PLANT A TREE
C 1 HOUR 5

Some public utility companies give away free trees.
They will also give suggestions on where to plant it
to take the best advantage of the shade when it grows tall.

- Dig a deep hole.
- Unwrap the bottom of the tree if needed and place in the hole.
- Fill in with dirt.
- Water.

205. SNAIL'S-EYE VIEW PICTURES
$$ 2 HOURS 4

Taking pictures from this angle will give you
a different perspective.

- Lie down on the ground and take pictures of different objects, people, pets, etc.
- Have the pictures developed.
- You will be surprised at the different views that will show up in your photographs!

206. THEME PHOTO BOOK
$$ 2 HOURS 5

- Take pictures of things that are the same color. For example, a red stop sign, apples, a wheelbarrow, and pizza sauce.
- Have the pictures developed.
- Mount the pictures with corner mounts on heavy paper like watercolor paper.
- Stack the mounted pictures.
- Place a plain sheet of paper on the top and bottom of the stack.
- Staple the pages together at the side or top.
- Write the title of your book on the front cover. If you chose red, you could write, "My Red Photo Book."

207. CRUISIN' CARDBOARD CAR
C 2 HOURS 4

• Find a box big enough to fit around your waist.
• Cut the flaps off the top of the box.
• Turn the box upside down on the floor.
• Cut a square hole in the middle of the bottom of the box. Make the hole big enough to easily stand in and be able to lift it up around your waist.
• Decorate the box like a car with crayons, small paper plates, etc. Make headlights and a grill on one end, and taillights and a license plate on the other end.
• Cut a piece of cardboard for a windshield and tape it in place in front of the square hole.
• Have fun and drive safely!

208. COLLECTIONS
$ ONGOING 1

• Start your own collection. For example, postcards, napkins, bugs, matchbook covers, driftwood, beads, stamps, coins, or keys.
• Display your collection or store it in a box.

209. CHILD'S TIMELINE
C ONGOING 2

• Tape a long piece of white butcher paper to a wall.
• Draw a line down the length of this paper.
• Write important dates, events, and accomplishments on the timeline. Start with the child's birth. Glue a picture of the newborn below the timeline. Draw and color a little picture of the important events.

210. MEMORIAL STONES
C ONGOING 5

In Joshua 4, the Lord told Joshua to gather stones
for a memorial so when the children of the Israelites asked,
"What do these stones mean to you?"
the parents could tell them of the things
the Lord had done for them.

• Whenever there is an answer to prayer, a special provision from the Lord, or victory over sin, add a rock to the pile.
• The pile could be by the mailbox, the front door, or in the corner of a room.
• Write one or two words on the rock that explain the reason for the stone. For example, "sickness healed," "test passed," or "traveled safely."

ACTIVITIES FOR MIDDLER CHILDREN
PAPER PROJECTS

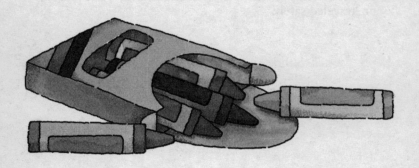

211. THANK YOU, JESUS!
C 15 MIN. 1

- Write a thank-you note to Jesus. Thank Him for all he has done for you. Include all the friends and things He has provided.
- Read the note to your family and Sunday school class.

212. RECORD-KEEPING NOTEBOOK
C 15 MIN. 1

- Fold a 12" x 18" sheet of construction paper in half the long way.
- Unfold and cut the paper in half, following the crease.
- Put a strip of glue down the sides and across the bottom of the 6" x 18" piece.
- Let dry. Turn over, and fold in half.
- Place 10–20 sheets of lined paper in the folder.
- Place a 12" x 18" sheet of construction paper on top.
- Staple down the left side of the notebook, making sure to catch the edges of the lined paper.

213. MISSIONARY PEN PAL
C 15 MIN. 1

- Write a letter to the child of a missionary your church or family supports.
- Tell the child about yourself, family, school, and favorite activities.
- Include a picture of yourself.
- Ask the child to write back and be your pen pal.

214. "TO" AND "FROM" TAGS
C 15 MIN. 1

- Collect used birthday and Christmas cards.
- Cut out the pictures and messages.
- Glue a picture or message to construction paper.
- Write on the paper "To:" and "From:".
- Trim the tag into a square, rectangle, or the shape of the picture or message, leaving a border of $1/4$"– $1/2$".
- Attach the tag to a gift with Scotch tape, or by punching a hole in the tag and tying it on the package with a ribbon.

215. SIMPLE MAT FRAMING
$ 15 MIN. 4

*This matting can be used for any piece of flat artwork
that you would like to frame.*

- Decide how wide the frame border should be. For example, 2".
- Cut a piece of construction paper or mat board 4" wider and longer than the artwork.
- Place the artwork, face down, in the center of the construction paper or mat board.
- Trace around the artwork.
- With a ruler, mark ¼"– ½" around the inside of the traced line.
- Connect the marks with a ruler.
- Lay the construction paper or board on a layer of newspaper.
- Lay a ruler along one inside line and cut with an X-Acto knife. Make the cut deep enough to go through the frame in one cut.
- Cut on all 4 lines.
- Lay the artwork face down on the frame and tape in place.

216. INTERLOCKING CHAIN
C 15 MIN. 3

*Start this chain on January 1,
and add to it throughout the year.
It is fun to keep track of your accomplishments.
Count the loops at the end of the year
to see how much you've done.*

- Cut 2" x 7" strips of different color construction paper or wrapping paper printed on both sides.
- Fold a strip in half, unfold it, and fold each end to the center crease.
- Fold again on the center crease, holding the two flaps in place.
- With the center fold on the left side draw a block style "C", making sure to leave some of the center fold.
- Cut out and unfold.

- Re-fold on the center fold to create double-sided oval.
- Make another loop.
- Thread the second loop through the first O.
- Place a small dot of glue on the right end of the second loop.
- Add a loop or chain every time you memorize a verse or read a book.
- Write the reference or book title on the loop.
- Hang on your bedroom wall.

217. POSITIVE AND NEGATIVE SHAPES
C 30 MIN. 1

- Draw a shape on a 6" x 9" sheet of construction paper.
- Cut out the shape.
- Fold a 9" x 12" sheet of construction paper in half.
- Glue the shape to one side. This is the positive shape.
- Glue the 6" x 9" frame the shape was cut from to the other side. This is the negative shape.
- To use as a card, decorate the front and write a message inside.

218. INDEX POSTCARD
C 30 MIN. 1

- On the front of a plain 3" x 5" index card, draw a picture and write a verse. For example: Draw a peaceful waterfall scene, and write the verse from Isaiah 26:3, "Thou wilt keep him in perfect peace whose mind is stayed on thee."
- On the back left side write a note.
- On the right side write the name and address of the person to whom the card will be sent.

219. GIGANTIC BIRTHDAY CAKE & CARD
$ 30 MIN. 1

The birthday person will really enjoy
receiving and reading this card!

• Draw the shape of a cake and candles on a sheet of poster board.
• Cut out the cake.
• Have each guest write a note and sign his or her name on the card.
• Present the card to the birthday person.

220. GIFT BAG
C 30 MIN. 1

• Trim the top of a brown lunch bag with pinking shears or special-edged scissors.
• Hole-punch several holes as far from the top edge of the bag as possible.
• Decorate the bag with stickers, crayons, markers, and glitter.
• Place a gift in the bag.
• Thread ribbon through the holes and tie the bag closed.

221. TRANSPARENT SNOWFLAKES
C 30 MIN. 4

• Cut 4" x 4" squares of bright tissue paper.
• Trim each square into a circle.
• Fold each circle in half 4 times.
• Trim off the point.
• Cut a small V down the center of the triangle-shaped tissue.
• Cut out shapes down each side.
• Open.
• Place a sheet of wax paper on a layer of newspaper.
• Arrange the snowflakes on top of the wax paper.
• Top with a second sheet of wax paper and a newspaper.
• Iron.
• Let cool.
• Cut around each snowflake.

- Poke a hole in the top and bottom of each snowflake.
- String together with clear thread.
- Hang in a window.

222. RECIPE CARDS
C 30 MIN. 1

- Decorate 3" x 5" index cards with rubber stamps and stickers, or draw your own designs.
- Decorate down one side or make a border all the way around the card.
- Near the top of the card write, "Here's What's Cookin'."
- Underneath write, "From the Kitchen Of:".
- Fill in the cards with your favorite recipes.
- Use the cards with the recipe box in Project #390.

223. GIANT SPORTS POSTER
$ 30 MIN. 1

- Cut out a large picture of your favorite sports figure.
- Glue the picture to a piece of poster board.
- Trim close around the picture.
- Write out the sports figure's name and team on the front.
- Write the statistics on the back.
- Hang or prop up in your room.

224. STUFFED QUILT SQUARES
C 30 MIN. 1

- Cut two 9" x 9" squares of white or newsprint paper.
- Draw a quilt pattern on one square. Color the square.
- Color a calico pattern on the second square. Do not color if using as a wall quilt.
- Glue the 2 squares together, colored sides facing out. Leave part of one side open.
- Stuff the square with small pieces of wadded-up newspaper.
- Glue the opening shut.
- Make a lot of squares and tape to a wall like a quilt.
- Or use one for a doll pillow and bed.

225. BOOK BORDER
C 30 MIN. 1

- Draw a shape on a 9" x 12" sheet of scrap paper. This will be the pattern. The shape could be an animal you love or a sports ball.
- Cut out the shape.
- Every time you read a book, trace the shape on a piece of construction paper and write the book title and author on the shape.
- Cut out the shape.
- Draw a little picture on the shape that illustrates a character or the best part of the book.
- Tape the shapes to your wall as a border or to your room door.

226. WINNER'S CROWN
$ 30 MIN. 3

When a person runs in a race, he runs to receive the prize—
1 Corinthians 9:24–27.
This is the way we should live our lives as Christians.
Paul said in 2 Timothy 4:7 that he had fought the good fight.

- Cut three lengths of raffia to fit around your head. Make the lengths a little longer to allow for braiding and sewing the ends together.
- Braid the raffia.
- Check for fit.
- Sew the ends together.
- Collect different types of leaves and flowers and push them into the braided headband.

227. CARTOON GIFT WRAP
C 30 MIN. 1

- Cut enough black and white cartoon newspaper sections to wrap a gift.
- Color the cartoons with crayons, markers, or colored pencils.
- Wrap the present.

228. WRAPPING PAPER GIFT BAG
$ 30 MIN. 3

- Lay a box on top of a sheet of wrapping paper and trim the paper as you would if you were wrapping the box.
- Fold the top edge of the paper down ½", then fold it down again 1".
- Place the box on the paper so the folded edge is a little below the top of the box.
- Bring the paper up over the sides of the box and tape. Do not tape the paper to the box.
- Wrap the bottom of the box.
- Slide the box out.
- Crease down the sides of the bag by pinching together the 2 top right corners, pushing the side in and creasing.
- Do the same on the left side.
- Cut a piece of cardboard to fit in the bottom of the bag.
- Cover the cardboard with gift wrap and place in the bottom of the bag.
- Hole-punch 2 holes at the top, on the front and back of the bag.
- Cut two lengths of yarn, ribbon, or raffia for handles.
- Place one end of the raffia through the front left hole and knot, then the other end through the right hole and knot.
- Repeat in the back holes.
- Fill the bag with tissue and a gift.

229. FAVORITE CHARACTER BOOKMARK
C 30 MIN. 1

- Cut out a 2" x 6" rectangle from a piece of poster board.
- On the bookmark, draw a favorite character from a book, or cut out magazine pictures that illustrate the story.
- For example, for *Curious George*, cut out a picture of a monkey, palm tree, a man, or anything that would help illustrate the book.
- Cover the bookmark with clear contact paper.

230. LION IN A CAGE
C 30 MIN. 1

*Daniel was thrown into a den of lions because he disobeyed a law,
but God closed the mouths of the lions to keep him safe.
Make this toy to see if a lion is in the cage.*

- Trace a mayonnaise lid twice onto lightweight cardboard.
- Cut out the 2 circles.
- With a hole punch, punch 2 holes in one of the circles, one on each side.
- Place the circle with the holes on top of the second circle and mark the holes with a pencil.
- Punch out the holes of the second circle.
- Draw and color a lion on the front of one circle.
- Draw a cage on the other circle.
- Glue the blank sides of the circles together.
- Tie a string through each hole.
- Twist the strings, then release them to see if the lion is in his cage.

231. CHARACTER MEDAL
C 30 MIN. 1

*Each person has many special gifts from God.
Make a medal to celebrate theirs—and yours!*

- Chose 3 colors of construction paper.
- Cut 3 squares: 5" x 5", 4" x 4", and 2" x 2".
- Fold each square in half and draw a curved line from corner to corner.
- Cut on the curved lines.
- Open each circle and trim off any points.
- Cut a design along the edge of each circle. Use regular scissors to cut out notches or use special scissors like pinking shears.
- Glue the middle-sized circle to the largest circle.
- Glue the smallest circle on top of the middle circle.
- Cut 3 "ribbons" from 2" x 4" pieces of construction paper.
- Trim the edges with scissors.
- Decorate the ends of each ribbon with small circles or flowers

cut from construction paper.
• Write a special character trait on each ribbon. Traits could include Friendly, Loving, Kind, or Generous.
• Award it to the deserving person!

232. POP-UP CARD
C 30 MIN. 1

This idea can be used to make a card for any occasion.

• Fold a 9" x 12" sheet of construction paper in half.
• With the fold on the left, make 2 cuts about 1" apart in the center of the fold. Each cut should be about 1" long.
• While holding the card like a tent, poke the cut part inside the tent.
• Hold the card so the fold is on the top.
• Open the card and the cut part (now on the inside) will pop out.
• Fold a second 9" x 12" sheet of construction paper in half. This sheet can be the same color as the first sheet or another color to complement the first. It will become the outside of the card.
• Open the first piece of cut construction paper.
• Glue the second piece on top of the first piece. Be careful not to glue the cut strip.
• Decorate the card for the occasion you are going to use it for.

233. FAMILY STAND-UPS
$$ 30 MIN. 3

People are very important to God, therefore
our friends and family should take priority in our lives.
In this project you will create a fun way
to show off your family and friends.

• Take pictures of your family and friends doing what they love. For example, playing baseball or soccer, working in the garden, or holding their favorite pet.
• Have the film developed.

- Cut out each person as close to the body as you can.
- Glue the pictures to foam board with rubber cement.
- Cut out the person again with an X-Acto knife.
- Make a stand for each figure by folding a strip of cardboard into a triangle and gluing it to the back.
- Stand up the figures on a table or dresser where they can be enjoyed.

234. PRINTED PAPER BAG
C 30 MIN. 2

Use this bag for lunch, to give a present,
or for the loaves and fishes from Project #483.

- Cut the rim off a small Styrofoam tray.
- Draw a simple fish on the tray.
- Cut out the fish.
- Paint one side of the fish with tempera or acrylic paint.
- Press fish paint side down onto a paper lunch bag. Continue printing until the bag is covered on both sides.

235. BUTTERFLY NAPKIN RING
C 30 MIN. 1

- Cut a 2" x 6" strip of green construction paper.
- Cut three 1" x 2" rectangles of white construction paper.
- Glue a white rectangle to the left end of the green strip.
- Skipping a green section, glue another white rectangle to make green and white checks.
- Bend the green and white strip into a ring and glue, over-lapping the ends.
- Fold a 3" x 3" piece of orange construction paper in half.
- Draw a butterfly wing starting and ending on the fold.
- Cut out the wings.
- Cut a long oval black body and glue in the center of the wings.
- Glue small scraps of triangular yellow construction paper to the wings.
- Glue the butterfly to your napkin ring.

236. BUTTERFLY CUP
C 30 MIN. 1

- Make a butterfly as in Project #235.
- Cut a green strip of construction paper long enough to fit around a glass or cup, then glue on the white squares.
- Bend the strip into a ring and glue, overlapping the ends. Make sure it fits around the glass or cup.
- Glue the butterfly to the ring.
- Place the ring around the cup.

237. STICK PUPPETS
$ 30 MIN. 1

- Use crayons or markers to decorate the top half of a brown lunch bag to look like a character in your favorite story.
- Make several characters.
- Fill each brown bag character with wadded-up pieces of newspaper.
- Insert a stick or dowel into the bottom of the paper bag.
- Gather the open end of the bag around the stick and tie closed with a ribbon.
- The stick will be the handle of the puppet.
- Put on a puppet show for friends and family.

238. WINTER SCENE
C 30 MIN. 1

- Cut pieces of construction paper into shapes of a winter scene, such as a snowman, snowflakes, a bare tree, and children sledding.
- Arrange the shapes on a 9" x 12" piece of blue construction paper.
- Glue the shapes down.
- Draw a line across the paper, a little above the bottom of the shapes, for the ground.
- Color from the line to the bottom of the paper with a white crayon.

239. SPRING SCENE
C 30 MIN. 1

- Cut pieces of construction paper into shapes of a spring scene, such as grass, a tree with buds or very small leaves, spring tulips, and baby rabbits and chicks.
- Arrange the shapes on a 9" x 12" piece of blue construction paper.
- Glue the shapes down.

240. SUMMER SCENE
C 30 MIN. 1

- Cut pieces of construction paper into shapes of a summer scene, such as a tree, children on bikes, a sun, grass, and a bee.
- Arrange the shapes on a 9" x 12" piece of blue construction paper.
- Glue the shapes down.

241. FALL SCENE
C 30 MIN. 1

- Cut pieces of construction paper into shapes of a fall scene, such as a tree with colorful leaves, leaves on the ground, and a pumpkin.
- Arrange the shapes on a 9"x 12" piece of blue construction paper.
- Glue the shapes down.

242. FOUR SEASONS POSTER
C 30 MIN. 1

- Arrange the four season scenes from Projects #238, #239, #240, and #241 on a large piece of poster board, leaving room at the bottom for a Bible verse.
- Glue the scenes down.

- Cut out letters from newspaper print to form the verse: Daniel 2:21, "And he changes the times and the seasons."
- Hang the poster.

243. "REMEMBER THE MISSIONARIES" FAN
C 30 MIN. 2

- Fold a 6" x 9" piece of construction paper in half.
- Cut in half along the fold.
- Draw a circle on one piece of paper.
- Holding the 2 pieces of construction paper together, cut out the circle.
- Holding both circles together, make fringe cuts about 1" long around the edge.
- In the center of one circle, put a strip of glue about one inch long.
- Lay a Popsicle stick in the glue.
- Put another strip of glue on the stick starting at the top and going about one inch.
- Put a few dots of glue on the circle inside the fringe lines.
- Lay the second circle on top of the first circle and stick.
- Let dry.
- Glue a picture of a missionary on the front and back.
- Let dry.
- Fold up every other piece of fringe and fan yourself.
- Remember to pray for the missionaries!

244. "GO" TRAFFIC SIGN
$ 30 MIN. 2

- Cut a 22" x 28" piece of white poster board in half.
- Draw a circle on one piece of board using as much of the board as possible.
- Cut out the circle.
- Cut a circle from green construction paper. Make this circle a little smaller than the white circle.
- Glue the green circle on top of the white circle.
- Cut, from black construction paper, the word "GO" in large letters.

- Glue the letters to the center of the green circle.
- On the back, write out the "Great Commission," found in Matthew 28:19–20.
- Hang the sign.

245. SHADED LEAVES
C 30 MIN. 1

- Lay several leaves on an orange piece of construction paper.
- Trace around each leaf with a pencil. Leaves can overlap.
- Trace over the pencil lines with fall color crayons. The lines should be thick and applied heavily.
- With an eraser, pull out the color of the line into the center of the leaf. This will create a shaded effect.
- Shake off any eraser crumbs.
- Draw veins with a crayon or marker.

246. FLAG OF ISRAEL
C 30 MIN. 1

The Israelites were God's chosen people, and in 1948,
they became a nation.
Make a flag to celebrate their nationhood.

- Cut 2 strips of blue construction paper.
- Glue to a 9" x 12" sheet of white paper, keeping one strip 1" from the top and the other 1" from the bottom.
- Cut 2 blue triangles about 2" x 3".
- Draw a triangle in the center of each blue triangle and cut out the middle triangle.
- Glue the triangles, with the center cut out, to the middle of the white background (one triangle glued inverted on top of the other).
- For an example, look up the flag in an encyclopedia.

247. WORD-SHAPED CARD
C 30 MIN. 1

This card can be used for almost any occasion.

- Fold a 9" x 12" sheet of construction paper in half, then in half again.
- Fold the top down to the bottom.
- Fold again taking the left side to the right.
- Open the card, and with a pencil, lightly draw an outline of a shape. For example, a cross for an Easter card, or a bell for a Christmas card.
- Write a message inside the shape, being careful not to go outside the pencil line. The words will need to be divided to fit inside the shape.
- Decorate the front of the card with crayon, marker, and construction paper.

248. DOT-TO-DOT LETTER
C 30 MIN. 1

- On a piece of scrap paper, print a short note to a teacher, grandparent, or friend.
- Place a piece of lined paper on the note and copy, making each letter in dot-to-dot form. Make sure to leave a space between each word.
- Send with another short note (in normal handwriting) explaining that the dots need to be connected to form letters and words.
- Connect some dots to form a few letters or a word to get them started.

249. SERVICE COUPONS
C 30 MIN. 1

- On index cards, write something nice you can do for your teacher, baseball coach, Sunday school teacher, or club leader.
- Service activities might include passing out papers, cleaning up, or loading baseball gear on the bus.

- Decorate each coupon with markers and stickers.
- Give it to the person to redeem.

250. JOKE CARD
C 30 MIN. 1

Everyone needs to laugh!
Send one of these cards to someone special in your life—
or someone in the hospital,
or someone celebrating a special day—
to put a smile on his or her face.

- Check out a joke book from the library.
- Pick out 3 to 5 jokes.
- Fold a 9" x 12" sheet of white construction paper in half.
- Divide the front into rectangles with a crayon or marker—one rectangle for each joke.
- Write a number in the top left corner of each section.
- Write a message, such as "Have a Great Day," on the inside right of the card.
- Write the first part of the joke in a section on the front of the card.
- Divide the inside left of the card like the front of the card and number the same way.
- Write the punch line of each joke in the corresponding section of the inside left of the card.

251. NO LONGER BLIND
C 30 MIN. 2

- Cut out a large picture of a man's or woman's face from an old catalog or magazine.
- Glue it to a sheet of construction paper, leaving about 2" at the bottom.
- Cut out 2 black construction paper circles or ovals a little bigger than the eyes of the person.
- Place one black shape over an eye, and with a paper fastener, poke a small hole through the papers, at the left edge of the left eye.

- Press down the prongs of the fastener on the back side.
- Cover the other eye, poking the hole at the right edge.
- At the bottom, write, "One thing I do know, once I was blind but now I see!"
- Move the eye shades to reveal a person who has accepted Christ and is no longer blind.

252. ARK ANIMAL STORY
C 30 MIN. 1

- Pretend that you were an animal on Noah's ark.
- Write a journal entry about your experience.
- Include emotions you felt, the smells, the rain, what you ate, who closed the door, etc.

253. LINE DESIGN
C 45 MIN. 1

- Draw lines with a ruler at different angles from the top to the bottom of a 9" x 12" sheet of white construction paper.
- Draw a second set of lines from side to side.
- Color in the shapes created by the lines. Only color the shapes that touch at the corners, not shapes that share a side.

254. CURSIVE COLOR
C 45 MIN. 1

- Fold an 8½" x 11" sheet of white construction paper in half the long way. Open the paper.
- Write your name, or a special phrase like "Merry Christmas," in the center of the top half of the paper.
- Trace over the word in heavy black crayon.
- Trace around the word(s) 4 or 5 times with a black crayon, following the shape of the letters.
- Color each ring around the words a different color. Make sure each ring has a heavy color.
- Fold the paper in half with the design on the inside.

- Rub over the colored portion with the back of a spoon. The design will transfer to the bottom half of the paper.

255. HOLE PUNCH PICTURE
C 45 MIN. 1

- Using a hole punch, punch out several dots from construction paper.
- Arrange the dots into a scene on a 9" x 12" sheet of construction paper. Make a flower garden, geometric design, or use your imagination.
- Glue down the dots by spreading an area with glue and laying the dots in the glue.
- Add any details needed with crayon, marker, or colored pencil.

256. TORN PAPER CORNUCOPIA
C 45 MIN. 1

- Draw a horn of plenty on a 9" x 12" sheet of tan or brown construction paper.
- Tear out the horn and lay it on a 12" x 18" sheet of orange construction paper.
- Draw fruits, vegetables, and nuts on colored construction paper.
- Tear them out.
- Arrange the food at the wide end of the horn of plenty. The food can overlap.
- Glue down the horn and food.
- Trace around the horn and food with the same color of crayon that the object is.
- Around the edge, print the verse from Philippians 4:19.

257. FLOWER VERSE CARDS
C 45 MIN. 1

• Cut 2" x 4" rectangles of spring-colored construction paper.
• Draw a flower on a 2" x 2" square of the colored construction paper.
• Cut out the flower.
• Cut out a small circle and glue to the center of the flower.
• Glue a flower to the left end of each 2" x 4" rectangle so the flower is part way off the edge of the card.
• Make several flower cards.
• Write a reference on each card for a verse that is about life. For example, Psalm 103:4, Matthew 6:25, John 3:16, John 6:35, John 15:13, Isaiah 40:31, and 2 Corinthians 5:17.
• Place the verse cards in the May Day Basket in Project #854.
• During dinner, pick a verse card from the basket, look it up, and read it out loud.

258. GIFT CONE
$ 45 MIN. 2

• Bend a small piece of poster board into a cone shape.
• Staple or tape closed.
• Decorate the cone with crayons, markers, glitter, sequins, and beads.
• Place a gift inside the cone.
• Cut long strips of 2"-wide tissue paper and glue across the opening of the cone. Trim off any extra length.
• Glue strips in the opposite direction, weaving them through the first set of strips.
• The receiver of the gift may open the cone by tearing the woven tissue paper away to reveal the gift.
• The cone can be used again by adding new tissue strips.

259. WIND SOCK
C 45 MIN. 2

- Draw a design on a 12" x 18" sheet of construction paper.
- Cut out the design with scissors or an X-Acto knife.
- Roll the paper into a tube and glue or staple.
- Hole-punch 2 holes at the top on opposite sides.
- Thread a long piece of yarn through the holes and tie the ends together.
- Cut 1" x 18" strips of tissue paper.
- Glue the strips around the inside bottom of the construction paper tube.
- Hang in the wind.

260. INDIAN HEADBAND
C 45 MIN. 1

- Cut a strip of 6" x 18" construction paper.
- Fit the strip around your head, adding about ½".
- If it is not long enough, glue 2 strips together.
- Draw and color Indian designs on the headband.
- Draw feathers on different colors of construction paper.
- Cut out the feathers.
- Draw a line down the center of each feather and diagonal lines from the center line up to the edge of the feather.
- Glue the feathers to the back of the headband. Make sure the feathers are placed so the vein lines face out.
- Staple the ends of the headband together.

261. FISH BOWL
C 45 MIN. 1

- Draw a fish bowl on a 9" x 12" sheet of light blue construction paper.
- Cut out the bowl.
- Outline this bowl with a blue crayon.
- Draw a line across the bowl ½" from the top and bottom.
- Draw 4 or 5 strands of seaweed in the bowl.
- Trace the seaweed with 2 different colors of green crayon.

- Draw small dots across the bottom of the bowl, with bright crayons, for rocks.
- Draw a fish on a 2½" x 3" piece of orange construction paper.
- Cut out the fish, outlining and adding details to it with a black crayon.
- Make one or two smaller fish.
- Glue the fish on the bowl.
- Outline the bowl with a thin strip of glue.
- Lay a sheet of plastic wrap over the bowl and press it into the glue.
- Let dry.
- Trim off the excess plastic wrap.

262. RUBBER STAMP DOOR GARLAND
$ 45 MIN. 2

- Cut a 24" length of ribbon.
- Ink a rubber stamp such as a scarecrow, angel, or an animal.
- Stamp onto stiff paper.
- Color in the stamped figure if needed.
- Cut out each figure.
- Tape the back of each figure to the ribbon, spacing them evenly apart.
- Tape to your room door.

263. INDIAN TEPEE
C 45 MIN. 1

- Cut a square of white or tan construction paper. The larger the square the larger the tepee will be.
- Draw a half-circle from the bottom left corner to the bottom right corner.
- Cut out the tepee.
- Decorate the tepee with Indian designs. The straight edge will be the top of the tepee.
- Paint with tempera paint or color the designs.
- Holding the tepee so the curved edge is down, fold the ends together to create a tepee shape.
- Staple.

• Cut tepee poles from brown construction paper and glue them to the inside top of the tepee so they stick out through the top.
• Make a whole village, or use as place cards.

264. KEY TO MY HEART
$ 45 MIN. 3

• Draw a large antique key on a piece of poster board. Use a picture as a drawing reference.
• Cut out the key with scissors and an X-Acto knife.
• In fancy letters, write, "Here's the key to my heart," and your name.
• Give to a parent on a special day.

265. SEE-THROUGH BIRTHDAY CARD
C 45 MIN. 2

• Fold a 9" x 12" sheet of construction paper in half.
• Open the card and draw several rectangles and squares, to represent presents, on the front.
• Cut out the shapes with an X-Acto knife or small scissors.
• Close the card and trace each present with a pencil onto the inside of the card.
• Cut tissue or construction paper a little bigger than the traced presents.
• Glue to the traced presents on the inside of the card.
• Draw bows on the outside and inside presents.
• Write "Happy Birthday" and a message on the card.

266. RELIEF CARD
C 45 MIN. 1

• Fold a piece of construction paper in half.
• Draw a design on the front. For example, big birthday candles.
• Trace the design with glue.

• Place yarn in the glue.
• Decorate and write a message on the inside of the card.

267. MENU CARD
C 45 MIN. 1

• With a pencil and using "fancy" lettering, write a menu on a
    4" x 5" piece of white paper.
• Trace over the lettering with a marker or colored pencils.
• Carefully erase any pencil marks.
• Mount the menu on a 5" x 6" piece of construction paper.
• Trim the edges with special-edged scissors.

268. THANK-YOU NOTE
C 45 MIN. 1

• Fold a 5" x 7" piece of construction paper in half.
• With the fold at the top, write, "Thank You" in fancy letters.
    Or, spell the words with alphabet stickers or letters cut from
    magazines or newspapers.
• Write a thank-you message inside.
• Sign your name and give or mail it to someone special.

269. CARBON PAPER PRINT
$ 45 MIN. 2

• Cut several sizes of hearts from lightweight cardboard.
• Build a press by placing a 9" x 12" piece of cardboard on a
    work surface.
• Arrange the hearts on the cardboard.
• Place a piece of carbon paper, carbon side up, on the hearts.
• Place a 9" x 12" sheet of white paper on the carbon paper.
• Rub the top sheet of white paper with the back of a spoon or
    roll it with a rolling pin. Make sure to press down hard.
• Remove the top sheet to view the heart transfers.
• In the blank spaces around the hearts or around the edge,
    write, "No one ever cared for me like Jesus."

270. SPRING TULIP CHALK DRAWING
C 45 MIN. 1

• With a pencil, draw different-sized tulips on a 9" x 12" sheet of black construction paper. Make the body of a tulip by drawing the letter U with a W across the top, connecting with the top of the U.
• Shade in each tulip with chalk.
• Draw a long green stem from each tulip to the bottom of the paper.
• Draw blades of grass along the bottom of the picture.
• Shade in blue sky, making sure to shade from the top of the paper all the way into the grass.
• Smooth the chalk with your fingers.
• Spray with hair spray to make the chalk adhere.

271. HAND FAN
C 45 MIN. 1

• Draw a fan shape on a 9" x 12" piece of lightweight cardboard.
• Cut out.
• Decorate by gluing pictures on both sides.
• Staple or glue a wooden tongue depressor or large Popsicle stick to one side of the fan.

272. PICTURE FRAME
C 45 MIN. 3

• Choose 3 pictures that are the same size or can be trimmed to the same size.
• Multiply the length of one picture by 3. For example: If each picture is 5" long, then 5" x 3" = 15".
• Do the same for the width.
• Add 2 inches to the length and the width.
• Cut 2 strips of construction paper the width and length measured.
• Lay the pictures on the strip of paper so they are evenly spaced.

- Trace around the pictures with a pencil.
- Cut ¼" inside each traced space. (This opening will be a little smaller than the picture.)
- Tape the pictures face down on the side where the pencil lines are.
- Glue on the back of the picture strip around the edges.
- Decorate the front of the frame with small shapes or dots punched with a hole punch.
- Fold the frame between the first and second picture and the second and third picture so it will stand up.

273. TISSUE PAPER BANNERS
$ 45 MIN. 2

These colorful banners can be used to decorate a room for a birthday, graduation, or a celebration of answered prayer.

- Fold tissue paper several times.
- Cut out shapes on the folds.
- Unfold.
- Make several banners.
- Fold down the top of each banner about ½".
- Unfold top.
- Cut string long enough to hold all the banners.
- Fold the top of the banner over the string and glue it down.
- Mount other banners along the string.
- Hang and enjoy!

274. CRAYON ETCHING
C 45 MIN. 1

- Using old crayons, cover a 9" x 12" piece of white paper with thick stripes.
- Polish with a tissue or paper towel.
- Color the whole striped paper with a thick coat of black crayon.
- Polish.
- With a nail or paper clip, scratch a design through the black

coat of crayon. The colors underneath will show through. A design could include a fish scene, flower garden, or different geometric shapes.

275. BUTTERFLY PLACE MAT
C 45 MIN. 1

• Starting in the upper left corner, glue a 1" x 1" square of white construction paper to a 12" x 18" piece of green construc-tion paper. Skip an inch of green and glue another white square.
• Continue gluing on white squares around the edges to create a checked border.
• Draw and color different sizes of butterflies on white con-struction paper.
• Cut out.
• Glue the butterflies to the green place mat.
• Use and enjoy at your kitchen table!

276. CARD BY THE YARD
C 45 MIN. 1

This could be made for any occasion.
A sick child would especially like this card!

• Cut a 9" x 12" piece of white paper into strips, 3" wide and 12" long.
• Glue the strips together, overlapping the edges about ¼".
• Decorate the strips starting at the left end with stickers, drawings, pictures, and words cut from old catalogs and magazines. You could also use rubber stamps.
• Sign the card at the right end of the strip.
• Roll the card starting at the right, or signed, end of the card.
• Tie with a pretty ribbon.

277. RAINY DAY NOAH'S ARK SCENE
$ 45 MIN. 1

- Brush water over a piece of heavy watercolor paper or art board.
- With chalk, draw a Noah's ark scene. Include Noah and his family, the ark, animals, and raindrops. If the paper dries, re-wet it.
- Let dry.
- Set the chalk by spraying the paper with hair spray.

278. GIFT CARDS
$ 45 MIN. 2

*These cards can be made for missionaries
to give to their native friends.*

- Make a card by folding a piece of 6" x 7" white paper in half to fit inside a small envelope.
- Decorate the outside of the card with crayons or watercolors. Cards could be decorated for special holidays like Christmas or Easter.
- Cut a piece of 2" x 4" felt.
- Put a strip of glue along the 2" side of the felt and glue it to the inside of the card.
- Let dry.
- Stick a few needles, pins, and safety pins through the felt.
- Give to the missionaries that visit your church or mail to the missionaries on the field. The missionary can write his or her own greeting on the inside of the card across from the needles and pins.

279. AN INVITATION
C 45 MIN. 1

- Fold a 12" x 18" piece of dark construction paper in half, then in half again.
- Draw a wavy design along the edges that are not folded.
- Cut out the design and open.

- Glue to a 12" x 18" sheet of light-colored construction paper.
- Write an invitation from Jesus in the center. For example, "Jesus invites you to . . . 'Come to Me all who are weary and heavy-laden, and I will give you rest.' Matthew 11:28 NASB."

280. CITYSCAPE
C 45 MIN. 1

- On a piece of classified newspaper, draw several sizes of buildings.
- Cut out the buildings.
- Glue to a 12" x 18" piece of black construction paper.
- Cut different sizes of windows from black and yellow construction paper.
- Glue the windows to the buildings.
- Draw doors in each building or use black or yellow paper and glue on the doors.
- Draw stars and a moon in the night sky with yellow or white crayons.
- Add any other details like a street lamp, fire hydrant, or road.

281. PRAYING HANDS
C 45 MIN. 2

- Fold a piece of construction paper in half. Trace your hand on the paper. (Fingers should be together, not spread out.)
- Cut out the hands.
- Glue the hands together.
- Draw lines to form fingers and thumb on each side of the hand.
- Write on each finger on one side, "ADORATION, CONFESSION, THANKSGIVING, SUPPLICATION."
- Write "1 Thessalonians 5:17: Pray without ceasing" on the opposite side in the middle of the hand.
- On the same side, write on the fingers people to pray for, such as relatives, the president, missionaries, etc.
- To make a stand for the hand, fold a strip of construction paper into a triangle and glue it together.
- Cut a slit in the top of the triangle. Insert the praying hands.

282. YIELD SIGN
$ 45 MIN. 2

- Cut a triangle from a piece of yellow poster board.
- Lay the triangle inverted so one point is down and the other two points are at the top.
- Round off the points with scissors.
- Cut out the word "YIELD" from black construction paper.
- Arrange the word "YIELD" on the poster board.
- Glue the word onto the board.
- On the back, write this verse of the hymn "Yield Not to Temptation": "Yield not to temptation, for yielding is sin. Each victory will help you some others to win. Fight manfully onward, dark passions subdue. Look ever to Jesus, He'll carry you through."

283. WILD ANIMAL PARK
C 45 MIN. 1

Silhouettes do not have to be cut from black and white paper. In this project, choose the colors that work well together.

- Cut out pictures of wild animals. Cut close to the subject so there is no background.
- Lay the cutout on a sheet of construction paper and trace.
- Cut out the construction paper animal.
- Arrange the animals on a 9" x 12" sheet of construction paper.
- Add other silhouettes like a moon and grass.
- Glue the silhouettes to the paper.

284. FALL REFLECTIONS
C 45 MIN. 1

- Fold a 12" x 18" sheet of light blue paper in half the long way.
- Open the paper and draw a fall scene just above the fold on the top half of the paper. The scene could include colorful fall trees, a barn, a fence, and pumpkins. Apply the crayon in a heavy layer.
- Fold the paper in half on the center fold so the crayon picture is on the inside.

- Rub the back of the crayon side with the handle of a pair of scissors or the back of a spoon.
- Open the paper to see the reflection transferred to the bottom of the paper.
- If needed, touch-up the top scene.

285. DOT-TO-DOT DRAWING
C 45 MIN. 1

- Cover a picture from a coloring book with a thin sheet of white paper. Pick a simple picture to start with.
- Make sure the coloring-book picture shows through.
- Tape around the edges so the white paper will stay in place.
- Place dots evenly along the lines of the picture on the white sheet.
- Number the dots.
- Remove the tape and send the dot-covered paper to a friend, or follow the dots yourself!

286. DINOSAUR HABITAT
C 45 MIN. 1

- Check out a book from the library about dinosaurs.
- Construct a dinosaur by cutting shapes from construction paper and gluing them to a 12" x 18" piece of paper.
- Use triangles for spikes, ovals for the body, brown triangles for background mountains, etc.
- Construct several dinosaurs and overlap them on the background paper. This will give your scene perspective and depth.
- Add details, like eyes, with crayons or markers.

287. HAPPY BIRTHDAY PUZZLE
C 45 MIN. 1

- Use crayons, glue, and glitter to decorate a 6" x 9" sheet of construction paper with the words, "Happy Birthday," a cake with the correct number of candles, and the person's name.

- Sign your name.
- Cut the paper into 9–12 puzzle shapes.
- Place in an envelope and give to the birthday person.

288. SNOWFLAKE PRINTS
C 45 MIN. 2

Psalm 139:14 states, "I will praise thee,
for I am fearfully and wonderfully made.
Marvellous are thy works."
Just as there are no two snowflakes exactly alike,
there is no one like you. You are special and unique.
Remember this as you make this project.

- Cut several sizes of construction paper circles.
- Fold each circle in half, then in half again.
- Cut out shapes on the folds.
- Open the snowflakes and coat one side with glue.
- Lay the snowflakes, glue side down, on a sheet of dark blue or black construction paper.
- Lift off the snowflakes.
- Sprinkle a mixture of powdered and white sugar onto the glue.
- Let dry.
- Shake off the excess sugar.
- Write "Psalm 139:14" down the side in white crayon.

289. SIN-BEARING CROSS
C 45 MIN. 1

- Draw a cross on a 6" x 9" sheet of red construction paper.
- Draw a hill on a 4" x 12" sheet of brown construction paper.
- Tear out the cross and hill.
- Glue the hill to the bottom of a 9 x 12" sheet of white construction paper.
- Glue the cross on the hill.

- Across the top, write, "My sin is nailed to the cross, and I bear it no more."
- On small strips of paper, write different sins.
- Place a small dot of glue on one end of each strip and glue it to the cross.

290. FOIL MIRROR
C 45 MIN. 1

- Draw a large mirror with a handle on a 9" x 12" sheet of construction paper.
- Trace it onto a second piece of construction paper and cut out.
- Cut out the glass area, leaving a 1" border.
- Cut a piece of foil a little larger than the hole. Glue to the top of the frame with the hole.
- Glue the second frame on top of the frame with the foil.
- On one side, on the handle and around the mirror, write "James 1:23–24" and on the other side write "1 Corinthians 13:12."

291. DAY AND NIGHT
C 45 MIN. 1

- Glue a 9" x 12" sheet of black construction paper to the right side of a 12" x 18" sheet of white construction paper.
- Cut out a sun from yellow construction paper.
- Glue the sun to the top left corner on the white side.
- Cut out a crescent moon and stars from white paper.
- Arrange on the black side and glue down.
- Glue down the stars and moon.
- On the white side, write "I love the law of the Lord and meditate on it day and night."

292. TRAVEL POSTER
$ 1 HOUR 1

- Write "Go ye therefore into all the world. . ." in block letters

on one end of a large piece of poster board.
• Cut out pictures of different places and people of the world.
• Cut out a picture of a globe.
• Arrange the pictures on the poster board.
• Glue the pictures to the poster.
• Color in the words or fill them in with a pattern.
• Hang in a Sunday school room or at home.

293. COLLAGE
C 1 HOUR 1

• Hunt around the house and yard for different textures that
  would make a good rubbing.
• Make a rubbing page by placing a sheet of paper on the object
  and rubbing it with a crayon. Bark, cement, brick, and coins
  make great rubbings.
• Tear each rubbing into a square or rectangle.
• Arrange the rubbings on a 9" x 12" sheet of construction
  paper. Rubbings can overlap or be arranged in rows.
• Glue down the rubbings.

294. PAPER FLOWER VASE
C 1 HOUR 1

• Cut flower shapes from different colors of construction paper.
• Cut stems from green construction paper.
• Glue the stems to the flowers.
• Roll a 9" x 12" piece of construction paper into a cone and
  staple.
• Place the flowers in the vase. If the flowers are too short, glue
  them to the inside of the vase so they stick out the top.

295. EARLY AMERICAN SAMPLER
C 1 HOUR 1

• Lightly draw a border of X's with a pencil around the edge of
  a 9" x 12" sheet of white construction paper.

- Print the alphabet at the top of the paper. Space the letters evenly in several rows.
- Under the letters, in the center, draw a house.
- Draw a heart on each side of the house.
- Under the house, print your name and the date.
- Near the name draw a flag.
- Over the alphabet, name, and date, with sharpened crayons or colored pencils, draw X's.
- Color in the pictures.
- Fill in more X's by the name, date, under the flag, and under the alphabet.

296. CHALK VERSE
C 1 HOUR 1

- Choose a favorite verse. For example, 1 John 1:9, James 1:5, Hebrews 4:12, or Psalm 130:3–4.
- On a sheet of scrap paper, write out the verse in different ways. Emphasize some words by making them big, little, or space out the words in different ways.
- On a sheet of black construction paper, write out the verse like your favorite practice one. Draw some words with fat or skinny letters. (The size of the paper will depend on the length of the verse.)
- Trace each word with a different color chalk using bright colors like yellow, green, blue, red, and orange.
- Color in the fat letters.
- Make a border around the edge of the black paper. Draw X's, hearts, or triangles.
- Spray the drawing with hair spray to adhere the chalk.

297. MILK CARTON CHURCH BANK
C 1 HOUR 2

- Tape the opening of a half-pint milk carton shut.
- Cover the sides of the carton with construction paper.
- Cover the roof with black construction paper.
- Cut a slit through one side of the roof to make a bank.
- Draw and color windows, a door, and flowers around the bot-

tom of the carton.
- Glue 2 pieces of Popsicle sticks into a cross and glue it onto the church.
- Save money for a special church project or for a missionary.

298. FAMILY MONEY
$ 1 HOUR 2

- Cut pieces of 2" x 6" construction paper.
- Photocopy small pictures of yourself and your family.
- Cut the pictures into ovals or squares.
- Glue a picture in the center of each bill.
- Decorate each bill with crayons, colored pencils, or markers.
- Add details like the dollar amount, a picture on the back, "In God We Trust," and the bill's origin.

299. THE HISTORY OF ME
C 1 HOUR 1

- Write your first name in big, fat letters on a 12" x 18" sheet of white construction paper. The letters need to connect to each other.
- Cut out the name.
- Write things about you on your name. For example, the sports you like, pets' names, your favorite foods, etc.
- Draw and color little pictures beside each word.
- Lay it on a newspaper and trace around the letters with a marker.
- Hang on your bedroom wall.

300. HEAVENLY SIGNALS
C 1 HOUR 3

- With a white crayon, draw an outline of a stoplight on a 12" x 18" sheet of black construction paper.
- Cut out the stoplight.
- Draw a circle on a 4" x 4" square of green construction paper.

- Cut out the circle.
- Trace the green circle on a 4" x 4" sheet of yellow and red construction paper.
- Cut out the circles.
- Glue the circles to the stoplight with red at the top, yellow in the middle, and green at the bottom.
- In the yellow circle, write, "Streets of Gold—Revelation 21:21."
- In the red circle, write, "Blood of Jesus—Ephesians 1:7."
- In the green circle, write "Grow in Knowledge—2 Peter 3:18."

301. SCRATCH LAMP PICTURE
C 1 HOUR 1

- Cover the top third of a 9" x 12" sheet of white paper with red, yellow, and orange stripes of thick crayon.
- Cover the middle third of the paper with a thick layer of gold or silver crayon.
- Cover the bottom third with orange crayon.
- Cover the whole paper with 2 thick layers of black crayon.
- Scratch out an Aladdin-type lamp in the middle third area.
- Scratch beams of light from the lamp to the top of the paper.
- Scratch out the verse Psalm 119:105 at the bottom.
- Glue the picture to an 11" x 13" sheet of red construction paper.

302. OWL PRINT
C 1 HOUR 4

- Draw a tree trunk and branch on a 12" x 18" sheet of blue construction paper. The trunk should be placed on the left and go from the top to the bottom of the page. Place the branch in the lower third of the paper.
- Color an owl on the rough side of a 3" x 5" piece of sandpaper. Put on the color in a heavy layer.
- Lay the blue paper on several layers of newspaper.
- Put the sandpaper owl face down so the owl is sitting on the branch.
- Cover the sandpaper with a sheet of newspaper.

- Iron the sandpaper so the crayon melts onto the blue construction paper.
- Re-color the owl and print again.
- Print 2 or 3 owls.
- Color a leaf on the rough side of a 1" x 2" piece of sandpaper.
- Print lots of leaves in the same way the owl was printed.

303. BUTTERMILK AND CHALK SCENE
$ 1 HOUR 2

- Using a pencil on a 12" x 18" sheet of thick white paper, lightly draw the scene from John 6:16–21, about Jesus' walking on the water. Watercolor paper works well with this.
- Do not make the boat and Jesus too small. Fill the paper with large shapes.
- Brush the paper with a thin coat of buttermilk.
- Let dry.
- Color the picture with chalk. The color of the chalk will be brighter because of the buttermilk.
- Write "It is I, do not be afraid!" in the top right corner. Smooth out the chalk with Kleenex or your finger.
- Spray with hair spray to make the chalk adhere.

304. GOOD BEHAVIOR CHART
C 1 HOUR 1

- Write your name in bubble letters across the top of a 6" x 9" sheet of construction paper.
- Fill in each letter with a different color and pattern, like stars and dots.
- Draw horizontal lines about ½" apart across the width of the paper to the bottom edge.
- Under your name at the left, write, "Date." In the middle, write, "Good Behavior/Good Deed."
- Draw a vertical line after Date and Deed to create columns.
- When you do a good deed or show a good behavior, write the date and behavior and put a special sticker beside it.
- Parents: When the chart is full, reward the child in a special way.

305. I AM. . .
C 1 HOUR 2

- Cut a 9" x 9" square of purple construction paper.
- Measure 4½" from the top and one side and mark a short line to form an X with a pencil. The center of the square will be where the lines cross.
- Bring each corner to the center and crease.
- With the corners folded down, write on each triangle one word of the phrase: Jesus said, "I am. . .", with marker or crayon. Form the words into a circle.
- Open one flap at a time and write a claim and its reference: The Resurrection, John 11:25; The Life, John 11:25; The Way, John 14:6; The Bread of Life, John 6:48; The Light of the World, John 8:12; The Door, John 10:9.
- Draw and color a small picture to go with each claim. For example, a sun for the Light of the World.

306. PRINTED TISSUE PAPER
$ 1 HOUR 2

- Thin some glue with a little water.
- Spread a wash of glue on a section of a 9" x 12" sheet of construction paper.
- Lay torn pieces of tissue paper in the glue. Smooth out the tissue paper with a paintbrush. It is all right if the tissue paper goes over the edge of the construction paper.
- Cover the whole sheet of construction paper with tissue.
- After the glue has dried, trim around the edges.
- Dip the end of a spool in tempera paint and print on top of the tissue paper.
- Make 10 to 15 prints over the entire paper.
- Let dry and hang as an art print.

307. KING OF KINGS TISSUE PRINT
C 1 HOUR 2

- Thin some glue with a little water.
- Spread a wash of glue on a section of a 12" x 18" sheet of construction paper.

- Lay torn pieces of tissue paper in the glue. Smooth out the tissue paper with a paintbrush. It is okay if the tissue paper goes over the edge of the construction paper.
- Cover the whole sheet of construction paper with tissue.
- After the glue has dried, trim around the edges.
- Cut a medium to large potato in half the short way.
- Draw a simple outline of a crown on one potato half and a cross on the other.
- Cut away the potato around the drawing, leaving the crown and cross above the edge of the potato.
- Dip the cross in tempera paint and print on a practice scrap of paper.
- Print on the tissue paper.
- Print with the crown, using a different color paint.
- Let dry and hang as an art print.

308. STORY COASTERS
C 1 HOUR 3

- Cut 4–6 pieces of 3" x 3" white paper.
- Read Daniel 3 and list 4–6 things that happened in the story. Be sure to include the response of Nebuchadnezzar near the end of the chapter. Write one event on each square.
- Draw a picture illustrating the things you listed on each square of paper.
- Color the pictures with colored pencils.
- Cut 4–6 pieces of 3" x 3" lightweight cardboard.
- Glue a picture to each piece of cardboard.
- Let dry.
- Spray with several coats of clear sealer, letting each coat dry before applying the next one.

309. TEMPLATE CHALK DRAWING
$ 1 HOUR 2

- Draw and cut out a shape, like a sailboat, on a 5" x 5" piece of heavy paper or lightweight cardboard.
- Lay the shape on a 9" x 12" piece of white construction paper.
- Rub the side of a piece of chalk from the inside of the shape

over the edge onto the construction paper.
- Holding the shape in place, smooth out the chalk with a tissue.
- Repeat several times to fill the paper.
- Mat, following the instructions of Project #215.

310. TISSUE AND FOIL SCENE
$ 1 HOUR 3

- Cut a 9" x 12" sheet of cardboard.
- Cover the cardboard with heavy-duty foil.
- Illustrate the story of the man lowered through the roof to Jesus, in Mark 2:1–12, by cutting or tearing colored tissue paper into shapes. For example, use brown for the house and tan for the roof.
- Arrange the tissue shapes on the foil.
- Glue the shapes on the foil with acrylic polymer mixed with a little water.
- More tissue can be layered on top for a textured effect.
- Let dry.

311. ART PORTFOLIO
$ 1 HOUR 1

- Place 2 sheets of poster board together.
- Put paper clips around 3 sides of the poster board.
- Staple around the 3 sides placing the staples about an inch apart.
- Remove the paper clips.
- Write the words ART PORTFOLIO and your name in big block letters on construction paper.
- Cut out the letters and glue to one side.
- Add any other decorations.
- Store your artwork inside.

312. "I CAN" BANNER
C 1 HOUR 2

- Cut two 1½" x 12" strips of yellow construction paper.
- Cut two 1½" x 18" strips of yellow construction paper.
- Trim the strips so they have wavy edges.
- Glue the strips ½" from the edges of a 12" x 18" sheet of black construction paper.
- Lightly write the words of Philippians 4:13 on a 9" x 12" sheet of red construction paper.
- Trace over the words with a dark marker or crayon.
- Cut around the verse in a wavy line, leaving a 1" border.
- Cut out different sizes of small circles from red and yellow construction paper.
- Place the verse in the center of the black paper and trim if necessary.
- Glue down the verse.
- Arrange the small circles on both sides of the yellow wavy lines.
- Glue down the circles.
- Hang the banner in your room or on your door.

313. MAKE-A-FACE
C 1 HOUR 2

- Cut an oval from a piece of flesh-colored construction paper, to serve as a face.
- Cut out several hairstyles, noses, and sets of eyes, lips, and ears, from appropriately-colored construction paper.
- Mix and match the various facial features to create different faces, à la "Mr. Potato Head."

314. WISE MAN/FOOLISH MAN REBUS
C 1 HOUR 3

In Matthew 7:24–27 and in Luke 6:46–49,
Jesus talks about the wise man compared to the foolish man.
Make this poster to illustrate these verses.

- Find a picture from an old catalog or magazine of a man you think looks wise. Maybe this man is smiling.
- Find a picture of a foolish man. Maybe he is frowning.
- Cut out the following pictures: two ears; two sets of feet; one house that looks strong and unmovable; one picture showing the effects of wind, rain, and flooding; one picture of a demolished house; one picture of sand and rocks.
- Trim the pictures.
- Write "The Wise Man vs. The Foolish Man" at the top of a sheet of construction paper or poster board. The size will depend on the size of the pictures.
- Write "Deuteronomy 32:29" at the bottom.
- Arrange the pictures into an equation. For example, put a plus sign between the picture of an ear and the feet and an equal sign between the wind picture and the house on the rock. (the firm foundation). Put a minus sign between an ear and feet and an equal sign between the wind and the demolished house.
- Glue down the pictures.
- Hang the poster.

315. BIRD'S EYE VIEW
C 1 HOUR 3

- Draw different sizes of rectangles and squares lightly with pencil on a 9" x 12" sheet of white construction or watercolor paper. This will be the fields.
- Color in each field with different shades of greens and browns and yellows. Use crayons, colored pencils, or watercolors.
- Outline each field with a slightly darker shade of color to form hedges or tree divisions.
- Cut a 3" x 6" piece of white paper and draw a picture of yourself flying.

- Cut out the picture and glue it to the field scene so part of it goes off the edge of the paper.
- Mount on a 11" x 14" sheet of black construction paper.
- Write "1 Thessalonians 4:17" on the top black border in white crayon.
- Write "I'll meet Him in the air!" in white crayon along the bottom border.

316. MAD HATTER
$ 1 HOUR 2

Dr. Seuss's Cat in the Hat wore a funtastic hat.
Make one yourself!

- Draw an outline of a funny-shaped hat on a sheet of newspaper.
- Cut out the pattern and lay it on a white piece of poster board.
- Cut out the poster board hat.
- Trace it onto a second sheet of poster board and cut out.
- Draw designs on the front and back in pencil—stars, stripes, huge dots, or flowers.
- Paint the hat with tempera paint.
- Let dry.
- Place the 2 hats together and staple around the edge, leaving the bottom open for your head.
- Put on the hat. If it is too large, staple some of the bottom shut, being careful not to make it too snug, which will cause the hat to tear.
- Have a funtastic time wearing your new hat!

317. KING DAVID BOOK
C 1 HOUR 2

Read about David in 1 and 2 Samuel.
This project can be enjoyed in several sessions.

- Draw a crown on a 9" x 12" piece of white paper. Use the whole paper.

- Cut out the crown. This will be your pattern.
- Trace the crown pattern onto 5 pieces of 9" x 12" yellow construction paper.
- Cut out the crowns.
- On the first crown, print the title "KING DAVID," with pencil, in block- or bubble-style letters.
- Trace the title with crayons or markers.
- Draw jewels on the crown and color.
- On the second crown, draw a picture of David tending his sheep.
- Turn over the second crown and draw David killing a bear or lion.
- Glue cotton to the sheep and brown felt to the bear or lion. Use small pieces of yarn for David's hair.
- On the third crown, draw a scene of David fighting Goliath.
- Turn over the third crown and draw and color a scene of David and Jonathan as friends.
- Decorate the third crown with yarn and felt.
- On the fourth crown, draw a picture of David as king.
- Turn over the fourth crown and write out a favorite psalm written by David.
- The fifth crown is the back cover.
- Stack the crowns in order and staple on the left side so it opens like a book.

318. 3-D PICTURE
$ 1 HOUR 2

- Pick out a sheet of gift wrap that has a design you really like. For example, horses, sports figures, Noah's ark, or fish. You will need enough wrapping paper to cut out three of each shape.
- Cut out the shapes
- Arrange one of each picture or design into a scene on a sheet of construction paper.
- Glue down each picture.
- Decide which picture(s) you want in the background and the ones you want to stand out or be in the foreground.
- Cut small pieces of construction paper and glue together until you have a small stack.

- Glue the stack to the pictures you want to stand out. If the picture is large, more than one stack will be needed.
- Put a dot of glue on top of each stack.
- Lay another of the same picture on top of the stack.
- If you want a picture to stand out even more, add more stacks and the same picture on top.

319. PINPRICK PICTURE
C 1 HOUR 1

- Choose a picture from a coloring book. The picture should have simple lines and not too much detail.
- With a colored pen or marker, put small dots ¼"–½" apart on every line.
- Cut a sheet of construction paper the same size as the coloring book picture.
- Lay the construction paper on top of an old magazine.
- Lay the picture on top of the construction paper.
- Tape down.
- With a push pin, poke small holes through each dot. Make sure the pin goes through the picture and construction paper.
- Tape to a window and let the light shine through the holes.

320. "GOD IS LOVE" POSTER
C 1 HOUR 1

- Using a ruler, divide a white piece of 12" x 18" paper into different-sized squares and rectangles.
- Starting at the top left space, write the letter "G" in block or script style with a black marker or crayon.
- After the word "GOD" is done in 3 different spaces, skip a few spaces and write the word "IS" in 2 more spaces.
- Continue with the word "LOVE."
- In some of the remaining spaces write the reference of a verse that talks of God's love. For example, John 3:16, 1 John 3:1, 1 John 3:16, and Romans 5:8.
- Using red and blue markers or crayons, fill in each space with dots, lines, hearts, and circles.
- Outline the letters in black.
- Hang your poster!

321. REBUS VERSE
C 1 HOUR 2

A picture that stands for a word is called a rebus.

• Read Joshua 6 about the capture of the city of Jericho.
• Decide what words you want to replace pictures with.
• At the top of a 9" x 12" piece of construction paper, write the title "Jericho Captured!" in bubble letters.
• Turn the paper over, and at the bottom draw the pictures and write the word it stands for underneath. For example, draw a picture of a trumpet, the city Jericho, priests, the number 7, a group of Israelites, a person shouting, and the woman named Rahab.
• On the front, write the story of the capture, replacing the words you chose with a small drawing.
• Add color to your story with crayons, watercolor paints, or markers.

322. CHAIR SLIPCOVERS
$ 1 HOUR 3

A fun way to help children memorize Bible verses!

• Cut 2 pieces of poster board 3" wider than the top of a kitchen chair and 14" long.
• Staple together the pieces on 3 sides.
• Slip over the top of the chair to check for fit.
• Choose the verse to be memorized. Decide how to divide up the verse. Make a slipcover for each word of the verse or write several words on each cover.
• Decorate the front and back of the cover, leaving room for part of the verses on the front.
• Write the verse and reference on the slipcovers.
• Place the slipcovers on the chairs.
• Have the children sit in the chairs, and when it is their turn, say the words that are on their slipcovers. Let each child change chairs to take turns saying different parts of the verse.

323. NEW LIFE VERSE BOX
C 1 HOUR 1

- Cut off the top of a pint or half-pint milk carton.
- Cut squares of construction paper to fit the sides.
- Glue a square to each side.
- On white paper, draw and color a spring picture for each side of the carton. For example, a baby chick, flowers, butterflies, and birds.
- Cut out the pictures and glue to each side of the carton. The picture can stand above the top edge of the carton.
- Write verses about new life on strips of paper. For example, Genesis 2:7, Psalm 103:4, Proverbs 4:23, John 5:24, Romans 6:4, 2 Corinthians 5:17, and John 3:16.
- Fold the verse strips and place them inside the carton.
- During a meal, have one person pick a verse strip, read it, then discuss its meaning.

324. NEIGHBORHOOD SCENE
C 1 HOUR 1

- Collect color newspaper comics and pictures.
- Make a neighborhood scene by cutting out pictures of things that make up a neighborhood. Pictures could include trees, fire hydrants, children, bicycles, an ice cream truck, houses, etc.
- Arrange the pictures on a 12" x 18" sheet of white paper. Leave room for the reference and verse, Galatians 5:14.
- Turn over one picture at a time and trace around it with a pencil.
- Remove the pictures and color in the penciled area with a white crayon.
- Place the picture face side down on top of the colored-in area.
- Rub the back of the picture with the handle of a pair of scissors. Use an even pressure, being careful not to rip the picture.
- Lift the picture to see the transfer.
- Continue tracing, coloring, and rubbing until all the pictures are complete.
- Add details with crayons and markers.
- Write the verse in the space left for it.

325. SPACE COLLAGE
C 1 HOUR 1

- Collect newspaper and magazine pictures of astronauts, rockets, planets, and stars.
- Carefully arrange and glue the pictures on a sheet of poster board. Leave room for the verse.
- On a separate sheet of paper, write out Psalm 8:3–4 (NIV): "When I consider your heavens, the work of your fingers, the moon and the stars, which you have set in place, what is man that you are mindful of him, the son of man that you care for him?"
- Glue the verse onto the space collage as a reminder of God's love.

326. FAVORITE PLACE PENNANT
C 1 HOUR 1

Do you have a favorite place that you like to go?
Here's a fun way to display some good memories.

- Draw a straight line from the bottom left corner of a 12" x 18" sheet of construction paper to the middle point of the right side of the paper.
- Draw a second line from the top left corner to the middle point of the right side, connecting in a point with the first drawn line. You should have a triangle-shaped pennant.
- Cut out the pennant.
- Divide the pennant into 3 different sections: one for the name of your favorite place, one for a picture of that place, and one for a written story of a visit to this place.
- Outline each section and the edge of the pennant with a black marker or crayon.
- Write the name of the favorite place in one section in block letters.
- Glue a picture of this place in a section.
- Write a story of a visit to this place on lined paper and glue it to the last section.
- Make small streamers by cutting 4 strips of 1" x 2" construction paper and gluing them to the back at each corner of

the left end of the pennant.
- Hang the pennant on your bedroom wall.

327. SANDPAPER FISH PRINT
$ 1 HOUR 4

In Luke 5:1–11, Jesus performs a
miracle for Simon, James, John, and Andrew.
Make this print to remember the call to be fishers of men.

- Cut a 4" x 5" sheet of sandpaper.
- Draw the outline of a fish on the rough side of the sandpaper with pencil.
- Color the fish with a very heavy layer of crayon. The fish could have spots or stripes.
- Color in some waves.
- Lay the sandpaper, crayon side up, on a layer of newspaper.
- Lay a 9" x 12" sheet of white paper on top of the sandpaper, then a layer of newspaper.
- Iron the sandpaper at a low heat until the crayon melts.
- Make several iron prints on the paper.
- The sandpaper may need to be colored again to make a nice print.
- Let cool.
- Write around the fish prints what Jesus said to Simon, "Do not fear, from now on you will be catching men."

328. PASSPORT
$ 1 HOUR 3

- Cut two 7" x 10" pieces of dark blue or black construction paper.
- Glue the 2 pieces together.
- Fold the papers in half.
- Cut ten 3" x 4" pieces of white paper.
- Stack the papers together so the edges are even, then place them inside the blue or black cover.
- Staple along the fold.
- Write "United States of America" on the front cover.

- Trace with a silver or white pen.
- On the first page, write: "Name:", "Birthplace:", "Date of Birth:", "Height:", "Weight:", "Address:", "Date Issued:," and "Date Expired:".
- Draw a line after each category.
- Write the appropriate information on each line.
- Glue a picture of yourself on the second page.
- Sign your name under your picture.
- Divide the rest of the pages into 4 squares by drawing a vertical line down the middle and a horizontal line through the center.
- When you visit a different state or country write its name in a square.
- Place a sticker in the square. For example, a cactus sticker after a visit to Arizona.

329. THE-LOVE-OF-GOD PUZZLE
C 1 HOUR 1

- Fold a 9" x 12" sheet of red construction paper in half the long way, like a hot dog.
- Starting at the top of the fold and ending at the bottom, draw one-half of a heart.
- Cut out the heart.
- Trace the heart onto a thin piece of cardboard.
- Cut out the heart.
- Glue the red heart to the cardboard.
- With a pencil, divide the heart into 12 puzzle shapes.
- Read Romans 8:38–39, and write something that cannot separate you from God's love in each puzzle shape. There are 10 things listed.
- Write, "Romans 8:38–39" in one shape.
- Write, "Nothing can separate me from God's love!" in the last shape or on the back.
- Trace over the writing and the lines with a dark marker or colored pencil.
- Cut the heart puzzle into pieces following the lines.
- Send to a friend or relative, or keep as a reminder to yourself of God's love for you.

330. DECORATIVE GARLAND
$ 1 HOUR 2

- Cut several 1" x 2" strips of colorful paper. The colors will depend on what occasion the garland will be used for.
- Fold a strip in half.
- Open the strip and fold the ends to the center fold mark.
- Fold in half again by matching the bottom to the top.
- To make the zigzag garland, poke the ends of a second strip through the folded ends of the first strip.
- Keep adding strips until the garland is the length needed.
- Decorate with glitter or stickers.
- Hang the garland.

331. SUNFLOWER PLACE MAT
C 1 HOUR 1

- Place a dinner or paper plate upside down on a large piece of brown paper.
- Trace around the plate with a pencil.
- Cut out the brown circle.
- Make fleck marks on the circle with a black crayon or marker.
- Draw a sunflower petal and leaf on a piece of scrap paper.
- Cut out the patterns and trace onto yellow and green paper.
- Cut out the petals and leaves.
- Place the brown circle face down and glue on the petals and leaves, face down around the circle so they stick out over the edge of the circle.
- Let dry and turn over.
- Make a place mat for each family member and guest.

332. "GOD IS LOVE POSTER"
C 1 HOUR 1

- In the center of a 9" x 12" sheet of white construction paper, write "GOD IS LOVE" in big block letters.
- Fill in the letters with pink and red crayons.
- Fold four 3" x 3" squares of red construction paper in half.
- Draw half a heart on each folded square and cut out, starting

and ending on the fold.
- Fold four 2" x 2" squares of white and pink construction paper in half.
- Draw half a heart on each folded square and cut out.
- Glue a small heart inside a large heart.
- Draw a long thin oval in the center of the glued-together hearts for the body of a butterfly.
- Re-fold the hearts.
- Arrange the hearts on each corner of the white paper.
- Place a strip of glue on the fold, on the back of each heart, and glue to the white paper. Do not glue the heart wings down.
- With a black crayon, draw antennas on the white paper above each heart butterfly.
- Cut out more hearts and glue them around the edge of the white paper.
- Hang the poster.

333. PEEKABOO ARK
C 1 HOUR 2

- Fold a 12" x 18" sheet of brown construction paper in half the long way, like a hot dog.
- Using the whole paper, draw an ark. Make sure the fold is the top of the roof.
- Cut out the ark.
- Draw a door and 3 levels or rows of windows on the front.
- Draw lines to show boards and the roof line.
- Open the paper and lay the front on several layers of newspaper.
- Cut the door and windows, on 3 sides only, with an X-Acto knife. This will allow them to open and close.
- Fold the ark and trace the door and windows onto the back part.
- Cut out pictures of people to depict Noah, his wife, his 3 sons and their 3 wives, as well as some of the animals that were on the ark.
- Glue the pictures on the traced windows and door.
- Peekaboo! Open the windows and door to reveal a person or animal.

334. TEXTURED SCENE
$ 1 HOUR 2

- Think of a scene. For example, George Washington crossing the Delaware, or the Good Samaritan from Luke 10:30–37.
- Cut simple shapes from different grades of sandpaper.
- Write a title at the top of a 9" x 12" sheet of construction paper.
- Arrange the shapes on the paper and glue them down.
- Let dry.
- Color the different shapes with a thick layer of crayon. Use old crayons.
- Add background details with crayon.

335. PARCHMENT COMMANDMENT
C 1 HOUR 2

- Round off the top corners of a 6" x 12" sheet of white typing or computer paper.
- Cover the work area with several layers of newspaper, then 3 layers of paper towels.
- Place the white paper on top of the paper towels.
- Put a small amount of cooking oil on the white paper and spread it around with a wadded-up paper towel.
- Cover both sides of the white paper with oil, adding more oil if needed.
- Wipe off any excess oil with a clean paper towel.
- Let dry. This might take several days.
- When dry, write the words and reference of Ephesians 6:1–3 on the "parchment" paper with a pencil.
- Trace over the words with a marker.
- Place the commandment on a textured surface, such as a sidewalk, and rub over it with the side of a gray crayon.
- Tape the parchment to a window or glass door.

336. MEMORY HEART POCKET
C 1 HOUR 1

- Draw a large heart on a paper plate.
- Place a second plate under the first plate and cut out the heart.
- Cut off the top of one heart and staple it to the bottom of the whole heart. This will form a pocket.
- Paint the heart with watercolor or tempera paint.
- Write "Memory Heart Pocket" on the pocket.
- Decorate with heart stickers, or glue on construction-paper hearts.
- Cut out hearts from 3" x 3" pieces of white paper.
- Write a verse that you'd like to memorize on each heart.
- Hang on the refrigerator and work on a verse at mealtime.

337. AARON'S ROD
C 1 HOUR 2

*God showed the leaders of Israel, in Numbers 17,
that he had chosen Aaron by causing his rod
to sprout and blossom.*

- Draw a rod on a 4" x 12" sheet of brown construction paper.
- Cut out the rod and glue it to a 5" x 15" sheet of light blue construction paper.
- Draw small brown branches coming out of the rod.
- Cut a notch in the end of a stick or dowel.
- Cut several ¼" x 6" strips of pink paper.
- Place one end of a pink strip in the notch and wrap it around the stick to form a blossom.
- Take the rolled strip off the stick and slightly indent the top.
- Place a small dot of glue on the loose end to secure.
- Make lots of blossoms and glue them to the small branches.
- Cut small leaves from green construction paper.
- Glue the leaves around the blossoms.

338. NAAMAN HEALED
C 1 HOUR 1

Read the story of Naaman in 2 Kings 5.

• Place a 9" x 12" sheet of white watercolor paper or construction paper vertically.
• Draw a 6" tall Naaman standing in the Jordan River.
• Add clouds and hills in the background.
• Paint with watercolor.
• Write, at the top or bottom, what Naaman said to Elisha after he was healed, "Behold now, I know that there is no God in all the earth, but in Israel." 2 Kings 5:15.

339. ANCHOR OF THE SOUL
$ 1 HOUR 3

• Draw a life preserver on a 15" x 15" sheet of white poster board.
• Cut out.
• Draw an anchor on an 18" x 18" sheet of blue poster board.
• Cut out.
• Glue the anchor at an angle on the life preserver.
• Cut lengths of white rope cording and glue it to the top of the anchor and the life preserver so it looks like it is wrapping around them.
• Around the edge of the life preserver, write "Hebrews 6:19."

340. GUARDIAN ANGEL
$ 1 HOUR 1

• Draw an angel on a 9" x 12" sheet of white construction paper.
• Add details, like facial features and hands.
• Color.
• Glue on cotton for the hair.
• Spread some glue on the body and sprinkle it with glitter, tapping off the excess.
• Cut out a crescent moon from yellow construction paper.

- Cut out different sizes of stars from white and yellow construction paper.
- Arrange the moon, stars, and angel on a 12" x 15" sheet of blue poster board.
- Glue the shapes down.
- With alphabet stickers, spell out "His Angels Will Guard Me." Psalm 91:11–12.
- Hang the guardian angel by your bed.

341. NEBUCHADNEZZAR'S DREAM
C 1 HOUR 3

- Read Daniel 2:25–49.
- Cut a 5" x 15" piece of white paper.
- Divide the paper into 5 sections.
- Draw and color King Nebuchadnezzar's dream in the 5 sections (2:31–35).
- Glue the drawings to a 7" x 16" piece of construction paper.
- Under each picture, write a part of Daniel's interpretation (2:37–45). For example, "God made you king and other kingdoms will come after you."

342. PEOPLE COLLAGE
$$ 1 HOUR 1

- Take pictures of your friends, family, neighbors, and people from church and school. Include people of different ethnic backgrounds.
- Have the pictures developed.
- Tape together two 12" x 18" sheets of construction paper.
- Cut out pictures of people and groups of people from old magazines and newspapers.
- Glue the magazine and newspaper people to the construction paper.
- Cut around the people in the photographs you took.
- Glue to the collage.
- Across the top or bottom write "God sees no color. Acts 10:34–35."

343. HANDWRITING ON THE WALL
C 1 HOUR 2

*Daniel was the only one who could interpret
the writing on the wall. Read this story in Daniel 5.*

• Draw a banquet scene of King Belshazzar, gold vessels or
   goblets from the temple, the handwriting on the wall, a
   lamp stand, Daniel, and the words written by the hand.
• On the back, write Daniel's interpretation of MENE MENE
   TEKEL UPHARSIN.
• Add texture to the scene by gluing on fabric, paper, and foil.
• Color the rest of the scene.

344. "JESUS SAID" CIRCLE
C 1 HOUR 2

• Draw a circle on an 8" x 8" square of orange construction paper.
• Cut out the circle.
• Trace onto a white piece of construction paper and cut out.
• Mark a dot in the center of the orange circle.
• Draw 4 lines from the dot to the edge of the circle to make
   equal-sized pie-shaped sections.
• Cut out one section.
• Write, "Jesus said. . .", on the edge of the orange circle, ending
   at the cutout section.
• Place the orange circle on top of the white one and trace the
   cutout pie-shaped wedge.
• Turn the orange circle and trace 3 more sections.
• Trace the lines on each circle with a black marker.
• Around the edge of the white circle, in each section, write
   something Jesus said and draw a picture to illustrate His
   words. For example, "It is finished!" John 19:30. Draw
   Jesus on the cross. Or, "Peace! Be still!" Mark 4:39. Draw
   the disciples and Jesus aboard a boat in a storm.
• Place the circles together.
• Poke a paper fastener or brad through the center dot.
• Move the orange circle to reveal one saying at a time.

345. CHALK PARROT
C 1 HOUR 1

- On a 9" x 12" sheet of white paper, lightly draw a large parrot perched on a tree branch. Find a picture of a parrot to use as a reference as you draw.
- Shade in the drawing with different colors of chalk.
- Shade in a blue background.
- Spray with hair spray to help set the chalk.

346. LAMP BOOK
C 1 HOUR 1

- Draw a lamp that was used in Bible times on a 9" x 12" sheet of brown construction paper. Find a picture to use as a reference in a pictorial Bible dictionary.
- Cut out the lamp.
- Trace the lamp onto another sheet of brown paper and 3 pieces of yellow construction paper.
- Cut out the lamps.
- Place the yellow lamps between the brown lamps and staple on the right side.
- Write on each side of a yellow lamp the things they symbolized in the Bible:
- God's Word—Psalm 119:105, 2 Peter 1:19.
- God's Guidance—2 Samuel 22:29, Psalm 18:28.
- God's Salvation—Isaiah 62:1.
- Man's Spirit—Proverbs 20:27.
- Prosperity—Proverbs 13:9.
- A son or successor—1 Kings 11:36, 15:4.
- With markers, write "Lamp Book" on the front cover.

347. TIME CLOCK
C 1 HOUR 3

- Draw the outline of an old-fashioned clock on a 9" x 12" sheet of brown construction paper.
- Cut out the clock.
- Cut a white circle and glue it to the top of the clock.

- Write the numbers 1 through 12 on the clock face.
- Draw the hands of the clock.
- Draw the pendulum on a piece of yellow construction paper.
- Cut out the pendulum and glue it hanging from the clock face.
- Write, "Now is the day of salvation. 2 Corinthians 6:2," on the pendulum.

348. WHEN I GROW UP
C 1 HOUR 1

- On lined paper, write about what you want to be when you grow up. Write at least 5 sentences.
- Cut off any leftover lines.
- Mount to a piece of construction paper that is a little bigger than your trimmed paper.
- Glue to the left side of a 12" x 18" sheet of white construction paper.
- Draw and color a picture on the right side of who you want to be.
- Or cut out pictures from catalogs and old magazines and make a collage on the right side.

349. HOLY BIBLE MOSAIC
C 1 HOUR 1

- Place a 6" x 9" sheet of white construction paper vertically.
- Write "HOLY BIBLE" in block letters, 2" from the top.
- Fill in the letters by gluing on little white squares of paper. The squares can overlap.
- Cover the remaining white Bible with small black squares.
- Outline the letters with a black marker.

350. CIRCLE AND TRIANGLE COLLAGE
C 1 HOUR 1

- Draw different sizes of circles with a compass on different colors of construction paper.

• Cut out the circles.
• Draw a dot in the center of each circle with a black marker.
• Draw lines from the dots to the edge of the circles, creating pie shapes.
• Arrange the circles on a 12" x 18" sheet of black construction paper. Overlap some of the circles.
• Glue down each circle.

351. "TOUCHY, FEELY" BOOK
C 1 HOUR 1

Children love making special things for friends.
This book would be a great gift for a young friend.

• Cut out pictures from old catalogs or magazines. The pictures could include animals, flowers, landscapes, or children from other countries.
• Fold 9" x 12" sheets of construction paper in half.
• Stack sheets with the folds on the left and staple down on the side.
• Decorate and title the front of the book.
• Glue pictures to the inside pages.
• Glue scraps of fabric, cotton, bark, foil, or anything with texture to the pictures. For example, glue a piece of brown felt to a picture of a bear, or foil to a mirror.

352. STUFFED SCARECROW
$ 1 HOUR 2

• Cut 2 sheets of white or brown butcher paper about 36" long.
• Draw a scarecrow on one of the sheets.
• Include details, like a hat with straw sticking out and a patch on the knee.
• Paint or color the scarecrow.
• Paper-clip the 2 sheets together.
• Cut out the scarecrow.
• Glue together the 2 scarecrows leaving an opening for the stuffing.

- Carefully stuff the scarecrow with small pieces of wadded-up newspaper or newsprint.
- Glue the opening shut.
- Display on the porch or in your home

353. APPLE SLICE MOBILE
C 1 HOUR 3

- Draw an apple on a 5½" x 5½" square of red paper.
- Cut out.
- Trace the apple onto two 5½" x 5½" squares of white paper.
- Cut out the white apples about ½" inside the traced line. This will be the inside of the apple.
- Glue a white apple to each side of the red apple.
- For the core, cut two 1½" x 3¾" rectangles of light green or yellow construction paper.
- Draw a long oval and cut it out.
- Cut out the center of the oval to make an O.
- Glue an O to the center of each white apple.
- Cut small brown seeds from construction paper and glue to each side of the apple inside the O.
- Cut 4 green leaves.
- Cut 4 small light green leaves.
- Glue the light green leaves to the green leaves.
- Cut a couple of ¾"-wide black stems.
- Glue the leaves and stem to each side of the apple at the top.
- Poke a hole in the stem.
- Tie yarn through the hole.
- Make 5 or 6 apples.
- Write a verse and its reference on the edges of 4 apples: Psalm 17:8, Proverbs 25:11, Zechariah 2:8, and Deuteronomy 32:10.
- Hang on a hanger, such as the one from Project #452.

354. NEWSPAPER HAT
$ 1 HOUR 2

- Layer 4 sheets of newspaper, laying each piece off center of the previous piece.

- Place it on your head.
- Have another person place several strips of masking or strapping tape around your newspaper-covered head.
- Roll up the edges of the newspaper all the way around.
- Decorate the hat with buttons, construction paper, feathers, tissue paper, etc.

355. NAMING THE ANIMALS
C 1 HOUR 3

In Genesis 2:18–20,
we are told that Adam named the animals God had created.
He must have been very smart!

- Draw and color Adam, some animals, and a garden scene on a 9" x 12" sheet of white construction paper.
- Draw a conversation bubble and write what Adam might have said. For example, "I'll call this big one an elephant!"
- Color the scene a second time so the crayon is thick. Make sure to leave some white paper.
- Place the scene on a layer of newspaper.
- Dilute black tempera paint with water.
- Brush the paint over the entire picture.
- The wax crayon will resist the paint and the scene will stand out against the black.

356. CHARACTER MOBILE
$ 1 HOUR 4

God wants us to have His character.
Here's a fun project to help us remember
what kind of people we should be.

- Make a list of the characteristics of God. For example, Kind, Slow to Anger, Forgiving, and Peaceful.
- Cut out different-sized shapes from white poster board.
- Make a hole in the top of each shape.
- Write a characteristic on each side.
- Trace around the words with black paint or marker.

- Paint or color each side with lines, dots, solid colors, etc.
- Tie a length of yarn from the middle of a short stick to the middle of a longer stick. Space the sticks 12" apart, farther depending on the size of the cardboard word shapes.
- Cut different lengths of yarn, and put an end through the hole in each shape and knot.
- Tie the shapes to the sticks.
- Tie a length of yarn to the middle of the short stick for a hanger.
- Experiment with balance by moving them around; perhaps put 2 small shapes on one end and a large one on the other.
- Hang near a window and watch its movement.

357. JOYFUL NOISE CHOIR PICTURE
C 1 HOUR 3

*Different colors are associated with emotions,
like blue for sadness. What color shows joy?
The Bible says in Psalm 66 to shout joyfully to God,
and Luke 15:7 states that there is joy in Heaven
when a sinner repents.*

- Draw 7 different sizes of human heads on white, brown, and black construction paper.
- Draw facial details and hair on each head shape. All the mouths should be drawn as small ovals and colored in black or light red to show that each person is singing.
- Lay a 9" x 12" sheet of orange construction paper horizontally, so the 12" length is at the top and bottom.
- Leaving 3" at the top of the orange paper, glue 4 heads in a row like a choir would stand. The heads should be placed at different heights to show that the people are different heights.
- On yellow construction paper, draw simple choir robes, starting with an upside down U shape.
- Glue a robe to the orange background paper so the top of the robe touches the chin of a head.
- Glue on 3 more heads in front of the first row of choir members, alternating between each one. These heads will be on top of the robes.
- Cut out 3 more robes and glue on.

- This overlapping will give the scene depth.
- Outline each robe with black.
- Draw simple hands on the choir members whose hands show.
- At the top, in a wavy line, write "Make a Joyful Noise unto the Lord!"
- Draw musical notes with a black crayon or marker around the title.

358. ABRAHAM'S JOURNEY COLLAGE
C 1 HOUR 2

In Genesis 12:1–5, God told Abraham to leave the country he was living in and go to a land that He would show him. God promised Abraham that He would become a great nation.

- Tear sheets of brown, blue, and white tissue paper into small pieces.
- Cut pictures from old magazines, newspapers, or greeting cards that would illustrate Abraham's journey. Find pictures of camels, goats, sheep, men, women, deserts, and mountains. Old *National Geographic* magazines are a great source of pictures.
- Pour some glue into a bowl and thin it with a little water.
- Brush some glue on a small section of a piece of cardboard. The size will depend on how large the pictures are.
- Glue pieces of tissue to the cardboard to form the sky and the desert floor.
- Glue the pictures on top of the tissue, overlapping them. This will give the scene perspective.
- Cover with a coat of thinned glue.

359. LIFE-SIZED JONAH
$ 1 HOUR 2

- Measure how tall you are, then add 6".
- Cut 2 lengths of white butcher paper this length.
- Lay one length of paper on the floor.
- Lie down on the paper with your arms away from your body.
- Have another person trace around you with a pencil.

- Lightly draw on clothes, facial features, hair, etc. Draw clothes that would be from biblical times such as tunics and sashes.
- Paint Jonah with tempera paints.
- Let dry.
- Lay Jonah on top of the other length of butcher paper and trace.
- Cut out the second Jonah.
- Place a line of glue around the legs and feet of the blank Jonah and lay the painted Jonah on top.
- Let dry.
- Wad up small pieces of newspaper or scrap paper and carefully stuff the feet and legs.
- Continue gluing together small sections and stuffing those until the whole figure has been stuffed.
- If a glued section pops open, re-glue and hold until it dries. (This section might have a little too much stuffing.)

360. DANIEL & THE LIONS DIORAMA
$ 1 HOUR 2

- Paint the inside and outside of a shoe box with tan tempera paint.
- Let dry.
- To make the box look like stone, wad up a paper towel and dip it into brown tempera paint. Tap off the excess paint onto a newspaper.
- Sponge-paint the box. Several paper towels may be needed. Do not cover all the tan paint.
- Sponge the box with a few dabs of black paint to make highlights.
- Draw and color Daniel on white paper. Make him smaller than the width of the box.
- Cut out and glue to thin cardboard.
- Cut out the mounted Daniel.
- Make a triangle stand from thin cardboard.
- Glue the stand to the back of Daniel.
- Stand the box on its side. Place Daniel inside the box.
- Put small lion figurines inside the box. Or draw and cut out lion pictures from magazines and mount like the Daniel figure.
- Draw an angel to mount and stand inside the box.

- Cut strips of black construction paper about ½" wide and long enough to go across the box opening.
- Glue the strips to the top and bottom of the box opening to look like prison bars.

361. 3-D POSTER
$ 1 HOUR 1

- Cut out construction-paper block letters for the phrase, "God loves you." Letters can be drawn freehand or traced with stencils.
- Make "stilts" for each letter by gluing together several layers of small construction paper squares or rectangles.
- Arrange the letters in the center of a large piece of poster board.
- Raise letters off the poster board by gluing at least 2 stacks of stilts to each letter then gluing it to the board.
- Cut out old catalog or magazine pictures of children from different cultures and glue to the board.
- Glue buttons, scraps of material, and yarn with the pictures of the children.
- Hang the poster in your Sunday school classroom.

362. PAPER RUG
$ 1 HOUR 3

- Cut strips of 2" x 36" paper. Use colored paper to match your room. You can also experiment with different kinds of paper. If you can't find 36" long paper, glue shorter lengths together.
- Fold each strip in half. This will give the rug some thickness.
- Glue together the ends of each strip.
- Lay 36 strips on a large table, or on the floor, to make the width of the rug.
- Weave a strip starting at either end, weaving under/over, under/over.
- Push the first strip to the end and paper-clip in place.
- Start the second strip, weaving over/under, over/under.

• Push the second strip up against the first strip.
• Continue weaving to the opposite end.
• Fold over the loose ends and glue on the back of the rug if needed. Or, glue the end of each strip.
• Glue the horizontal strips at the top and bottom.
• Paper clips will help hold the ends until the glue dries.
• Place in your room on the floor or hang on the wall.

363. MIRACLES MILK CARTON
C 1 HOUR 2

• Draw a 3¼" x 4¼" window near the top of each side of a half-gallon milk carton.
• Cut out the windows.
• Cut four 3" x 4" pieces of white paper.
• Draw and color a different miracle of Jesus on each paper. Miracles could include turning water into wine from John 2:1–11; the miraculous catch of fish from Luke 5:1–11; healing of a blind man from Mark 8:22–26; and the raising of Lazarus from the dead in John 11:17–46.
• Paint the carton with 2 coats of acrylic paint.
• Put a strip of glue on the front of each picture around the edges.
• Glue each picture inside the carton so the picture is facing out.
• On the carton under each picture, write a title and the Bible reference with a marker.
• On one side of the carton write THE MIRACLES OF JESUS.
• Staple the top closed.

364. EMOTIONS BOOK
$ 1 HOUR 3

Colors can be used to show emotion.
Red, pink, or yellow for happiness; black, brown, or gray for sadness;
and green or blue for peacefulness.
The Bible is full of emotions.

• Cut seven 4" x 12" sheets of watercolor paper or thick white paper.

- Paint each sheet with watercolor.
- Black on the left side of the sheet, faded to gray on the right side—Mark 1:15.
- Yellow—Luke 15:7.
- Green—Romans 14:17.
- Red—Proverbs 8:32.
- Pink—Proverbs 3:13.
- Orange—Psalm 1:1–3.
- Blue—Philippians 4:6, 7.
- Let dry.
- Fold the right side of each sheet to ½" from the left side.
- If the sheets are warped, place under heavy books to flatten them.
- On the right side of the fold line, write the verse and the reference with markers or colored pencil.
- Cut out a picture from a magazine that shows the emotion and glue it on the left of the fold. For example, a child jumping for joy or crying for sadness or repentance.
- Cut two 4½" x 7½" pieces of construction paper.
- Stack the folded emotions sheets.
- Place a piece of construction paper on the top and bottom of the stack.
- Staple down the left side, being careful not to catch the folded-over pages.
- Open each flap to view the whole page.

365. TOWER OF STRENGTH
C 1 HOUR 2

- Paint a Pringle can with tan tempera or acrylic paint.
- Near the bottom, on one side, paint a black door.
- Above the door, paint a window.
- Cut a 5" x 5" square of black construction paper.
- Cut off the corners to make a circle.
- Make a cut from the edge of the circle to the center.
- Fold the circle into a cone and tape or glue it shut.
- Draw lines on the can to create stacked stones.
- Trace the lines with a black or brown marker.
- Cut a small triangle of construction paper.
- Glue it to the end of a toothpick by folding the wide end over the toothpick.

- On one side of the flag, write "Proverbs 18:10."
- Write out the verse on one side of the can with a marker.
- Place the black cone on top and insert the flag.

366. MY COUNTRY POSTER
C 1 HOUR 3

- Draw a large star on a 7" x 7" square of red paper.
- Cut out the star.
- Trace the star on a square of white paper.
- Cut the white star ¼" inside the traced line.
- Glue the white star to the red star.
- Draw and cut out different sizes of smaller blue and red stars.
- Draw a simple outline of the Statue of Liberty on a 5" x 8" sheet of blue construction paper.
- Cut out the statue. Write, "Psalm 33:12: Blessed is the nation whose God is the LORD," on the statue.
- Write the first verse from the song "My Country, 'Tis of Thee" on the white star with the red background.
- Place a 12" x 18" sheet of white construction paper horizontally.
- Arrange the song star on the left and the statue on the right.
- Arrange the smaller stars around the song star and the statue. The shapes can overlap.
- Glue down the shapes.
- Draw lines coming out from the points of the stars with red and blue crayons.

367. TISSUE RAINBOW
$ 1 HOUR 2

- Cut a rainbow shape from 4½" x 6" lightweight cardboard.
- Draw 5 rainbow stripes on the cardboard.
- Cut 1" x 1" squares of red, orange, yellow, green, blue, and violet tissue paper.
- Cover the top stripe with glue.
- Place the eraser end of a pencil in the center of a tissue square and wrap the tissue around the pencil.

- Place the tissue in the glue and lift out the pencil.
- Cover each stripe with one color of the rainbow.
- Hang on your bedroom wall or window.

368. BIBLE STORY MURAL
C 2 HOURS 2

- Decide what story to illustrate. For example, the story of Joseph, David, or Jesus.
- Cut a long length of butcher paper.
- Start at the far left with the earliest mention of the character and create scenes from his life.
- Cut out pictures from old Sunday school papers, workbooks, bulletins, or magazines, and glue them to the mural.
- Add backgrounds, like pyramids, if illustrating Joseph.
- Add scraps of fabric, twigs, leaves, and yarn for more detail.
- Make several scenes along the length of the mural.
- Write any important verses on the mural.
- Hang on a wall.

369. ROAD MAZE
$ 2 HOURS 2

- Cut a 3" x 5" rectangle of lightweight cardboard to use as a pattern.
- Trace the rectangle 60 times onto poster board.
- Cut out the rectangles.
- Draw a section of a road on each rectangle, starting and ending in the middle of a side.
- Draw the center dividing line on each road section.
- Draw 2 roads intersecting.
- Make the same number of each card.
- Leave 10 blank cards.
- Draw a car on 2 road cards. One will be the start card and the other one the finish card.
- To construct a maze, shuffle the cards and place them face up.
- Draw a card and place it next to the start card. If it doesn't fit, draw another card.
- Add cards to create a maze.
- Then follow the maze with your finger or a Matchbox car!

370. PAPIER MÂCHÉ PENGUIN
$ 2 HOURS 4

- Partially fill a liter bottle with sand or dirt.
- Form a penguin head and beak by wadding up some foil.
- Tape the head to the top of the bottle.
- Form a tail by wadding foil into a thick triangle
- Tape the tail to the back bottom of the bottle.
- Form 2 feet with flat, wadded up foil and tape to the bottom of the bottle.
- Form two wings or fins from foil and tape to the sides of the bottle.
- Make sure the penguin stands.
- Cover the penguin form with four layers of newspaper strips dipped in a mixture of wallpaper paste and water.
- Cover the form with 2 layers of blank newsprint paper.
- Let dry overnight.
- With a pencil, mark a line for the white chest and neck areas of the penguin.
- Paint the penguin with acrylic paints. A picture of a penguin would be a helpful guide while painting. Some penguins have a little yellow on their chests and necks, and orange on their beaks.

371. SPRINGTIME FLOWER GARLAND
$ 2 HOURS 2

- Fold several different colors of 9" x 12" construction paper in half, then in half again.
- Open the paper and cut on the fold lines.
- Draw a flower shape on each paper.
- Cut out each flower.
- On green construction paper, draw and cut out leaves. Do not make them too small.
- With a few different shades of green crayon, draw lines on the leaves.
- Outline the edge of each flower with a contrasting color. For example, outline a yellow flower with an orange crayon.
- Glue several leaves, veins facing up, to the back of each flower.
- For each individual flower, cut out a black or brown center.

- Glue to the center of each flower.
- Some flower centers can be made by gluing a small paper muffin cup to the middle of the flower and filling with some cotton. Brown or black construction-paper seeds can be glued to the cotton.
- Make a loop for the back of each flower by gluing together the ends of short piece of construction paper then gluing the loop to the back of the flower.
- String all the flowers on a strong of piece of yarn and hang.
- To make the flowers stay on a certain spot on the string, use a little tape.

372. LAYERED TISSUE GRAPES
$ 2 HOURS 3

- Cut enough grapes for one bunch from both blue and purple tissue paper. Each grape should have 2 purple circles and one blue tissue circle.
- Cut vines, fence posts, and grape stems from brown tissue paper.
- Cut leaves from green tissue paper.
- Thin some glue with a little water.
- Brush some glue on the white paper and arrange the first layer of tissue shapes.
- Start with a purple circle for the grapes, then the blue, and another purple on top.
- Layer each shape 3 times.
- Glue down all the shapes.
- Cut pieces of white and blue tissue and glue down for the sky, layering the pieces.
- Cover with a wash of glue.
- Let dry.
- Along the bottom write "Jesus said, I am the true vine."

373. FRUIT OF THE LAND
$ 2 HOURS 3

*When the Israelite spies came back from the land of Canaan,
they returned with grapes, pomegranates, and figs.
Numbers 13:17–33.*

- Make grapes, pomegranates, and figs by rolling foil into the
  fruit shapes. For pictures of these fruits, check out a book
  from the library.
- Cover each shape with small pieces of newspaper dipped in a
  mixture of wallpaper paste and water.
- Cover the fruit with 3 to 4 layers of newspaper and one layer
  of newsprint.
- Let dry overnight.
- Paint the fruit with tempera or acrylic paint.
- Glue the grapes together in a cluster.
- Glue or tie on a short stick with thin florist's wire for a stem.
- Tie your fruit onto a stick with wire like the Israelite spies tied
  theirs to a pole to take back to camp.

374. STAINED GLASS WORDS
$ 2 HOURS 5

- Obtain a 9" x 12" sheet of white tissue paper.
- Tape together two 9" x 12" sheets of wax paper.
- Lay the tissue paper on the wax paper.
- Tear colored tissue paper into medium and small pieces.
- Brush a small section of the white tissue with glue thinned
  with water.
- Lay the torn tissue in the glue.
- Cover the whole sheet with colored tissue.
- Let dry.
- With a piece of white chalk, draw a border ½" from the edge
  of a 9" x 12" sheet of black construction paper. Draw all the
  way around the edge.
- Inside the white border, draw at least 8 sections of a stained
  glass window with the chalk.
- Cut away the black outside the white lines with an X-Acto
  knife to leave black lines like stained glass, leaving the white
  chalk lines.

- Place thin strips of glue along the cutout black frame and the black stained glass lead.
- Turn over the frame onto the tissue paper design.
- Let dry.
- With a marker, write a word from this sentence in each stained glass section: "Redeemed with the precious blood of the Lamb."

375. WALL JOURNAL
C ONGOING 2

- Tape a large sheet of paper to the wall.
- Let each family member write and draw small pictures on the paper.
- For example, after a great day at the lake you might draw a picture of a fish jumping out of the water and write, "We really had a great time at Lake Tahoe today. The water sparkled and the clouds were big and fluffy!"
- Or "I was baptized today," and draw a picture.
- Write dates beside the pictures.

ACTIVITIES FOR
MIDDLER CHILDREN
PAINT PROJECTS

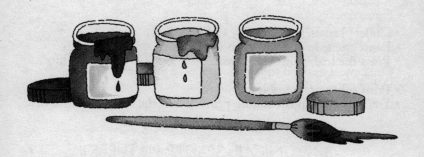

376. SPIN PAINTING
$ 15 MIN. 2

- Poke a pencil or stick through the center of a small box.
  (Scissors can be used to start the hole.) Do not make the
  hole too big.
- Cut a piece of construction paper to fit inside the box.
- Poke the paper over the pencil or stick so it lies flat on the
  bottom of the box.
- Drop in globs of thinned tempera paint.
- Spin the box.
- Remove picture, let dry, and hang!

377. SUNSET PICTURE
C 30 MIN 1

- Wet a 9" x 12" sheet of white construction or watercolor paper with a brush or sponge.
- Fill the paper with stripes of red, yellow, and orange water-colors to paint a sunset. The watercolor will bleed together. Add more water if needed.
- Let dry.
- With a marker, print, "You make the dawn and the sunset shout for joy. Psalm 65:8 NASB" over the watercolor.

378. NATURE PRINTS
C 30 MIN. 1

- Collect leaves, rocks, twigs, and grass.
- Paint one side of a leaf with watercolor.
- Press the leaf, paint side down, on a 9" x 12" sheet of white paper.
- Print other nature objects.
- You can overlap the nature prints when the first prints are dry.

379. UNIQUE SPATTER PICTURES
C 30 MIN. 2

- Cut desired shapes from white paper, such as stars or flowers.
- Dampen a piece of colored or white construction paper.
- Place the shapes onto the damp paper. The shapes should be flat against the background paper.
- Dip a toothbrush into blue watercolor paint and spatter paint onto the paper by raking your thumb or a Popsicle stick across the toothbrush.
- If a shape does not stay down, hold it while you spatter the color on the paper.
- Clean the toothbrush and spatter on red watercolor paint.
- Let dry.
- Lift the shapes off the paper.
- Outline each shape with a thin line of glue.
- Sprinkle red and blue glitter in the glue.

- Shake off excess glitter.
- Hang as a mobile or ornament, or show it off on the refrigerator.

380. STENCILED STATIONERY
C 30 MIN 2

- Draw a small cross on a piece of scrap paper.
- Cut out this cross pattern with an X-Acto knife. The cross-shaped hole in your paper is a stencil.
- Lay the cross stencil on a piece of writing paper.
- Wad up a piece of paper towel.
- Dip the paper towel in watercolor or acrylic paint.
- Dab the paper towel on newspaper to remove excess paint.
- While holding down the stencil, dab the paper towel around the stencil opening. If the stencil moves, tape it down.
- Lift off the stencil and enjoy your work. Repeat if you'd like.
- Stencil on an envelope, too, so you have a matching stationery set!

381. ADDRESS MARKER
$ 30 MIN. 2

- Paint a large rock with white outdoor paint.
- Paint your house number on the rock with black paint.
- Spray with clear sealer.
- Place near the street, the end of the driveway, or on the front porch.

382. STAR GIFT WRAP
$ 45 MIN. 1

- Draw several sizes of stars on lightweight cardboard.
- Cut out the stars.
- Tape the stars to white or brown butcher paper.
- Dip a sponge in poster or acrylic paint.
- Sponge-paint over and around the stars.
- Let the gift wrap dry, then sponge on a different color.

383. PHARAOH'S DREAM PAINTING
$ 45 MIN. 2

Read about Pharaoh's Dream in Genesis 41.

- Using tempera paints, paint a picture about Pharaoh's dream on a 12" x 18" piece of heavy white paper. The painting could include the Nile River and ears of corn.
- Allow to dry.
- Color over different areas of the scene with a contrasting color of crayon.
- With a wet sponge, wipe the painting until the tempera paint begins to flake off, but do not wipe off all the paint.

384. SPRING STRING DESIGN
C 45 MIN. 1

Spring is a wonderful time of renewal and new life.
Celebrate springtime flowers by using them in this project.

- Press several spring flowers between sheets of paper towels and a few heavy books.
- Let the flowers press for at least a week.
- Cover your work area with newspaper.
- Place a 9" x 12" piece of white construction paper on top of the newspaper.
- Dip a long piece of string in thinned tempera paint, leaving one end uncoated.
- Lay the string on the white paper in twists and curves. Let the unpainted part of the string hang off the edge of the paper.
- Lay another piece of paper over top.
- Cover this paper with a piece of cardboard a little bigger than the paper.
- Hold in place with one hand while pulling the string with the other. Don't hold the cardboard too tightly.
- Separate the paper.
- Let dry.
- Arrange dried, pressed flowers on the pulled string design and glue down.

385. MINIATURE SPOOL CANDLE
C 45 MIN. 1

- Paint small wooden spools with acrylic paint.
- Paint with holiday or checkerboard designs.
- Seal with a clear sealer.
- Place a miniature candle in the spool.

386. FREE-FORM FLOWERS
$ 1 HOUR 1

- Fold 2 or 3 sheets of 9" x 12" white paper in half.
- Open the paper and place blobs of yellow and red tempera paint on one side of the fold.
- Fold the paper and rub gently to smear the paint around.
- Open the paper and let the paint dry.
- Repeat with other colors like red and blue, blue and yellow.
- Repeat with green paint.
- Cut flower stems from the green blob paper.
- Cut flowers and butterflies from the other painted papers.
- Glue stems, flowers, and butterflies to a 12" x 18" sheet of blue construction paper, overlapping the stems and a few flowers.

387. GARDEN MARKERS
C 1 HOUR 1

- Sponge-paint smooth rocks by dipping a sponge into acrylic paint, dabbing off the excess paint on a newspaper, then dabbing the sponge on a rock.
- Let dry.
- Sponge a small amount of another color on top of the first color.
- Do a very small amount of sponging for the second color.
- Using a thin paintbrush, print the name of a garden plant on the rock with acrylic paint. For example, Tomato, Basil, Green Pepper, etc.
- Place the rock markers in the garden.

388. COLOR WHEEL
C 1 HOUR 2

- On a 12" x 12" sheet of white paper, draw 6 small circles, in a circle, with a protractor. Space the circles evenly.
- Number the circles, starting at the top circle with number one and numbering clockwise.
- Starting with the primary colors, watercolor-paint the number one circle red, the number 3 circle blue, and the number 5 circle yellow. The less water that is mixed with the paint, the brighter the color will be. A primary color is a color that cannot be mixed from any other color.
- Paint the secondary colors orange, green, and violet (purple) by mixing two primary colors together. Paint the number 2 circle purple, the number 4 green, and the number 6 circle orange. On a separate sheet of white paper, test the color that has been mixed.
- Label each circle by writing the color name underneath.

389. PIPE CLEANER PRINTS
$ 1 HOUR 3

- Draw a simple design on a 4" x 4" square of heavy cardboard.
- Bend pipe cleaners into the shape of the design.
- Trace the cardboard design with glue.
- Lay the pipe cleaners in the glue and press down until they stay in place.
- Allow to dry.
- Paint the pipe cleaners with tempera or acrylic paint with a brush or small ink roller. Be careful not to get any paint on the cardboard.
- Print the design several times on a 9" x 12" sheet of colored paper.
- Let dry.
- To frame the print, lay it in the center of a 12" x 15" sheet of construction paper and trace around it.
- Draw another line, about ½" inside the traced line.
- Poke a hole in the center of the sheet and cut out the center rectangle, cutting on the inside line.
- Lay this frame face down with the traced lines up.

- Put a strip of glue around the center cutout.
- Lay the print face down on the frame and press down.
- Wipe off any excess glue.
- Top with a heavy book and let dry.
- Turn over to view the print.

390. RECIPE BOX
$ 1 HOUR 2

*This could be for yourself or given as a gift
along with some of your favorite recipes.*

- Spray-paint a small metal file box.
- Cut out designs from wrapping paper.
- Glue them to the box.
- Seal with a clear spray sealer.

391. FLAME OF GOD
C 1 HOUR 3

- Draw a flame of fire on a 9" x 12" sheet of thick watercolor paper. Make the bottom as wide as the paper.
- Fold a 9" x 12" sheet of watercolor paper in half and cut on the fold.
- Draw 2 more flames.
- Brush the large flame with water.
- Brush on orange, red, and small amount of black watercolor paint onto the wet flame.
- Let dry.
- Follow the same step for the 2 smaller flames, but use only yellow and orange watercolor on these flames.
- Glue the small flames to the bottom sides of the large flame.
- With a black marker, write, "Exodus" on the left small flame and "3:5" on the right.
- Neatly write the text of the verse on the large flame.

392. WATERCOLOR STARS
C 1 HOUR 1

- Write the phrase, " 'He made the stars,' Genesis 1:16," in block letters, in the middle of a 9" x 12" sheet of white paper.
- Draw stars around the phrase. The stars can overlap and be placed in different positions.
- Paint in the stars and words with watercolor paints.
- Mount on an 11" x 14" sheet of black construction paper.

393. POSTAGE STAMP PRINT
$ 1 HOUR 3

- Cut a smooth Styrofoam tray into a 4" x 5" rectangle.
- Draw a design on the tray with a pencil. The design could be a large flower or fish, or have the name of a place like Nazareth, where Jesus grew up, across the top or down one side. The word and each letter must be written backwards.
- Write a monetary value like ".20" backwards in the upper left corner.
- Trace hard over the lines of the design with a pen so the design cuts deeper into the foam.
- Roll acrylic or tempera paint onto the Styrofoam with a small ink roller.
- Lay a piece of 4" x 5" paper on the inked plate.
- Gently rub the paper.
- Peel the paper off the Styrofoam.
- Re-ink to print again.

394. BURNING BUSH MONO PRINT
$ 1 HOUR 3

- Draw a simple shape of a burning bush on a 4" x 5" sheet of lightweight cardboard.
- Cut out the bush.
- Ink a small ink roller with red or orange paint.
- Place the bush template on a layer of newspaper and ink.
- Place the template ink side down on a 9" x 12" sheet of white paper. Gently rub the back of the template, being careful

not to move it.
- Complete the scene by drawing mountains in the background and Moses near the bush.

395. WATER FROM THE ROCK
C 1 HOUR 3

In Exodus 17:1–7,
God provided water for the Children of Israel.

- Cover the work area with newspaper.
- Mix ⅓ cup blue tempera paint and a spoonful of dish soap in a bowl.
- Put a straw in the bowl and blow some bubbles. Add more water for bigger bubbles and more paint for a darker color.
- When the bubbles are above the rim of the bowl, place a 9" x 12" sheet of white paper on the bubbles. Be careful not to touch the paper on the rim of the bowl.
- Repeat until the whole paper is covered with bubble print.
- Let dry.
- Repeat with purple paint.
- Lay a 12" x 18" sheet of white paper horizontally.
- Draw big rocks on the left side.
- Color and shade in the rocks.
- Cut the bubble-printed paper like a waterfall and a stream running from the rocks.
- Glue down the water.
- Draw and color Moses striking the rock with his staff.
- Draw and color a crowd of Israelites.
- Write "Exodus 17:1–7" and "Water from the Rock" at the top or bottom of the scene.

396. ANGEL MONO PRINT
$ 1 HOUR 3

- Draw an angel on a 4" x 5" piece of lightweight cardboard.
- Cut out the angel.
- Place the angel on a layer of newspaper.
- Ink a small ink roller with white paint.

- Ink the angel, too.
- Lay the angel, paint side down, on a 9" x 12" sheet of dark blue or black construction paper.
- Gently rub the back of the angel, being careful not to move it.
- Lift the angel off the paper.
- Place the angel on another part of the paper.
- Gently rub.
- Re-ink the angel and print the whole paper.
- Some of the angels can go off the edge of the paper.
- Paint tiny white stars in the empty spots around the angels.
- Let dry.
- Mount on a 10" x 13" sheet of white paper.

397. OUTLINE PAINT PICTURE
$ 1 HOUR 2

- Choose a picture from a Bible story coloring book or a card, or draw a picture illustrating a Bible story, such as Paul and Silas in jail.
- Cut a piece of cardboard the same size as the picture.
- Glue the picture to the cardboard with rubber cement.
- Outline each object in the picture with dimensional or puff paint. If the paint gets clogged in the tip, use a toothpick or straight pin to clean it out.
- Glue a picture hanger on the back and hang.

398. WINDOW PAINTING
$ 1 HOUR 3

- Decorate a window or sliding glass door for any holiday, birthday, or special occasion with tempera paint.
- To protect the area around the window, cover it with drop cloths, old sheets, or shower curtains.

399. PSALM 121 PLAQUE
$ 1 HOUR 3

- Purchase a piece of slate at a lumberyard or home supply store.
- Write, "Psalm 121:1–2" down the side or across the bottom with acrylic paint or marker.
- Paint a mountain scene on the slate with acrylic paints.
- Spray with a clear sealer.

400. TORN PAPER ILLUSTRATION
C 1 HOUR 1

- Write "Noel, Born Is the King of Israel" on the right side of a 12" x 18" sheet of construction paper.
- Cut from construction paper things about the birth of Jesus from the song "The First Noel." For example, from verse one, an angel, shepherds in a field, the star, and sheep. From verse four, baby Jesus in a manger.
- Arrange the torn shapes and glue them down to make your illustration.

401. OVERFLOWING MUG
$$ 1 HOUR 4

- Wash and dry a plain coffee mug.
- Use Perm Enamel paints to write, "My Cup Overflows with God's. . .", around the bottom in a straight or wavy line.
- Write words on the sides of the cup that complete the sentence. For example: Love, Peace, Goodness, etc.
- Between the words paint a favorite shape, such as teddy bears, baseballs, hearts, or dots.
- Bake or dry according to paint package instructions.
- Every time you use your special mug think about what God has done for you!
- This mug would make a great birthday, Christmas, Mother's Day, or Father's Day gift, too. Personalize it for whomever you're giving it to.

402. SWEATSHIRT DESIGN
$$ 1 HOUR 4

• Think of a design to put on a sweatshirt. For example, a manger scene, flowers, lines and shapes, or a phrase from your favorite Bible verse.
• Place a piece of cardboard inside the shirt.
• Draw and decorate your design with dimensional or puff paint.
• Let dry overnight.
• Wear and enjoy!

403. CLOWN PARTY-FAVOR HOLDER
$ 1 HOUR 2

• Draw a simple shape of a clown on a 9" x 12" sheet of light-weight cardboard.
• Cut out.
• Trace onto a second piece of cardboard and cut out.
• Paint the back of each clown with tempera paint.
• Let dry.
• Paint the front of the clown, adding details like dots cut from shiny paper and a pom-pom at the top of the hat.
• Paint a box the same color as the back of the clowns.
• Glue the clowns to opposite sides of the box.
• Fill the box with shredded tissue paper.
• Place wrapped party favors, one for each guest, in the tissue.
• Use as a centerpiece.

404. WATERCOLOR COLLAGE
$ 1 HOUR 2

In the Bible, the ocean is described as
"the deep," "breakers," "waves," and "billows."

• Cut a 9" x 12" piece of medium-weight cardboard.
• Cover a 9" x 12" sheet of watercolor paper with water.
• Paint the top one-third of the watercolor paper with different

shades of black, orange, and yellow watercolor in strips of colors.
- Paint the remaining two-thirds with shades of blue and purple.
- Let dry.
- Plan out a stormy ocean scene.
- Tear the watercolor into pieces and glue to the cardboard. Form waves with the different blue and purple pieces.
- Make stormy clouds with the black, and a setting sun with the yellow and orange pieces.
- Overlap the pieces to cover the entire cardboard. Paint more paper if needed.
- On the back, write these words from the hymn "It Is Well with My Soul": "When sorrows like sea billows roll, whatever my lot, Thou hast taught me to say, 'It is well, it is well with my soul.'"

405. ANIMAL CARICATURE
$ 1 HOUR 3

- Draw a simple outline of your favorite animal on a large piece of cardboard (the side of a refrigerator box would work well).
- Draw a circle for the face.
- Cut out the circle.
- Paint the animal with tempera paint.
- Prop up the animal.
- Put your face through the circle and have someone take your picture.
- Another use would be to take pictures of your friends at your birthday party.

406. COPY OF A PAINTING
$ 2 HOURS 2

- Copy a painting such as Vincent van Gogh's "The Starry Night," or Claude Monet's "Rue Montorgueil" onto a sheet of poster board.
- Use tempera paint and large brushes.

- Let dry.
- Frame the painting by cutting out the center of a second piece of cardboard, leaving a 2" border.
- Lay the painting face down on the back of the frame and tape the edges all the way around.
- Hang the painting.

407. SELF-PORTRAIT
C 2 HOURS 3

- Lightly draw your head, face, and shoulders on a 9" x 12" sheet of white construction paper or watercolor paper.
- Paint your portrait with watercolors.
- Paint the background.
- Let dry.
- Write the date and your age on the back.

408. BLOCK-PRINTED STORY RUG
$$ 2 HOURS 4

- Cut a piece of canvas 2" longer and wider than the desired size of the rug.
- Fold over each side 2".
- Trim each corner.
- Glue down the folded edges.
- Gather blocks of wood or small boxes.
- Cut Styrofoam food trays to fit each block or box.
- Draw simple shapes on the Styrofoam and cut out. For example, for Noah's ark, the shapes could include raindrops, an ark, animals, people, mountains, etc.
- Glue the shapes to the wood or box.
- Plan out the rug design. For example, will you print just around the border, randomly, or in order of the story? For the theme of Noah's ark, might there be raindrops in the center?
- Place some acrylic paint on an old cookie sheet.
- Ink a small ink roller by rolling it back and forth in the paint. Make sure the roller is evenly covered with paint.
- Ink the Styrofoam by rolling the small ink roller over it several times in different directions.

- Clean off any paint that might have gotten on the wood or box.
- Press the block, ink face down, onto the canvas.
- Repeat with all the shapes.
- Let dry.
- Brush the canvas with a coat of varnish.
- Let dry.
- Lightly sand with fine-grit sandpaper.
- Wipe off the dust.
- Repeat with several coats of varnish.

409. VICTORIAN BOOK
$ 1 HOUR 3

- Paint the inside and outside covers of an old cloth-covered book with acrylic paint.
- Let dry.
- Holding the pages of the book together, paint the edges with gold acrylic paint.
- Lay fern leaves on a layer of newspaper and paint with a slightly darker shade than the color of the cover.
- Lay the fern on the book and carefully press.
- Lift off the fern.
- Print the front and back covers.
- Let dry.

ACTIVITIES FOR MIDDLER CHILDREN

CRAFT PROJECTS

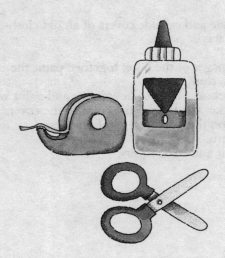

410. LETTER HOLDER
C 15 MIN. 2

- Cut a pie tin in half.
- Place one half upside down on another pie tin.
- Glue or staple the edges together. This will create a pocket.
- Hook a paper clip through the back for a hanger.
- Decorate with markers.
- Hang the holder.

411. HIDDEN GIFT
C 15 MIN. 1

*The person who receives a gift wrapped this way
will have fun opening box after box!*

• Gather different sizes of boxes.
• Place the gift in the smallest box and wrap.
• Place the wrapped gift in the next size of box and wrap.
• Wrap in as many boxes as you want.

412. FAMILY MAGNET
$ 30 MIN. 1

• Cut out pictures of your family, pets, or a favorite vacation
spot from leftover snapshots. Cut close to the subject so
there is no background.
• Glue to a thin piece of cardboard.
• If the picture starts to buckle, press it under heavy books.
• Glue a magnet or small magnet strip to the back.
• Display on the refrigerator.

413. PRESSED WILDERNESS
C 30 MIN. 1

• Gather grass, leaves, weeds, petals, and flowers.
• Press by placing them between two layers of paper towels.
Stack several books on top.
• Press for about a week.
• At the top of a 12" x 18" piece of construction paper, neatly
print 1 Corinthians 13:2 NIV, "If I have a faith that can
move mountains, but have not love, I am nothing."
• On the paper, arrange the pressed items into a mountain scene
with trees, flowers, and a sun.
• Glue down.

414. CRUCIFIXION SCENE
C 30 MIN. 2

*Read about the crucifixion and resurrection of
Jesus in Matthew 27 or in Mark 15.*

- Cook spaghetti noodles.
- Drain and rinse with cold water.
- On a 9" x 12" sheet of black construction paper arrange
  spaghetti into a crucifixion scene. Cut the spaghetti into
  different lengths with a table knife. The scene might
  include three crosses on hills, people at the foot of the
  crosses, and clouds.
- Cover the picture with wax paper to preserve.
- Place a heavy book on top of the wax paper. The spaghetti
  will stick to the construction paper even when it's dried.

415. RESURRECTION SCENE
C 30 MIN. 2

- Cook spaghetti and other pasta shapes.
- Drain and rinse with cold water.
- On a 9" x 12" sheet of blue or green construction paper
  arrange the pasta into a resurrection scene. The scene might
  include wagon wheel pasta for the rock that was rolled away
  from the opening of the tomb, spaghetti for people, grass,
  and flowers.
- Cover the picture with wax paper to preserve.
- Place a heavy book on top of the wax paper. The spaghetti
  will stick to the construction paper even when it's dried.

416. CRYSTAL GARDEN
$ 30 MIN. 5

- Combine ¼ cup each of salt, bluing, and ammonia in a glass
  jar.
- Place 5–8 charcoal briquettes in an aluminum pie pan.
- Sprinkle several drops of food coloring on the charcoal.

- Pour the ammonia mixture over the briquettes.
- Crystals will begin to grow in a day.
- Every few days, pour more ammonia mixture over the briquettes.

417. CLAY
$ 30 MIN. 5

- Mix 2 cups cornstarch and 4 cups baking soda in a pan.
- Add 2 cups cold water.
- Stir over medium heat until it has the consistency of mashed potatoes.
- Remove from the pan and place in a bowl.
- Cover with a dish towel and let cool.
- Knead for 6–8 minutes.
- Store in an airtight container.
- Make ornaments, pottery, or sculptures.
- Dry at room temperature for 3–4 days, or bake at 225° for 1–3 hours.
- This clay can be painted using acrylic paint.

418. BEESWAX CANDLES
$$ 30 MIN. 2

- Cut a length of candle wicking as long as the short side of a sheet of beeswax.
- Lay the wicking along the short edge and fold the wax over, pressing or pinching to help secure the wick.
- Carefully roll the sheet into a candle.
- Cut shapes with small cookie cutters from another sheet of beeswax.
- Press the shape onto the candle.
- Place in a holder.

419. PIE TIN TIMBREL
$ 30 MIN. 4

In the Bible, musical instruments were used to
help worship and praise the Lord. Read Psalm 150.

• Poke holes around the edge of a pie tin with a nail and hammer. Place the holes evenly and away from the edge.
• Tie a bell to every other hole with thin wire.
• Tie long ribbons to the remaining holes.
• Use the timbrel when singing together at home as a family or at Sunday school.

420. DANDELION CHAIN
C 30 MIN. 1

• Collect dandelions.
• Break off the flower.
• To start the chain, connect the stems by inserting one inside the other.
• Add a link by putting another stem through the first link and connecting the ends.
• Keep adding links until you run out of dandelions.
• Count how many links you have in your chain.

421. POTPOURRI
$ 30 MIN. 1

• Gather different types of flowers.
• Dry them by hanging upside down in a dark closet.
• Dry thin slices of oranges, lemons, and apples by placing on newspaper for at least a week. Turn the slices over onto a fresh newspaper every day.
• Place the dried flowers and fruit slices in a bowl.
• Try different combinations of flowers and fruits for different scents.

422. WALNUT LOCKET
C 30 MIN. 2

- Carefully open a walnut, preserving the shell shape.
- Clean out the walnut meat and let dry.
- Using 2 photos small enough to fit in the walnut shells, trace the shape of the shell halves on top of each photo.
- Cut out the photos.
- Glue the photos onto the walnut shell halves.
- Using a 1" x 1" piece of felt, glue it to the back of each walnut shell half to form a hinge, holding the halves together.

423. PIPE CLEANER NAPKIN RINGS
$ 30 MIN. 2

- Make a napkin ring by cutting a pipe cleaner in half and twisting the ends together.
- Twist more pipe cleaners into interesting shapes, leaving an end to twist around the napkin ring. For example, for Valentine's Day, twist a red and white cleaner together, then shape it into a heart and attach it to the ring.
- Small pieces of pipe cleaners can be used to attach the shapes to the ring.
- Or twist together several different-colored pipe cleaners and form them into a ring.

424. PLAY MASK
C 45 MIN. 2

- Draw a bubble letter B on a 4" x 8" sheet of lightweight cardboard.
- Lay the cardboard on several layers of newspaper to protect the work surface.
- Cut out the holes of the B with an X-Acto knife. These will be the eye holes.
- Cut out the B.
- Poke 2 holes at each end near the eyes.
- Decide what type of mask you want. For example, an animal, clown, king, or queen.

- Paint the front of the mask.
- Decorate with stripes, dots, plastic jewels, and glitter.
- Cut a thin length of elastic to fit around the back of your head.
- Thread each end of the elastic through the back of each hole and knot the ends.
- Have fun being the character of the mask!

425. DOVE OF PEACE
C 45 MIN. 1

*A dove is mentioned twice in Genesis 8
when Noah sent one out to see if
the water had abated from the Earth.
The Spirit of God descended as a dove when Jesus
was baptized in Matthew 3:16 and John 1:32.*

- Draw a simple outline of a dove in flight on a piece of scrap paper. Look at a picture of a dove to help in drawing.
- Cut out the dove.
- Trace the pattern onto a piece of Styrofoam.
- Cut out the dove.
- Poke a hole near the middle top of the dove.
- Cover a small section of the dove with glue.
- Sprinkle white sugar in the glue.
- Cover the whole dove with sugar.
- Push two cloves into the head for eyes.
- Spray with a clear sealer.
- Thread a piece of ribbon through the hole and knot.
- Hang.

426. LOVE SHOESTRINGS
$ 45 MIN. 1

- Cover the work area with newspaper.
- Lay out a plain white shoestring and tape both ends down. Tape down the string in several places in the middle.
- Decorate the shoestring with fine tip permanent markers.
- Draw a heart, then write, "God loves me," then draw a heart, etc.

- Hearts and words can be the same or different colors.
- Decorate the second shoestring.

427. NEW YEAR'S BLESSING
$ 45 MIN. 1

- Decorate cannelloni noodles by gluing on glitter or painting with acrylic paint.
- Write a blessing on strips of colorful paper. For example, use part of the blessing in Numbers 6:24–26 or Deuteronomy 28.
- Fold up the blessing strip and place inside a noodle. One blessing per noodle.
- Place in a bowl on the table on New Year's Eve and let each family member or friend pick one or two.
- Or before placing the blessing inside, thread a ribbon through and tie the ends. Hang on the doorknobs of each family member's room or friends' houses.

428. EGG PEOPLE
C 45 MIN. 2

- Poke a hole in both ends of an egg and blow out the contents.
- Rinse shell with water and let dry.
- Make an egg holder by rolling a 2" x 7" strip of construction paper and gluing the overlapping ends.
- Decorate the egg to look like a character from the Bible. Add hair, eyes, and clothes with marker, paints, and scraps of material and yarn.
- Write the name of the character on the egg holder.

429. BARRETTE HOLDER
$ 45 MIN. 3

- Loosely braid together 3 strands of unfolded raffia. The length will depend on where the holder will hang.
- Wrap some raffia around each end of the braid to secure.
- Cut a 12"-long length of raffia.

- Unfold the length.
- Tie into a bow.
- Attach the bow to the top of the braid with glue or needle and thread.
- Thumbtack the braid to the wall.
- Clip barrettes to the braid.

430. SPRING 3-D SCENE
C 45 MIN. 1

Spring reminds us of new things.
When Christ comes into our life, we are new on the inside!

- Glue spring blossoms to the corners of a deep, white Styrofoam tray.
- Decorate the bottom of the tray by gluing on small twigs and blossoms for tree branches.
- Cut butterflies from construction paper and glue them to the tray.
- Make a chick with pussy willows and construction paper beak and eyes. Draw the legs and feet on the tray with a marker.
- Write the verse or a phrase from 2 Corinthians 5:17 NIV, "If anyone is in Christ, he is a new creation; the old has gone, the new has come!"

431. CAT OR DOG COLLAR
$ 45 MIN. 2

- Measure around the neck of your pet and add a few inches.
- Cut 3 strands of cord or yarn.
- Knot together one end of each strand.
- Braid.
- Add beads to the strands as you braid.
- Knot the end.
- Tie the collar around your pet.

432. SWISS CHEESE CANDLE
$$ 45 MIN. 5

- Grease the inside of a quart or half-gallon milk carton.
- Cut a piece of candle wicking about 2" longer than the carton.
- Tie one end of the wicking around a weight like a small pebble.
- Tie the other end of the wick to a pencil.
- Place the wick inside the carton and rest the pencil across the top. If the wicking is too long, cut it shorter. It should be fairly straight.
- Place wax in an old pan.
- Put the pan of wax in an electric skillet filled with water.
- Carefully melt the wax. Do not get it too hot because it will flame.
- Place the carton in an old pan or on a cookie sheet.
- Fill the carton with ice cubes.
- Pour wax into the milk carton.
- Let cool.
- Tear away the carton.

433. SNOW GLOBE
$ 45 MIN. 2

- Glue several miniature plastic figurines to the inside of a clear glass jar lid to create a nativity, baseball, animal, or people scene.
- Let dry.
- Fill the jar with water.
- Put moth flakes in the water for snow.
- Put glue on the inside of the lid where it screws to the jar to keep it on tightly.
- Put the lid on the jar.
- Wipe off any excess glue.
- Let dry.
- Shake the jar to make it snow.

434. TOTEM POLE
C 45 MIN. 1

- Draw 2 or 3 faces in a row on one side of a paper towel roll.
- Add Indian details like arrows and suns.
- Cut 2 slits about 1" long on the sides near the top and 2 near the bottom.
- Cut 2 wings about 1" x 7".
- Decorate the wings.
- Color or paint the totem pole and wings.
- Push the wings through the slits.

435. YARN VASE
$ 45 MIN. 1

- Spread a layer of glue all the way around the bottom of a glass jar.
- Wrap different colors of yarn around the glued area of the jar. Use a toothpick to push yarn tightly in place.
- Continue gluing and wrapping yarn all the way to the top.
- Let dry.
- Fill with water and flowers.

436. POTPOURRI-FILLED HEART
$ 45 MIN. 2

- Dry your own potpourri by gathering flowers, such as roses, marigolds, carnations, and lilacs.
- Gently pull apart the petals and lay them on a sheet of newspaper.
- Let the petals dry for one to two weeks, turning every few days.
- Leaves, orange and lemon peels, and herbs can also be dried.
- When the potpourri is dried, place in a large bowl and sprinkle with a spice, such as cinnamon. Then stir the mixture.
- Cut 2 hearts from a piece of red felt.
- Sew around the edge leaving an opening about 1".
- Turn the heart right side out.

- Fill with potpourri.
- Sew the opening closed.

437. CROSS NECKLACE
C 45 MIN. 2

- Color 5 toothpicks with a brown marker.
- Lay 2 toothpicks side by side and 3 side by side on wax paper.
- Cover the 2 sets of toothpicks with glue. Make sure the glue runs between the toothpicks.
- Let dry.
- Carefully peel each set off the wax paper.
- Lay the set of 3 toothpicks vertically on the work surface and the other set horizontally over the vertical set.
- Tie the sets together with thin florist's wire, wrapping the wire around the crossing point several times.
- Leave the end long enough to wrap around a piece of yarn.
- Cut a length of yarn long enough to fit over your head and hang down a little bit.
- Tie the ends together.
- Attach the cross to the center of the necklace by wrapping the end of the wire around the yarn a few times till it's secure.
- Hang the cross around your neck.

438. BIG COINS
$ 45 MIN. 1

- Cut different sizes of circles from heavy cardboard for half dollars, quarters, dimes, nickels, and pennies.
- Cover each coin with silver or copper foil.
- Use a permanent marker to decorate each coin with the amount; the phrase "In God We Trust"; and a picture.
- Draw lines on the side of the coin to resemble the lines on a real coin.
- Use the coins for decorations or as play money.

439. CORNCOB GIRAFFE
C 45 MIN. 4

- Cut off 2"–3" of the pointed end of Indian corn. This will be the head.
- Cut another piece of corn in half.
- Stick four 2"-long dowels or sticks into one side of a half of Indian corn to form legs.
- Test the body to see if it will stand, adjusting the legs if necessary.
- Glue the longer corn piece on the body for the neck, or attach it by sticking a dowel into the body and neck.
- Glue the small pointed piece on top of the neck for the head. The pointed end is the nose.
- Glue small pebbles or nuts to the head for eyes.
- Glue corn silk on the neck for a mane and on the body for a tail.

440. CLAY TRIVET
$$ 45 MIN. 3

- Purchase non-baking clay at a craft supply store.
- Roll out the clay with a rolling pin.
- Place a bread plate on top of the clay and trace around it with a pencil.
- Remove the plate and cut off the excess clay with a table knife.
- Press pieces of small mosaic tile into the clay. Make a design, like a flower.
- Press tiles around the edge for a border.
- Let dry according to package instructions.

441. SAND PAINTING CANDLE
$ 45 MIN. 5

- Mix dry, clean sand with powdered tempera paint.
- Cut a 5" length of wicking and place it in the middle of a medium-sized baby food jar.
- Tape the top of the wicking to the top of the jar.

- Place a layer of colored sand in the baby food jar, working around the wick.
- Put another layer of a different color of sand on top.
- Continue layering the sand to about 1" from the top of the jar.
- Run a thin stick or opened paper clip down the side of the jar through the sand to create a design.
- Fill the remaining space with melted wax.
- Trim the wick if necessary.

442. FRIENDSHIP PRAYER WREATH
$ 45 MIN. 2

- With scissors, trim close around pictures of friends.
- Glue to construction paper with rubber cement.
- Trim the mounted pictures with special-edged scissors, leaving at least an inch at the top of each picture.
- Hole-punch a hole through the top of each picture.
- Tie the pictures to a small grapevine wreath with different colors of ribbon or yarn.
- Hang the wreath.
- Whenever you see the wreath, pray for one of your friends.

443. PIPE CLEANER PICTURE
$ 1 HOUR 2

- Cut out a 9" x 12" piece of lightweight cardboard.
- Glue a 9" x 12" sheet of construction paper to the cardboard.
- Bend different colors of pipe cleaners into shapes and glue them to the cardboard, creating a scene. For example, bend red and yellow pipe cleaners into tulips, and green into stems and leaves. Form white pipe cleaners into clouds.
- Hold the pipe cleaners down until the glue dries.

444. RUBBER BAND DESIGNS
$ 1 HOUR 4

- Cut a 12" x 12" piece of wood.
- Sand the edges of the board.

- Using a compass, draw a large circle on the board.
- Mark a dot every ½" on the circle.
- Pound a small nail into the board at every dot.
- Use different colors of rubber bands to stretch from nail to nail.
- Experiment making different designs.

445. CINNAMON WAX PINECONE
$ 1 HOUR 5

- Melt wax, red crayons, and a few drops of cinnamon oil in a coffee can placed in an electric skillet partially filled with water.
- Tie a string to each pinecone.
- Dip the pinecone in the melted wax. Be careful; it is very hot.
- Lift out the pinecone and let it drip back into the can.
- Set the pinecone on wax paper.
- Let cool.
- Dip the pinecone in the wax a second time.
- Repeat until the pinecone has a nice smooth coating of wax.
- The pinecone will not only look pretty, but smell good, too!

446. WELL-CHOSEN-WORDS PLAQUE
$ 1 HOUR 2

- Cover a large Styrofoam tray with aluminum foil.
- Cut out 2 apples from gold foil.
- Arrange the apples inside the tray.
- Spell out the words of Proverbs 25:11 with small alphabet macaroni.
- Lay the letters on a piece of wax paper and spray-paint gold.
- Arrange the macaroni verse in the tray.
- Glue apples and verse down.
- Poke a hole in the 2 top corners.
- Thread the ends of a length of yarn through the front of the holes and knot.
- Hang the plaque.

447. MIRACLES OF JESUS CHARM BRACELET
$ 1 HOUR 5

• Draw simple shapes of objects on a plastic meat tray that depict a miracle. For example, a water barrel from Jesus' first miracle of turning water into wine, or loaves and fish from the feeding of the 5,000.
• Outline each shape with a black ballpoint pen.
• Add any details, like eyes or stripes, with a black pen or permanent marker.
• Poke a hole at the top of each shape.
• Cut out and place on a foil-lined cookie sheet.
• Bake in the oven at 325° to 350° for approximately 2–4 minutes. (If the pieces curl, the oven is too hot or the time in the oven is too long.)
• Remove them from the oven and let cool.
• Attach a jewelry ring to each shape.
• Attach the shapes to a bracelet bought at a craft store.

448. POPSICLE STICK CHURCH
$ 1 HOUR 1

• Fill a half-pint milk carton with rocks or sand.
• Tape the opening closed.
• Cover the carton with Popsicle sticks. Some of the sticks might have to be cut to size.
• Make a cross and glue to the church.
• Paint the church with acrylic or tempera paint.
• Let dry.
• Paint on windows and a door.

449. SEASHELL CANDLES
$ 1 HOUR 2

• Glue a small candle to a small glass or ceramic plate.
• Glue seashells to the plate, overlapping and layering around the base of the candle. Use a hot glue gun or tacky glue.
• Glue a few small shells to the candle.

450. JONAH BEAN BAG
C 1 HOUR 2

• Draw a simple outline of a man on a 6" x 9" sheet of scrap
   paper.
• Cut out the man.
• Fold a piece of plain fabric in half.
• Place the Jonah pattern on the fabric and trace.
• Cut out Jonah.
• Turn one fabric Jonah over and decorate with markers. Add a
   face, hair, clothes, etc.
• Place the decorated Jonah face down on top of the plain
   Jonah and then pin together.
• Stitch around the doll, about ¼" from the edge. Leave a small
   opening.
• Clip around the edge, being careful not to cut through the
   stitching. This will make turning easier.
• Fill with beans or rice and stitch the opening shut.

451. SHIELD OF FAITH
C 1 HOUR 1

Take up the shield of faith, with which
you can extinguish all the flaming arrows of the evil one
(Ephesians 6:16 NIV).

• Draw a shield on a large piece of cardboard.
• Cut out the shield.
• Wrinkle up big pieces of brown paper bags or butcher paper.
• Un-wrinkle the paper and smooth flat.
• Glue the paper to the front of the shield overlapping
   the edges. If the paper bag has printing on it, glue the
   printed side down. This will give the shield a leatherlike
   look and texture.
• Write the word "FAITH" in bold, block-style lettering on yel-
   low construction paper.
• Cut out the letters.
• Glue the letters to the front of the shield on a diagonal.
• Outline the shield and letters with black marker or paint.
• Cut off the top of a laundry detergent box that has a handle.

• Glue the box top with the handle to the back of the shield.
• Cover the back of the shield with wrinkled brown paper. Cover over the box top so only the handle shows.

452. YARN HANGER
$ 1 HOUR 1

• Wrap a hanger with yarn. Start where the main body of the hanger and the neck of the hook meet.
• Place a small dot of glue on the hanger and start wrapping the main body.
• When the main part is wrapped, wrap the neck and hook.
• Glue the end of the yarn or tuck it in.
• The hanger can be wrapped with one or several colors of yarn.
• Hang your favorite outfit on this special hanger.

453. JONAH'S BIG FISH
C 1 HOUR 2

• Draw a whale on a large piece of cardboard.
• Paint the whale with gray tempera paint.
• Cut out the whale.
• Cut out a mouth.
• To make the whale stand up, cut 2 or 3 cardboard strips and bend into a triangle shape and staple the ends together.
• Glue one side of each triangle to the back of the whale.
• To illustrate the Bible story, toss a Jonah bean bag into the mouth of the whale (project #450).

454. PENCIL HOLDER
$ 1 HOUR 1

• Cover a small tin can with glue all the way around.
• Place a piece of yarn in the glue and wrap the yarn around the can.
• Push the yarn together.
• Continue gluing on yarn until the can is completely covered.

- A design can be made with the yarn by making wavy lines, or by forming the yarn into circles or mountain peaks. Use your imagination!

455. BENDING BIBLICAL CHARACTERS
$ 1 HOUR 4

- Draw hands, feet or shoes, a head, and a body on a sheet of scrap paper.
- Cut out and trace onto lightweight cardboard.
- Cut out each cardboard piece.
- Glue the cardboard to felt. Use flesh-colored felt for the head and hands, brown for the shoes, and different colors for the body. For example, purple for the body of a king or queen.
- Trim around each piece.
- Punch 2 holes near the top sides and bottom of the body.
- Punch a hole near the wrist of each hand and the ankle of each foot.
- Cut two 4"-lengths of pipe cleaner for the arms and two 5"-lengths for the legs.
- Poke one end of each arm pipe cleaner through the top 2 holes of the body and bend over.
- Repeat with the leg pipe cleaners.
- Poke the other ends of the pipe cleaners through the front of the hands and feet and bend over.
- Glue the end of the pipe cleaners to the felt. Hold with a paper clip or clothespin.
- Allow to dry.
- Glue on any felt details, like hair, facial features, a crown, a skirt to show a woman, etc.
- Act out a Bible story with the character, bending the arms and legs as needed.
- Make several bendable characters!

456. PRAYER PLAQUE
C 1 HOUR 1

- Cut a piece of construction paper to fit inside a Styrofoam meat tray.
- Write in block letters, "Pray Without Ceasing. 1 Thessalonians 5:17."
- Fill in the letters with patterns of stripes, flowers, dots, etc., using markers.
- Glue the verse to the bottom of the tray.
- Cut out construction-paper flowers.
- Glue the flowers around the edge of the tray.

457. GREETING CARD FLOWER POT
$ 1 HOUR 1

This cute flower pot makes a great gift or centerpiece.

- Cut a one-quart milk carton down to 6" tall.
- Glue a greeting card to each side.
- Cut lengths of thin ribbon and glue them around the edge of each side of the carton.
- Fill with potting soil and a flower or plant.

458. DESK PAD
$ 1 HOUR 2

- Cut a 22" x 28" piece of poster board in half.
- Cut four pieces, each 4" x 11½".
- Glue together 3 sides of 2 pieces, 4" x 11½".
- Place a strip of glue on the top, bottom, and left side of one 4" x 11½" piece.
- Slip pieces onto the ends of the 11" x 14" piece.
- Repeat with the other 2 pieces.
- Decorate the top of the side pieces by gluing on yarn to match the pencil holder in Project #454.
- Slip the pieces onto the ends of the 11" x 14" piece of poster board.

459. HEARTSTRINGS PICTURE
C 1 HOUR 1

- Cut different-sized hearts from pink and red construction paper.
- Glue the smaller hearts inside the larger hearts.
- Glue the hearts inside a white Styrofoam meat tray.
- Thread 2 needles, one with pink yarn, the other with red. Knot the ends.
- Poke holes around the edge of the tray with a nail.
- Sew the yarn from edge to edge over the hearts to create a design.
- Secure the ends of the yarn to the back with tape.

460. ROYAL KING MASK
C 1 HOUR 2

There are many kings mentioned in the Bible.
Use this mask to act out a Bible story.

- Open a grocery bag; the bottom will be the top of the mask.
- Cut away a 3" strip from the two sides and the back. Leave the front panel of the bag.
- Cut pieces of brown or yellow construction paper to fit the sides and back.
- Glue the construction paper about 2" from the top of the sides and back. Place glue along the top edge only.
- Cut the construction paper into 1" strips for hair up to where it is glued to the bag.
- Roll each strip around a pencil toward the top of the mask to create curled hair.
- Try on the mask and mark where the eyes should be.
- Cut out the eyes.
- Decorate the face of the mask with eyebrows, nose, and mouth.
- Color a beard the same color as the hair.
- For a crown, cut a strip of construction paper 3" wide and long enough to fit around the top of the mask.
- Cut the top of this strip to form a crown border.
- Decorate the crown.
- Glue it to the top of the mask.

461. NOAH'S ANIMALS
$ 1 HOUR 2

Make several animals to act out the story of Noah and the ark.

• Twist pipe cleaners together to form a body and head of an animal.
• Add legs and feet by cutting pipe cleaners to length and wrapping one end around the body. Secure tightly.
• Place a cotton or fabric ball in the head and body.
• Wrap yarn around the animal. Cover the entire animal. This will take a lot of wrapping.
• Glue the end of the yarn to the body.
• Add details like spots and eyes with small scraps of felt.

462. SALT DOUGH VOTIVE CUP
$ 1 HOUR 5

• Mix together 2 cups flour and 1 cup salt. Stir in 1 cup water. If the dough is too sticky add a little flour.
• Knead for about 7 minutes.
• Roll out the dough on a floured surface.
• Cover a small oatmeal container and its bottom with foil.
• Cover the container and its bottom with a sheet of dough. Use a little water to connect the dough.
• Smooth out any seams. Do not overlap the top edge.
• Use a table knife to cut out small shapes like triangles. Use a straw to cut out circles.
• Cut out shapes along the top and bottom, and create patterns on the sides.
• Bake at 325° for 30–40 minutes. Prick any bubbles.
• Check the oatmeal box while baking. Turn down the overn if the box begins to turn black.
• Let cool.
• Remove the oatmeal box and foil.
• Place a medium candle inside the votive.

463. PERSONALIZED WASTEPAPER BASKET
$ 1 HOUR 1

- Decorate a paper paint bucket to match your room by using leftover wallpaper and border.
- The bucket can also be decorated with stickers, markers, or baseball cards.

464. SALT DOUGH MOUSE FAMILY
$ 1 HOUR 4

A picture of a mouse will help in forming these whimsical mice.

- Mix together 2 cups flour and 1 cup salt. Stir in 1 cup water.
- Knead for about 7 minutes. The dough should not be sticky; if it is, add a little more flour.
- Form small balls of the dough into pear shapes.
- Pull out the top of the pear to form the head and nose of the mouse.
- Add legs, feet, eyes, and a tail with small pieces of dough. Use a little water when attaching small parts.
- Poke small holes around the nose with a toothpick. After baking whiskers will be added.
- Make a whole mouse family.
- Bake at 325° for 30–40 minutes. Cover small parts with foil if these areas are baking faster.
- Let cool.
- Paint the mice with acrylic paint.
- Seal with clear spray sealer.
- With a toothpick, put a small dot of glue in the holes around the nose, then place a strand from a paintbrush in each hole for the whiskers.

465. PAUL AND SILAS
C 1 HOUR 1

Read an exciting story in Acts 16 about two people being thrown in prison and what happened to them and the jailer.

• Cover toilet paper rolls with construction paper for the bodies of Paul and Silas.
• Add clothing details with scraps of fabric.
• Cut a small circle for the face and draw on facial features.
• Glue the face on the tube body. The face should not stick up above the top of the tube.
• Measure a strip of construction paper around the tube and make fringe cuts for hair.
• Glue hair to the tubes.

466. MOUSE HOUSE FURNITURE
C 1 HOUR 1

• Cover an oatmeal box lid with natural material for a picnic table.
• Use matchboxes glued together for dressers and bookcases.
• Glue sticks together for beds and chairs.
• Make a mirror by gluing foil to a stick frame.
• Move your furniture into your mouse tree house from Project #511.

467. HAPPY MEMORIES KEEPSAKE FRAME
$$$ 1 HOUR 2

• Collect mementos while on a family vacation or day outing. These could include an especially pretty leaf, a shell, a napkin from a restaurant, a postcard, sand from a beach, or a piece of gift wrap.
• Buy a keepsake frame.
• Glue your special finds to a piece of medium-weight cardboard cut to fit inside the frame.
• Let dry.

- Slip the cardboard into the frame.
- Hang your keepsake, or place it on a table, desk, or bureau.

468. WOVEN PLACE MAT
C 1 HOUR 1

*God has provided us with many different types of food.
Make a place mat with your favorite foods on it.*

- Cut pictures of your favorite foods from old cookbooks, catalogs, or magazines.
- Glue the pictures on a 12" x 18" piece of white construction paper, overlapping the pictures.
- Let dry.
- Cut the collage into 1"-wide vertical strips. You will have 18 strips. As you cut, carefully lay in order or number each one on the back.
- Fold a piece of 12" x 18" construction paper in half.
- Starting at the fold make a cut every inch. Cut to within ¼" of the edge.
- Starting with the first strip from your food collage, weave under, over, under, over . . . until strip one is done.
- Weave strip #2 over, under, over, under. . . .
- Weave strip #3 under, over, under, over. . . .
- Keep alternating until all 18 strips are woven in.
- Glue down the end of each strip to secure.

469. TWIG PICTURE FRAME
C 1 HOUR 2

- Gather twigs.
- Lay the picture to be framed on a large piece of heavy cardboard and trace around it.
- Inside this line, about ¼", draw another line with a ruler.
- Cut out the inside line.
- Paint the cardboard frame with brown tempera paint.
- Cut the twigs to size.
- Glue the twigs to the frame. Fill in the entire frame.
- Tape the picture to the back.

- Make 2 small triangles of a thin strip of cardboard.
- Glue them to the back of the frame on either side of the picture.
- Display the picture!

470. HEART WREATH
$ 1 HOUR 3

- Poke a hole near the top of a Styrofoam heart wreath
- Cover a small area of the wreath with glue.
- Place moss in the glue. Do not cover the hole.
- Glue on dried rosebuds, petals, and flowers.
- Cover the entire wreath.
- Hang by threading a ribbon through the hole and tying the ends.

471. BOOKENDS
$ 1 HOUR 2

- Fill 2 empty oatmeal containers with sand.
- Tape the lids shut.
- Cover the containers with white paper.
- Decorate the bookends with acrylic or tempera paint to look like a favorite Bible character or a character from a favorite book. For example, Joseph in his coat of many colors, or Pippi Longstocking.
- Add yarn for hair.
- Place the bookends on a shelf with your favorite books.

472. STAINED GLASS CHURCH
$ 1 HOUR 2

- Draw a church with a steeple and a big stained glass window on a 9" x 12" sheet of white construction paper.
- Outline the church with a black marker.
- Leave the church white.
- Color the sky and ground around the church.

- Divide the window into large sections.
- Trace the window and sections with a black marker.
- Spread glue on the inside of several window sections, starting at the top of the window.
- Sprinkle a spice, such as cinnamon or oregano, onto the glue.
- Let the glue dry.
- Tap off any excess spice.
- Cover the whole window with different spices.
- Brush off any smeared spices with a paintbrush.

473. SIGNET RING
C 1 HOUR 3

- Cut a length of wire a little bit bigger than your ring finger. Make it long enough to twist the ends together and to wrap yarn around it.
- Try on the ring. Make sure it is loose.
- Wrap yarn around the wire ring, gluing down the end.
- Trace a penny, twice, on a thin piece of cardboard.
- Cut out the circles.
- Poke two holes in the center of one circle, like button holes.
- Attach the cardboard button to the ring with needle and thread.
- Glue on the second circle.
- Glue the penny to the cardboard button.
- Seal a secret letter by dropping wax from a lit candle onto the back of the envelope and pressing the penny into the wax.

474. KIT GIFT
$$ 1 HOUR 3

- Gather items for the kind of kit you want to give. For example, paper, glue, crayons, and colored pencils for an art kit; or string, beads, and stones for a jewelry-making kit.
- Place the kit items in a special container, like a lunch box or a decorated shoe box.
- Wrap and give as a gift.

475. POPSICLE STICK PLAQUE
C 1 HOUR 1

- Glue 3 Popsicle sticks together to form a triangle.
- Let dry.
- Place the triangle on a sheet of white paper and trace the inside triangle with a pencil.
- Cut out the paper triangle, about ¼" outside the trace line.
- Draw a picture of what you think Joshua might have looked like, using Bible story books or reference books for ideas.
- Color the picture.
- Place a line of glue around the edge of the triangle picture and lay the Popsicle triangle on top.
- Let dry.
- Write, "Joshua 1:9" on the Popsicle sticks with a marker.

476. DECOUPAGE STAMP BOX
$ 1 HOUR 1

- Collect canceled postage stamps. If you want to make a special theme for the box, just use all flags, animals, people, etc., stamps.
- Glue the stamps to a wooden or plastic school box.
- Cover the entire box, overlapping the stamps and all the edges.
- Thin some glue with a small amount of water and coat the box.
- Let dry.
- Apply several more coats.

477. ROCK BABIES
C 1 HOUR 2

- Collect and clean different sizes of rocks and pebbles.
- Glue the rocks together with a glue gun or tacky glue, using large rocks for the body, a smaller rock for the head, and small rocks for feet and arms.

• Paint rocks with acrylic paint.
• Seal with a clear sealer.
• Add yarn, scraps of fabric, movable eyes, or buttons for details like diapers, hair, and clothes.

478. ALPHABET THUMBTACKS
$ 1 HOUR 1

Here's a fun way to dress up your bulletin board!

• Paint alphabet pasta with acrylic paints. Use the letters of your name or the whole alphabet.
• Glue to the thumbtack.
• Seal with a clear sealer.

479. TOWER OF BABEL
$$ 1 HOUR 2

*Read about the Tower of Babel
and the people's pride in Genesis 11:1–9.*

• Cut a 12" x 12" piece of heavy cardboard.
• Mark a 6" x 6" square in the middle.
• Glue sugar cubes around the edge of the square.
• Glue another layer of cubes on top.
• Cut a thin piece of cardboard a little smaller than the square formed by the cubes.
• Glue the thin cardboard on top of the cubes.
• Glue on 2 more layers of cubes, a little inside the first layers to create a small step.
• Glue on another thin piece of cardboard.
• Continue layering sugar cubes to the height you want.
• Paint with gray tempera paint.
• Cut out pictures of people from different countries and glue them to the thick cardboard base.

480. ANGEL DIORAMA
C 1 HOUR 2

- Paint the inside and outside of a shoe box with black tempera or acrylic paint.
- Cut small stars and a moon from white and yellow construction paper.
- Glue to the inside back, top, and sides of the box.
- Draw and color on thin cardboard several small angels, lambs, and a shepherd.
- Add cotton for hair.
- Tape the end of a short string to the back of each angel.
- Hang each angel by taping the other end of the string to the inside top of the box.
- Stand up the sheep and shepherd by gluing a strip of thin cardboard from the back of each figure to the box.

481. YARN-WRAPPED CARDBOARD PUPPETS
$ 1 HOUR 2

- Choose a Bible story or Mother Goose rhyme to act out.
- Cut the characters from stiff cardboard.
- Glue a tongue depressor to the back of the cardboard figures.
- Wrap the figures in different colors of yarn.
- Tuck the ends of the yarn under or glue them down.
- Add any details, like eyes or spots, by gluing on small scraps of felt.
- Perform the story for friends and family.

482. "FRUIT OF THE SPIRIT" BANNER
$ 1 HOUR 2

- Cut an 18" length of yarn.
- Tie one end of the yarn to the end of a 12" stick and the other end of the yarn to the opposite end.
- Poke 3 pieces of yarn through the top of a 9" x 15" piece of burlap and tie to the stick to hang.
- Using a marker, write the words "Love, Joy, Peace, Patience,

Kindness, Goodness, and Faithfulness," on different colors of felt.
- Cut out the words and arrange on the burlap.
- Draw different kinds of fruit on felt with a marker and cut them out.
- Arrange the fruit around the words.
- Place a sheet of wax paper under the burlap. This will keep any glue that seeps through the burlap from getting on the work surface.
- Glue the words and fruit to the burlap.
- Hang your banner.

483. SALT DOUGH LOAVES & FISHES
$ 1 HOUR 3

Many stories from the Bible,
like the feeding of the five thousand in John 6,
can be illustrated using a simple salt dough.

- Mix 2 cups flour and 1 cup salt. Stir in 1 cup water.
- Knead for about 7 minutes. If the dough is too sticky, add flour; if it is too dry, add a little water.
- Using $5/7$ of the dough, form 5 loaves of bread. For example, flat and round, braided, or French-shaped loaves. Lay loaves at least 2" apart on a cookie sheet.
- Brush loaves with egg whites.
- Form the remaining dough into 2 fish shapes. Fish should be about 2" x 3".
- Place the loaves and fishes on a cookie sheet.
- Bake at 350° for 30–40 minutes.
- Check the project during baking. If a puffy area forms on the dough, prick it with a pin. If an area is browning faster than other areas, cover it with foil. Baking time will vary depending on the actual thickness of the piece.
- Let cool.
- Paint fish with acrylic paint.
- Spray the loaves and fishes with a clear sealer.
- Put the loaves and fishes in the printed bag from Project #234.

484. WOODEN POTPOURRI BOX
$ 1 HOUR 2

- Paint a small wooden box and lid with acrylic paint.
- Make a paper pattern to fit on the inside of the lid and the bottom of the box.
- Trace the pattern onto calico material.
- Cut out the material and glue it to the inside bottom of the lid and box.
- Cut a length of ribbon long enough to wrap around the outside of the box.
- Glue the ribbon to the box, making sure to place it low enough that the lid will still fit on the box.
- Cut a length of ribbon to fit across the lid, and glue it on.
- Glue a few dried rosebuds to the lid.
- Fill the box with potpourri.

485. BASEBALL DIORAMA
C 1½ HOURS 1

- Paint the inside and outside of a shoe box with blue acrylic or tempera paint.
- Glue baseball cards to green construction paper. Trim to fit the outside of the box.
- Glue the cards to the outside of the box.
- Decorate the inside of the box to resemble a baseball park with paint, construction paper, and magazine pictures.
- Add baseball figurines.

486. KING ARTAXERXES' CUP
C 1 HOUR 2

Nehemiah had a very important job in King Artaxerxes' court.
He had to taste the wine before the king did
to make sure it had not been poisoned.
Nehemiah had this position for a reason.
Read about this reason in Nehemiah 1–2.

- Cover a plastic cup with 3 or 4 layers of newspaper strips dipped in wallpaper paste. Make the edge of the cup as

even as possible.
- Cover the cup with a layer of plain newsprint. Try to make the sides and top of the cup even.
- Let dry.
- Cover the cup with small squares of one color of tissue paper by thinning glue with a little water, applying the glue to the cup, and laying the tissue in the glue.
- Glue a strip of another color of tissue paper around the top of the cup.
- Let dry.
- Cover the cup with a coat of sealer.

487. MAGAZINE ANGEL
$ 1 HOUR 3

- Fold down the top right corner of every page of a thick magazine.
- Bring the ends together and staple. This forms the body of the angel.
- Cover the body with several coats of white or gold spray paint.
- Glue a Styrofoam ball to the top of the body for the head. Make sure the ball is in proportion to the body and not too small.
- Cut eyes and a mouth from construction paper and glue them to the head.
- Glue cotton to the head for hair.
- Cut 2 wings from thin cardboard.
- Spread glue on the wings and sprinkle with glitter.
- Shake off the excess glitter.
- Fold the wide end of the wings, not the tips, and glue to the magazine body. Hold until the glue dries.
- Use different sizes of magazines for different sizes of angels.

488. LIFESAVER BULLETIN BOARD
$$ 1 HOUR 4

- Cut a piece of plywood to fit the space where the bulletin board will be hung.
- Sand the edges of the board.

- Glue squares of cork to the front of the board.
- Attach 2 picture hangers on the back, 1"–2" from the top and 3" from the sides.
- Glue-gun or tacky-glue the lifesavers, stacking and layering them all around the edge.
- Coat with several coats of varnish or polyurethane.
- Hang on a wall.

489. PUZZLE BULLETIN BOARD
$$ 1 HOUR 4

- Cut a piece of plywood to fit the space where the bulletin board will be hung.
- Sand the edges of the board.
- Glue squares of cork to the front of the board.
- Attach 2 picture hangers on the back, 1"–2" from the top and 3" from the sides.
- Glue-gun or tacky-glue puzzle pieces, stacking and layering them all around the edge.
- Coat with several coats of varnish or polyurethane.
- Hang on a wall.

490. BASEBALL CARD BULLETIN BOARDS
$$ 1 HOUR 4

- Cut a piece of plywood to fit the space where the bulletin board will be hung.
- Sand the edges of the board.
- Glue squares of cork to the front of the board.
- Attach 2 picture hangers on the back, 1"–2" from the top and 3" from the sides.
- Hot glue-gun or tacky-glue baseball cards, stacking and layering them all around the edge.
- Coat with several coats of varnish or polyurethane.
- Hang on a wall.

491. BIBLE BOX
$$ 1 HOUR 1

The Pilgrims kept their Bibles in decorative wooden boxes.
Some of the boxes had a carved lion on the lid
as a symbol for England.

- Purchase a wooden box big enough to hold your Bible without bending its cover.
- Paint the box with several coats of acrylic paint, letting each coat dry before applying the next one.
- Decorate your box by gluing on pictures of flags and eagles.
- Coat with several layers of clear spray sealer or varnish.
- Or, paint small wooden shapes with acrylics, seal or varnish, then glue to the box.

492. DECORATED LAMPSHADE
$$ 1 HOUR 4

- Paint a cloth or paper lampshade with acrylic paints to match your room. Make sure the shade does not have a gloss finish.
- Cut out designs from your room's wallpaper and glue to the lampshade. Or, glue on stickers, buttons, or baseball cards.
- Cover the shade with 2 or 3 coats of thinned glue or Mod Podge.
- Mount the shade on your lamp and enjoy the new look!

493. VINTAGE SEED POT
$ 1 HOUR 2

- Cut the front off vintage seed packets.
- Clean a terra-cotta pot. Make sure the pot is taller than the seed packets.
- Paint the pot with several coats of acrylic paint.
- Glue the seed packet fronts to the pot.
- Put on several coats of varnish, letting it dry between coats.
- Fill the pot with soil and a plant or flower.

494. BIBLE CHARACTER FINGER PUPPETS
$ 1 HOUR 3

Read about Gideon in Judges 6 and 7.

• Draw Gideon, a fleece, a pitcher, a torch, a warrior, and a trumpet on 3" x 3" squares of thin cardboard. Make sure to leave some cardboard around each shape.
• Color with markers.
• Cut around each shape, leaving about ½" cardboard border.
• Bend up the small end of a pop-top tab and glue to the back and bottom of each puppet.
• Let dry.
• Put your finger through the tab and tell the story of Gideon. Put puppets on both hands.

495. SNOWBALL CANDLEHOLDERS
$ 1 HOUR 4

• Add small amounts of water to Ivory soap flakes.
• Form into large balls.
• Place on wax paper.
• Carefully dig out a hole big enough for a votive candle. Or, make the snowball large enough to hold and balance a taper candle.
• Sprinkle glitter on the snowball and gently press it into the surface. If the snowball is dry, spread a little glue thinned with water on it and sprinkle with glitter.
• Let dry.
• Place candles in the snowballs.

496. LOVE WREATH
$$ 1 HOUR 5

• Make a batch of salt dough (as described in Project #500).
• Divide the dough in half.
• Roll out the dough and use a heart cookie cutter to cut out 18 hearts.
• Place the hearts on a cookie sheet.

- Poke 2 holes at the top of each heart with a knitting needle or toothpick. Make sure the holes go all the way through and are large enough to be threaded with ribbon.
- Bake at 350° for about 20 minutes, or until lightly golden.
- Let cool.
- Paint with red, white, and pink acrylic paint.
- Write or paint "LOVE" on one heart and "IS" on another heart.
- Tie the hearts to the top of a grapevine wreath with ribbon or yarn.
- Write the 16 characteristics of love found in 1 Corinthians 13, one on each heart.
- Thread the hearts with ribbon or yarn and hang them on the wreath.
- Hang the wreath.

497. STYROFOAM SHEEPFOLD
C 1 HOUR 2

In John 10, Jesus tells the parable of the sheepfold.
He is the Good Shepherd,
and He knows and cares for His sheep.

- Color the textured side of a Styrofoam tray brown.
- Cut the colored tray into 2" wide strips.
- On a 9" x 12" sheet of white construction paper, draw hills and color them green.
- Color the sky blue.
- Glue the strips of brown Styrofoam into a square on the green hills to form the sheepfold. Cut the strips if they are too long. Leave an opening for the gate.
- Spread a layer of glue over the gate area.
- Lay toothpicks in the glue, touching each other to form the gate.
- Draw several fluffy bodies of sheep on a white Styrofoam tray.
- Cut out.
- Glue onto the construction paper in different areas.
- Add small black rectangles for legs.
- Draw a head on each sheep.
- Draw a shepherd on a white tray and color.
- Cut out and glue the shepherd to the scene.

498. BONGO DRUM
$ 1 HOUR 4

- Find a plate or lid 2"–3" larger than the top of a medium-sized flower pot.
- Trace the plate or lid on a brown paper bag 4 times and cut out.
- Paint the pot with 2 to 3 coats of acrylic paint.
- Paint on designs.
- Let dry.
- Seal with a clear sealer.
- Place one paper circle over the opening of the flower pot and wrap the edge over the top of the pot.
- Glue the paper to the pot, folding the paper so it lies flat.
- Place a rubber band or tie a string around the paper to hold it until the glue dries.
- Remove the band or string.
- Spread glue on the paper top and place another paper circle on and glue down the edge.
- Secure with a rubber band or string.
- Repeat until all 4 circles have been glued to the pot.
- Various sizes of pots will make different bongo drum sounds.

499. AUTOGRAPH PILLOW
$ 1 HOUR 2

- Cut 2 pieces of plain cotton fabric into a square or animal shape.
- Place the fabric right sides together and pin.
- Stitch all the way around the edge leaving an opening for stuffing.
- Clip all the way around the pillow, making sure not to clip through the stitching.
- Turn the pillow right side out.
- Stuff with old pantyhose or batting.
- Sew the opening closed.
- Have your friends autograph the pillow with pens or markers.

500. WALNUT MOBILE
$ 1 HOUR 3

*Some of the disciples and many others
in the time of Jesus were fishermen.
Make this mobile to illustrate an important occupation.*

• Carefully crack open 3 walnuts and dig out the meat.
• Fill each walnut half with a salt-dough mixture. (To make the
    salt dough, mix together 2 cups flour and 1 cup salt. Mix in
    1 cup of water to make a dough. It should not be sticky.)
• Cut small triangles from colored construction paper.
• Glue a toothpick to each sail by laying a glue strip on the sail
    and placing the toothpick in the glue. The toothpick should
    go above the top of the sail, so a string can be attached to it
    to hang.
• Let dry.
• Write the name of a disciple on both sides of each sail.
• Stick a sail into the salt-dough mixture of each walnut.
• Tie 2 sticks together in the center.
• Tie each walnut sailboat by the top of the toothpick mast to
    one of the sticks.
• Hang the mobile by attaching a string to the end of each stick
    or from the center where the sticks cross.

501. CORK COASTERS
$ 1 HOUR 2

• Cut four 3" x 3" squares from a sheet of cork.
• Draw a simple design on each coaster.
• Color the designs with a permanent marker.
• Seal with a clear spray sealer.
• Glue a piece of felt on the back of each coaster.

502. MACARONI BOOKENDS
$$ 1 HOUR 5

- Purchase metal bookends at an office supply store.
- Cut 2 blocks of wood a little bigger than the upright side of the bookends.
- Paint the wood blocks with several coats of acrylic paint, letting each coat dry before applying the next coat.
- Lay out a macaroni design on a piece of wax paper cut to the same size as the wood block. For example, flowers, cars, or strips of different shapes of macaroni.
- Paint the macaroni with acrylic paints.
- Glue the macaroni onto the blocks according to the design planned.
- Cover with a clear sealer.
- Glue the wood blocks to the metal bookends.
- Place your Bible and favorite books between the bookends on a shelf.

503. VERSE BLOCK PUZZLE
$$ 1 HOUR 3

- Purchase 6 plain wooden blocks of the same size.
- Stack the blocks in 2 rows of 3 blocks each.
- Cut 12 pieces of white paper a little smaller than the side of a block.
- On 6 pieces of paper, write a verse—several words per paper.
- Repeat with the other 6 pieces of paper.
- Decorate and color each verse paper.
- Glue the 6 pieces of one verse on the same side of the 6 blocks.
- Glue the second verse on the opposite side of the blocks.
- Mix up the blocks and try to put the blocks together to form a verse.

504. WORLD'S GREATEST FRIEND
C 1 HOUR 1

- Draw a figure of a boy or girl on a piece of cardboard. Cut out.
- Cover a section of the figure with a thick layer of glue.
- Lay different colors of yarn in the glue to create clothes, hair, skin, etc.
- Cover the whole cardboard figure with yarn.
- Cut a small square of cardboard that fits on the back of the figure.
- Trim the edge of the square with a piece of yarn.
- In the center of the square, write "World's Greatest Friend," and "Proverbs 17:17."
- Glue the sign to the back of the figure.
- Write: "To:" and "From:" on the back.
- Mail or give to a friend!

505. BRAIDED HOT PLATE
$ 1 HOUR 3

- Cut 3 strips of fabric 3" wide and 36" long.
- Safety-pin the 3 ends together and weigh down with a heavy weight or tie to a drawer handle.
- Braid the 3 strips of fabric together.
- Sew together the 3 strips of fabric at each end of the braid.
- Starting at one end, coil the braid and sew each coil together.
- Continue coiling and sewing.
- Tuck in the end of the braid and sew in place.
- Place on the table under a hot dish.

506. SWORD OF THE SPIRIT
C 1 HOUR 1

This piece of the armor of God is His Word, the Bible.

- Draw a sword on a large piece of heavy cardboard.
- Paint the handle with brown or black acrylic paint.

- Cover the sword with several layers of foil.
- Cut out small pictures of Bibles and glue them to the sword.

507. HELMET OF SALVATION
$ 2 HOURS 3

- Find a plastic bowl or bucket that fits on your head, but doesn't cover your eyes. Cover the bowl or bucket with a thin coat of Vaseline.
- Cover the bowl with 5 to 6 layers of newspaper strips dipped in a mixture of water and wallpaper paste. Make the bottom rim as even as possible.
- Cover with one layer of plain newsprint paper.
- Let dry overnight.
- To make horns for the helmet, use two pieces of lightweight cardboard rolled into a cone shape.
- Tape them to the helmet.
- Cover with 3 layers of newspaper strips and one layer of plain newsprint dipped in wallpaper paste. Let dry.
- Paint the helmet with acrylic paint.
- Paint the horns with gray or white acrylic.
- Write the word "Salvation" across the front of the helmet.

508. TOPIARY
$ 2 HOURS 5

- Fill a flower pot with Sahara Dry Flo Brick or green foam block.
- Dig out the center and fit a thick stick in the hole. Make sure the hole is a little smaller than the thickness of the stick. This will ensure a secure fit.
- Dig out a small hole in the bottom of a Styrofoam ball and fit the ball onto the top of the stick.
- Glue dried flowers onto the ball with a hot glue gun. Cover the entire ball.
- Fill in the top of the pot with more moss.

509. "THIS IS THE DAY" PLAQUE
$ 2 HOURS 1

• Print neatly Psalm 118:24 on a 6" x 9" sheet of white paper. Emphasize certain words, like "day," with a different color or style of lettering.
• Glue the verse to a 10" x 12" sheet of green poster board.
• Glue the poster board to a thick piece of 10" x 12" cardboard.
• Glue large seeds around the verse and the edge of the green poster board to create a border.
• Fill in the remaining green poster board by gluing on bits of dried moss, eucalyptus leaves, flowers, and grasses.
• Glue a hanger on the back.

510. CLAY LAMP
$$ 2 HOURS 5

Place this lamp on your desk or dresser to remind yourself of God's light and goodness in a sinful world.

• In a pictorial Bible dictionary, find a picture of a lamp that was used in Bible times.
• Form a large ball of oven-bake clay into the oval shape of a lamp, with one pointed end and a hole for the wick.
• Bake according to the clay package instructions.
• Cut flames from yellow and orange tissue paper.
• Cut one flame from yellow construction paper.
• Write "2 Samuel 22:29" and the words of the verse on the construction-paper flame.
• Glue the flames inside the wick hole so the verse can be read.

511. MOUSE TREE HOUSE
$ 2 HOURS 2

• Draw a U on the front of a large oatmeal box. Start the U at the top and touch the curve of the U about ½" from the bottom. The U should be about 5" wide.
• Cut out the U.

- Repeat with a small oatmeal box. Do not cut off any of the bottom.
- Fit the small box inside the large one. The bottom of the small box will be the second story of the mouse house.
- Tape the box in place.
- Roll up one-quarter of a sheet of newspaper and tape around the bottom of the box. This will cause the outside of the box to taper out at the bottom like a tree.
- Roll several one-quarter sheets of newspaper into a tube and tape vertically on the outside of the tree box to form bark.
- Cover the outside of the box with strips of newspaper dipped in a mixture of wallpaper paste and water.
- Cover the edges of the U-shaped openings and the bottom edge of the small box.
- Cover with 3 layers of newspaper strips.
- Let dry.
- Cover the outside of the tree with a layer of tacky glue and press moss and other dried natural material such as bark, seeds, and leaves into the glue.
- Work on a small section at a time.
- Cover the first and second story floors.
- Cover the inside of the box with dried leaf "wallpaper" or other natural materials.
- Play house with the mouse family from Project #464.

512. SALT DOUGH PLAQUE
$ 2 HOURS 4

- Mix 2 cups of flour and 1 cup salt together. Stir in 1 cup of water.
- Knead for about 7 minutes.
- Pick an encouraging phrase, such as, "God loves you," or "The Lord is good."
- Flatten the dough with your hands or a rolling pin on a cookie sheet. Dough should be 1" thick.
- Draw the letters of the phrase in the dough with a pen or toothpick. The letters should connect.
- With a table knife, cut out the phrase following the outside line. Cut out any holes like the center of an O or a space between the letters where they don't touch.

• Bake at 325° for 30–40 minutes. Prick any bubbles.
• Paint the plaque with acrylic paint.
• Outline the words in black marker.
• Hang the plaque with a ribbon.

513. SODA CAN ROBOT
$ 2 HOURS 2

• Collect used soda cans.
• Tape the cans together with electrical tape to make a robot.
• Tape the cans several cans wide for the body.
• Make sure the robot has good proportions. For example, the legs are bigger than the arms.

514. SPECIALIZED SUITCASE
$$ 2 HOURS 2

• Purchase an old hard-sided suitcase at a thrift store or garage sale.
• Cut out pictures from old magazines. Use pictures of things you enjoy, like animals, flowers, Bible story pictures, or pictures and words from travel brochures.
• Lightly sand the outside of the suitcase and wipe it clean.
• Spread a layer of glue on a small section of a side.
• Arrange the pictures in the glue.
• Cover the whole case with a collage of pictures.
• Let dry.
• Coat the case with several coats of varnish, letting each coat dry before applying the next coat.

515. WAXED LEAF WREATH
$ 2 HOURS 5

• Melt some wax in a pan placed in an electric skillet filled with water. Be careful not to get the wax too hot because it will start to burn.
• Cover the leaves by dipping them into the melted wax.
• Lay on wax paper to cool.

- Cover a straw wreath by attaching the leaves with glue gun.
- Hang.

516. MINIATURE QUILT
$ 2 HOURS 4

- Cut scraps of fabric into 2" x 2" squares.
- Pin the right sides of 2 squares together.
- Sew down one side, about ¼" from the edge.
- Open the squares and iron the seam flat.
- Pin another square to the double square and sew one edge. This will be a column of 3 squares.
- Open and iron the seam flat.
- Sew together 2 more columns of 3 squares each.
- Sew the 3 columns together. This will form the top of the quilt.
- Cut a square of fabric and batting the same size as the front.
- Lay the quilt right side up.
- Top with the backing fabric, right side down, so the right sides of the top and the back are together.
- Top with the batting.
- Pin together.
- Sew around 3 sides.
- Turn the quilt to the right side.
- Sew the opening shut.
- Tie the quilt by threading a needle with a short length of yarn and poking the yarn through the quilt so both ends are loose on the front of the quilt.
- Tie the ends together, twice, into a knot.
- Tie yarn at each corner of each square.

517. BATIK HEART PILLOW
$$ 2 HOURS 5

- Tack a piece of white cotton or silk fabric to a wooden frame. Wooden stretchers can be found at a craft store.
- Draw a large heart on the fabric, leaving a ½" border.
- Draw several small hearts inside the large heart.
- Fill an old egg poacher or a 6-cup muffin tin with small pieces

of red and pink wax crayons. Keep the colors separate.
- Place in an electric skillet.
- Fill the skillet half full of water.
- Melt the wax.
- Paint each small heart with red melted wax.
- With a different brush, paint the large heart pink.
- Let dry.
- Take the fabric off the frame and cut out the heart, leaving $\frac{1}{2}$" border.
- Place the heart between layers of newspaper and press with an iron.
- Wash the heart in soapy water.
- Rinse and iron.
- Iron off all the wax, using more newspaper if necessary.
- On a second piece of fabric, trace the heart and cut out.
- Pin right sides together.
- Sew around the edge, leaving a $\frac{1}{2}$" border. Leave an opening.
- Clip all the way around the heart, being careful not to clip through the stitching.
- Turn the pillow and stuff.
- Sew the opening closed.

ACTIVITIES FOR
MIDDLER CHILDREN

GAMES

518. I-LOVE-MY-PARENT GAME
C 15 MIN. 1

This is a fun game to play on Mother's Day or Father's Day.

• One child starts by saying, "I love my mother (or father) because she/he is. . . ." Fill in the blank with a descriptive word that begins with the letter A. For example, "I love my mother because she is Able to take care of me."

- The next child might say, "I love my mother because she is Beautiful."
- Continue taking turns using the next letter of the alphabet.
- Some of the answers might become very funny, especially at the end of the alphabet!

519. BEAN-BAG OBSTACLE COURSE
C 15 MIN. 1

- Set up an obstacle course.
- Time each child while he runs through the course with a bean bag balanced on his head.
- If the bag falls off, the child must stop and put the bag back on his head, then continue through the course.
- The child with the best time wins.

520. UNDER AND OVER BALLOON RELAY
C 15 MIN. 1

- Divide into 2 teams.
- Each team lines up behind a leader.
- Give each team a blown-up balloon.
- At the start signal, each team leader passes the balloon over his head to the next player.
- The second player then passes the balloon through (under) his legs to the third player.
- Continue passing the balloon over/under, over/under to the last player in line.
- When the balloon reaches the last player he then runs, with the balloon, to the front of the line and passes the balloon over his head and under/over to the last player.
- The first team to get the leader back to the front of the line wins!

521. DON'T-SPILL-THE-BEANS RELAY
C 15 MIN. 1

- Divide into 2 teams.
- Mark a start line and place 2 chairs toward the far end of the

room or yard.
- Give the first player on each team a paper plate with 5 dried beans on it.
- At the start signal, the first player must hold up his plate like a waiter and walk or run around the chair and back to the start line without spilling any beans.
- If beans are spilled, the player must stop and put them back on the plate, then continue toward his line.
- The first team to have every player run the course wins.

522. CANDY HEART RELAY
$ 15 MIN. 1

*This is a fun game to play at
a Valentine's Day or Christmas party.*

- Divide into 2 teams.
- Give each player a spoon. Give the player at the head of the line a red candy or chocolate foil-covered heart to place on his spoon.
- At the start signal, the player must pass his candy to the next person.
- The first team to pass its candy to the end of the line and back to the beginning wins.
- After the relay, let everyone have some candy!

523. JUMPING ROPE CONTEST
C 15 MIN. 1

- See who can jump rope the longest.
- Play music to see if the rhythm helps you jump longer.

524. FOUR CORNERS
C 15 MIN. 1

- This game requires at least 5 players.
- A player stands at each corner of a large square or room.

- One blindfolded player stands in the center as *It*.
- As *It* counts to 5, the players can change corners.
- *It* calls a corner and the player in that corner is out.
- *It* counts to 5 again and the players switch corners.
- *It* calls a corner and that player is out.
- The last player left is the winner and becomes *It*.

525. DOUGHNUT ON A STRING
$ 15 MIN. 2

- Hang a string across the room at a little above head height.
- Hang one doughnut per player from the string.
- At the start signal, see who can eat his doughnut first (no hands allowed).
- Let everyone finish his doughnut.

526. JUMP ROPE
C 15 MIN. 1

- Take turns holding the rope and jumping.
- Make up a rhyme using a story from the Bible. For example, "Once there was a man named Saul and he wasn't very tall. He heard the call of the Lord and his name became Paul. . . ."

527. HOLD YOUR BREATH
C 15 MIN. 1

- One person says "GO!" and the other players see how long they can hold their breath.
- Use a watch to time how long the breath is held.

528. AVOID-A-WORD GAME
C 15 MIN. 1

- Pick a word that cannot be said for a set amount of time, like 15 minutes.

- The word should be one that is frequently used, such as "the" or "and."
- It can be fun to try to trick another person into saying the word.

529. BIBLE SENTENCE
C 15 MIN. 1

*This project is a fun way to learn
the books of the Bible and their spellings.*

- Pick a book from the Bible and make a sentence out of the letters in the name. For example, for Matthew, "My Aunt Thelma Teaches History Every Week."

530. SONG CHARADES
C 15 MIN. 1

- One player is chosen as *It*.
- *It* chooses a song to act out. For example, "This Little Light of Mine," "Deep and Wide," or "The B-I-B-L-E."
- *It* acts out the song, and the other players try to guess the title.
- The player who guesses is the next *It*.

531. COMPOUND WORD GAME
C 15 MIN. 1

*A compound word is made up of two separate words.
For example, "blackboard" and "baseball."*

- Have each individual choose a favorite book.
- Set a time limit for playing the game.
- See how many compound words you can find in the text of your book before the time runs out.
- The person who finds the most compound words wins.

532. PAPER BAG SKIT
C 15 MIN. 1

• Place several items in a paper bag, such as a scarf, rock, or palm branch.
• Open the bag and take a few minutes to think of a Bible story to act out.
• Act out the story.
• For a group of Sunday school or youth group kids, divide into teams and use several bags of items.
• This is fun for birthday parties, too!

533. FILL-THE-CUP RACE
$ 15 MIN. 2

• Divide into teams.
• For each team, place a plastic cup, 2 pencils, and 10 objects, like lifesavers, jellybeans, or peanuts, on a table.
• Upon the start signal, one person from each team fills his cup with the objects, using the pencils like chopsticks, and then dumps them out of the cup for the next person.
• Then, the second person fills the cup.
• Continue to play until every person on the team has had a chance to fill the cup.
• The team done first wins.
• Or play by yourself and try to beat your best time of putting the objects into the cup.

534. EGG RACE
C 15 MIN. 1

• Mark a starting line.
• Place items such as chairs, an old tire, and a box as objects to crawl through or run around.
• Place a raw egg on a serving spoon.
• See who can run through the obstacle course the fastest, without dropping and breaking the egg!

535. BLADE WHISTLE
C 15 MIN. 1

• Pick a thick blade of grass.
• Place the blade between your thumbs, parallel to the thumbs.
• Blow between your thumbs to make a whistling noise.

536. BUBBLE-BLOWING CONTEST
$ 15 MIN. 1

• Divide into teams.
• Give each player 2–3 sticks of bubble gum.
• The first person in each line blows the biggest bubble he can.
• Give a point to the biggest bubble.
• When all the players have blown a bubble, add up the score.
• The team with the most points wins.

537. TOPPLING DOMINOES
C 15 MIN. 1

• Stand up dominoes in a long curved row, in a square pattern, or in any configuration.
• Topple the dominoes by pushing down the first one.

538. TELEPHONE GAME
C 15 MIN. 1

• Have the players sit in a circle.
• The first person whispers a sentence or a verse to the second player, who then whispers it to the next person.
• Continue passing on the message to the last person.
• The last person tells the group what he was just told, which might be very different than what the first person originally said.
• The change in the message can be very funny!

539. FILL-IN-THE-BLANK GAME
C 15 MIN. 1

- One player starts by making a statement, like, "As green as a _____."
- The second player finishes the statement: "As green as a pea."
- Take turns starting a riddle and finishing it.

540. BIBLE I SPY
C 15 MIN. 3

- Make a list of things to find in the Bible. For example, animals, people, places, numbers, and type of weather, like rain and wind.
- Give each child the same list.
- Use the concordance in the back of a Bible to find a word from the list, then a reference that has the word in the verse.
- Write down the reference beside the word.
- The first child to find everything on the list wins.
- Look up the references. This will help the child learn where the books of the Bible are and how to find a chapter and verse.

541. ACROSS THE YARD
C 15 MIN. 1

- Upon the start signal, each player must walk to the opposite end of the yard in exactly 3 minutes without the use of a watch.
- One player times the walkers and writes down the time each player reached the end of the yard.
- The player who arrives at the opposite end closest to 3 minutes wins.
- Players may walk and stop however they want as they try to reach the opposite end of the yard in what they think is 3 minutes.

542. TUG-OF-WAR
$ 30 MIN. 2

- Divide players into 2 teams.
- Tie an old scarf in the middle of a long, thick rope.

- Mark a line on the ground 60" (5') from the scarf on each side.
- At the start signal, each team tries to pull the other team over their line.
- To make this game more interesting, create a mud puddle in the center so the players are pulled toward the mud.

543. CODED TELEGRAM
C 30 MIN. 1

Jonathan and David were the best of friends.
Read about them in 1 Samuel 13–23.
They had to be careful because
Jonathan's father, King Saul, hated David.

- Make a telegram that David might have sent to Jonathan.
- Use the first letter of each word to spell out a place they could meet in secret.

544. WALKING MAP
C 30 MIN. 5

Children love going for walks and exploring places!

- Take a clipboard, blank paper, pencil, and eraser along on a walk through your neighborhood.
- Mark on the sheet of paper your street, house, and any cross streets or landmarks. For example, a friend's house, a large oak tree, stop signs, etc.

545. COIN HORSE RACE
$ 30 MIN. 1

- Place five 50-cent pieces in a cross shape.
- Place 4 quarters between each 50-cent piece, forming an outside circle.
- Place 4 nickels in the middle between the quarters and the 50-cent piece in the center.

235

- Give each player 3 markers that are distinguishable from those of their opponents.
- To play, a player rolls a die and moves one of his markers, or "horses," onto a 50-cent piece on the outside of the circle. Advance the horse according to the number on the die.
- Move the horse clockwise around the circle.
- A horse can be moved through the center of the circle if it has landed on a 50-cent piece.
- If a horse lands on an opponent, the opponent's horse goes back to start.
- The first player to move his horses around or through the circle back to his beginning 50-cent piece wins.

546. PLEDGE OF ALLEGIANCE
C 30 MIN. 1

- Make up your own pledge of allegiance to God.
- Include phrases like, "God of the Universe," and "I give my all."
- The first line might go something like this: "I pledge my allegiance to the God of the Universe. . . ."

547. GUESS THE SONG
C 30 MIN. 1

- Choose one player to be *It*.
- *It* taps out the rhythm of a well-known chorus or hymn on a table with chopsticks or by clapping his hands.
- The other players try to guess the song.
- The player who guesses the correct song is the next *It*, and taps or claps out a new song.

548. PICTURE CHARADES
C 30 MIN. 1

- Divide into teams.
- Set a 3-minute time limit.
- One player from each team draws a picture of a person, place, or thing.

- The other team members try to guess what the drawing is.
- When 3 minutes are up, the other team takes a turn.
- Play until each team member has had a chance to draw.
- The team that guessed the most pictures wins.

549. HOME 20 QUESTIONS
C 30 MIN. 1

- Choose a player to be *It*.
- *It* thinks of an object in one of 4 rooms in the house: the kitchen, family or living room, a bedroom, and the bathroom.
- The other players ask yes-or-no questions to figure out the object *It* has chosen.
- The player who guesses the answer becomes the next *It* and chooses a new object.
- If the players have not guessed the object in 20 questions or less, the same player continues to be *It*.

550. BIBLICAL CHARACTER 20 QUESTIONS
C 30 MIN. 1

- Choose a player to be *It*.
- *It* thinks of a biblical character, like Naomi.
- The other players ask yes-or no-questions to figure out the person.
- Only 20 questions can be asked.
- The player who guesses the character becomes the next *It* and chooses a new character.
- If the players have not guessed the character in 20 questions or less, the same player continues to be *It*.

551. RUBBER BAND GUITARS
C 30 MIN. 1

- Stretch different types and sizes of rubber bands across different objects like boxes, an oatmeal container, terra-cotta pots, etc.
- See how many different types of sounds you can make.

552. NUMBER SEQUENCE GAME
C 30 MIN. 1

This is a great memory builder.

- One player starts by saying a number, such as "5."
- The next player says "5" and another number. For example, "5 and 2."
- The next player says "5, 2, and 22."
- Keep adding numbers until you can't remember their order.
- See who can remember the most numbers!

553. FILL-IN-THE-ANSWER GUESSING GAME
C 30 MIN. 2

- One player is chosen to be *It*.
- *It* picks a man or woman from the Bible and gives a clue. For example, "I am in an Old Testament book."
- Player #1 would make a guess of either a man or woman.
- *It* would then give another clue. For example, "I talked with Ruth."
- Player #2 would take a guess.
- Continue giving clues and trying to guess the answer until 10 clues have been given.
- Give 5 points to the player who guesses the answer.
- The player who guesses the answer gets to chose a new person and give clues.
- The player with the most points wins.
- Make sure every player has a chance to give clues.

554. LICENSE PLATE GAME
C 30 MIN. 1

- While riding in a vehicle, each person tries to guess the state that the next car that comes into view will be from.
- Players can guess the same state.
- Award one point for a correct answer.
- The person to reach 20 points first wins.

555. WHO WOULD YOU BE?
C 30 MIN. 1

- Each player takes a turn asking the other players what famous person they would be. For example, Moses, Eve, Abraham Lincoln, or Laura Ingalls Wilder.
- The other players answer why they would be the person they chose.

556. BLINDFOLDED DRAWING
C 30 MIN. 1

- The first player picks an object to draw. For example, a car.
- Each player, including the player who chose the object, will close his eyes or be blindfolded and attempt to draw the object.
- When every player is finished with his drawing, show the pictures.
- Let each player have a turn at picking an object to draw.

557. DRESSING CONTEST
C 30 MIN. 1

- Divide into teams.
- Provide a set of clothes for each team.
- The first players in line run to their pile of clothes and put them on.
- When they have taken the clothes off and run back to their lines, it is the next person's turn.
- The first team done wins.

558. EXERCISE CHART
C 30 MIN. 1

- Make a list of various exercises like sit ups, leg lifts, push ups, etc.

- Make a chart with the exercises written across the top.
- Down the left side, write numbers for the days of the month.
- When an exercise is completed, write the number of times it was done, or the number of minutes, beside the date.
- Try to exercise every day or three times a week.

559. VERSE SCAVENGER HUNT
C 30 MIN. 1

- Pick a verse from the Bible.
- At the start signal, find the words of the verse from old newspapers, catalogs, or magazines.
- Cut out the words and tape them to a piece of paper.
- The first person or team with a completed verse wins.

560. DIAMOND HOPSCOTCH
C 30 MIN. 1

- With chalk, draw large diamonds on the patio or sidewalk in the pattern of: 1 diamond, 2, 1, 2, 1. The sides should touch.
- Place a small stone for the marker on the first diamond.
- Hop over the marker, landing with 2 feet on 2 diamonds and one foot on the single diamonds.
- At the end, turn around and hop back, picking up the marker and moving it to the next diamond.
- Do not land on the diamond with a marker.

561. DOTS AND LINES GAME
C 30 MIN. 1

- Draw a grid of dots on a piece of paper. The dots should be evenly spaced and be arranged in rows.
- Each person draws a horizontal or vertical line from one dot to the next.
- Then the next player draws a line.
- Players continue taking turns until a box is formed. When a

player forms a box he writes his initial in it.
- A player may continue making boxes until no more can be made.
- The person with the most boxes wins.

562. RHYMING STORY
C 30 MIN. 1

- Make a list of nonsense words that rhyme. For example, apple, bapple, sapple. . . Dinosaur, linosaur, kinosaur. . . , etc.
- Make up a nonsense fantasy story!

563. MUMMY WRAP
$ 30 MIN. 1

- Divide into teams.
- Set a time limit, like 20 minutes.
- Pick one person from each team to be the mummy.
- Team members wrap the person with toilet paper.
- The best-looking mummy wins.

564. WALL SHADOWS
C 30 MIN. 1

- Place a light near the wall or use a wall that the sun is shining on.
- Use your hands to create shadows on the wall.
- Practice making a sailboat, a cross, people, or animals.

565. MUSICAL GLASSES
C 30 MIN. 1

- Fill 8 glasses with different amounts of water.
- Tap on the side of each glass with a spoon.
- Each glass will have a different tone.
- Tap out a song on the glasses.

566. PING-PONG TOSS
$ 30 MIN. 1

- Line up 5 containers, such as a bucket, oatmeal box, etc., in a row, one behind the other.
- Mark a line to stand behind.
- Give a point value to each container. For example, the closest container could be worth 5 points, while the farthest one could be worth 30 points.
- Stand behind the line with 5 balls and toss a ball into a container.
- Add up the points.
- Try to beat your best score or play with a friend!

567. ODD ONE OUT
C 30 MIN. 1

- One player lists 3 or 4 things with one item that doesn't belong.
- Another player states which item doesn't belong in the group.
- For example, apple, hammer, banana, grapes.
- As the players become better, they will create harder puzzles.

568. DESCRIBING GAME
C 30 MIN. 1

- One player starts by picking an object or person and states one descriptive word used in a simple sentence. For example, "Jesus was perfect."
- The next player adds another descriptive word, such as, "Jesus is eternal."
- Keep adding as many words as you can think of.
- Or, a player may state, "A tree is green." The next player might add, "A tree is tall."

569. PENNY HOCKEY
C 30 MIN. 1

- Try to flick a penny through 2 objects used as goal posts, such as another player's fingers.

- Give each person the same amount of tries.
- The one with the most goals wins.

570. ALPHABET CARD GAME
$ 30 MIN. 1

- Place a deck of alphabet flash cards face down.
- Decide on a category like Bible names, colors, food, toys, etc.
- Turn over the top card so a letter shows.
- The first one to shout out a word that starts with that letter gets the card.
- Continue through the deck until all the cards are used.
- The child with the most cards wins.

571. HEADS UP, 7-UP
C 30 MIN. 1

This game is for a larger group.

- Seven players are chosen to be *It.*
- All the other players lay their heads down and close their eyes and hold one thumb up.
- The *It* players walk around and each touches the thumb of one player.
- The *It* players return to their spot and everyone raises his head.
- The players whose thumbs were touched try to guess who touched their thumb. If they guess correctly, they become one of the *It* players and the first *It* sits down in his seat.
- Play for a set amount of time.

572. PRODIGAL SON ACROSTIC
C 30 MIN. 2

- Read Luke 15:11–32.
- In a book, like the one in Project #771, write, "THE PRODIGAL SON" in capital letters in a column going down.

- Beside each letter, write a word that describes a part of the story. For example, for the "P," write "pods" and for the "O," write "The father went out to talk to his older son."

573. GROCERY STORE
C 30 MIN. 1

- Save all kinds of containers, cereal and Jell-O boxes, soup cans, shampoo bottles, etc.
- Arrange the boxes and cans on shelves or crates.
- Use play money to go shopping at your grocery store!

574. HAIRSTYLING DAY
C 30 MIN. 1

- Gather brushes, combs, barrettes, elastic bands, and curlers.
- Let the children style each other's hair or the parents' hair.

575. BOBBING FOR APPLES
$ 30 MIN. 3

- Fill a big, clean bucket or pail with water.
- Place apples in the water.
- Try to grab an apple in your mouth or with your teeth. Do not use your hands.

576. FOUR-SQUARE GAME
C 30 MIN. 1

- Draw a large square on the cement or blacktop with a piece of chalk.
- Divide into 4 squares.
- Mark each square A, B, C, or D.
- One person stands in each square.
- To play, the player in square A hits the ball into another square. The person in that square hits the ball back or to another person in another square.

- The ball must hit the ground.
- If the ball bounces twice in a square, that player is out and the players move up one square if there are more than 4 players.
- If there are only 4 players the last person left is the winner.

577. DICE SPELLING
C 45 MIN. 1

- Write down the letters of the alphabet on a sheet of paper.
- Beside each letter, write a number in corresponding order, starting with A = 1, B = 2, etc.
- Take turns rolling 5 dice.
- Decide what word to roll for. For example, roll for "heaven," or use a dictionary to find an unfamiliar word.
- Read the definition, then roll for the letters.
- Each player will need a pencil and paper.
- A player may use the number of dots on a die for a letter, such as 5 for the letter E, or may add his dice together to get a letter. For example, 5 + 3 to get 8 for the letter H.
- All or several of the dice can be added.
- A player may have up to 5 letters per roll.
- The first player to spell the agreed-upon word wins.
- Or choose several words to work on at once.

578. KICK THE CAN
C 45 MIN. 1

- Choose a person to be *It*. *It* counts to 50.
- The other players hide.
- *It* tries to find the other players.
- *It* then runs to a tree and covers his eyes and counts to 50.
- The other players then try to run in and kick the can. If they do they are safe. After a player kicks the can, he must put it back in the original spot.
- If *It* tags a player before he can kick the can, that player is out.

579. DODGEBALL
C 45 MIN. 1

- Divide into teams.
- One team stands in front of a wall.
- Using one or 2 balls, the other team stands behind a line and tries to hit the other team with the balls.
- When a player is hit with the ball he is out.
- When all the players are out, switch sides.

580. WATER BALLOON FIGHT
$ 45 MIN. 3

- Fill balloons with water.
- Outside, on a hot day, have fun throwing water balloons at each other.

581. PRESENT TREASURE HUNT
C 45 MIN. 1

This is a fun way to give a gift for any occasion!

- Hide a gift somewhere in the house.
- On a card, write a clue for the gift recipient to solve to find the next clue.
- Hide other clues throughout the house, yard, and garage.
- The last clue reveals the location of the gift.

582. GUESS WHICH ONE?
C 45 MIN. 1

This is a fun game to play at a birthday party.

- Lay out 9 magazines or books on the floor in 3 rows of 3.
- The emcee will pick another child who secretly has been told how to play the game.

- The child chosen says, "I can guess, every time, which magazine has been picked."
- Send the chosen child out of the room.
- A child in the audience will pick a magazine to be guessed.
- The chosen child comes back into the room.
- The emcee, using a yardstick, will point to a magazine and ask, "Is this the one?" The child answers yes or no.
- The trick is that the emcee will point to a magazine and the area pointed to will indicate which magazine is to be guessed. For example, if the magazine in the upper left corner is chosen, the point of the yardstick will be placed on any magazine at the upper left corner. If the center magazine has been chosen, the point of the yardstick will be placed in the center of any magazine.
- The emcee will continue asking "Is this the one?" until he points to the magazine chosen and the child says, "Yes that's the one!" Remember, the first magazine pointed to will tell the one guessing which magazine was chosen. This first magazine could also be the one chosen. The emcee must indicate which one was chosen on the first magazine pointed to.

583. ALPHABET TOSS
C 45 MIN. 1

Play this game when you need to practice spelling words for school, or when you're learning to spell the books of the Bible.

- Draw a grid of 36 squares (6 by 6) on the sidewalk with chalk.
- Draw a big letter in each square, starting with "A" at the top left.
- Write more vowels and the most-often-used consonants (R, S, T, L, N, M) in the leftover squares.
- Give each player the same spelling list, a pencil, paper, and enough pebbles for the longest word.
- Give each player 3 extra pebbles.
- Each player has the number of turns equal to the number of spelling words.
- Player #1 decides which word he will try to spell on the sidewalk grid.
- Player #1 will then throw his pebbles one at a time, trying to

land them on the correct letters.
- If he spells the word, he receives 10 points.
- After player #1 has removed his pebbles, player #2 takes his turn.
- The player who has the most points, after everyone has had his turns, wins.

584. ZOOLOGICAL SCAVENGER HUNT
C 4 HOURS 5

- Make a list of animals found at the local zoo.
- Divide the list among the children. Do not let the children know which animals the other children have.
- Using an encyclopedia, make a list of clues for each animal.
- Write the list of clues for each animal on separate index cards.
- Exchange cards.
- Visit the zoo and have each child find the animals based on the clues.
- Write the name of the animal on the card.

585. SIDEWALK SQUARES GAME
C 45 MIN. 1

- Draw a grid of squares on a sidewalk or patio so there are 5 rows of 5 squares each.
- Shade in the middle square and the middle square of each side.
- The center square is the finish.
- The middle square on each side is the players' starting square.
- This game can be played with 2 or 4 players.
- Give each player 5 markers that can be distinguished from the markers of the other players.
- Place the markers outside the shaded square on each player's side.
- To play, each player rolls two dice and moves one marker along the square, the number of the dice. The shaded square on each player's side will be counted as the first space he moves his markers onto.
- The markers move clockwise around the grid. When a marker

goes around the grid and returns to the starting square, the marker is moved up to the square above the shaded square. The shaded square is only counted once as the markers are moved onto the board.
- If a marker lands on a square already occupied by an opponent's marker, the opponent must move his marker back to the beginning.
- To win, a player must move all his markers to the center square by rolling the exact number to land on the square.
- If a player does not roll the exact number he must either move another marker or wait for his next roll.
- When a marker has landed on the center square it is removed from the board.

586. HEADS OR TAILS
C 45 MIN. 1

- Guess how many times a coin will land on heads or tails after 10, 20, 50, or 100 tosses.
- At the top of a piece of paper, write "Heads or Tails," the number of times the coin will be tossed, and your guess of heads and tails.
- Toss the coin and make a mark under the appropriate title how the coin fell.
- Try to toss the coin the same way each time.

587. DRAW THE STORY
C 45 MIN. 3

- Choose a well-known story from the Bible. For example, the story of Esther.
- Give everyone a pencil and a sheet of blank paper.
- The first "story teller" begins the story by talking about the first scene. For example, King Xerxes (Ahasuerus) was angry with Queen Vashti because she refused to come when he called for her.
- Each person draws what he thinks the scene would look like.
- The next person might say, "The king asked beautiful ladies to come before him so he could pick a new queen. Esther was one of these ladies."

- Everyone draws Esther before the king.
- Each person gets at least one chance to add to the story.
- Examine the drawings at the end of the story. How did each person show Esther as queen?, etc.

588. BIBLE WORD DRAW
$ 45 MIN. 1

- Cut index cards in half, then in half again.
- On a piece of paper, write out 20 verses and phrases that relate to God and the Bible. For example, "We love Him because He first loved us," "Oh, how He loves you and me," or "I am the Alpha and the Omega."
- Each phrase should be 8 words or less.
- Print each word of each verse or phrase on a separate card.
- To play, shuffle the cards and place them face down in a pile in the center of the table.
- Each player draws 8 cards and tries to make a sentence about God and the Bible. It can be a sentence on the list or a new one.
- Players are allowed to look at the list.
- If a player makes a sentence with the first 8 words, he is awarded 5 points.
- If no one makes a sentence, one player starts by drawing another word card.
- When a player keeps a card drawn from the pile, he must discard one.
- When one player forms a sentence, all the players turn in their cards. The cards are shuffled and the players draw 8 more.
- When every player has had the same number of turns, the player with the most points wins.

589. H-O-R-S-E BASKETBALL
C 45 MIN. 1

- One player starts by taking a shot near the hoop.
- If he makes the shot, the second player tries to make a basket from the same spot.
- If he missed the first shot, the ball is passed to the next player.

- If the second player misses the shot, he then gets the letter H.
- The player who shoots first does not earn a letter if he misses.
- The second player shoots first after the first player has missed a shot.
- Shots get progressively more difficult.
- The first player to spell the word HORSE, by missing shots, loses.

590. ABC ZOO GAME
C 45 MIN. 1

- Choose someone to be *It*.
- This person says, "I'm the zookeeper and I'm thinking of an animal that starts with the letter A."
- Each player gets to guess an animal.
- The one who guesses the correct animal is now *It* and continues with the next letter.
- Each player gets 5 guesses.
- If the animal is not guessed, *It* goes on to the next letter after giving the name of animal.

591. CHARADES
C 1 HOUR 1

- Pick a category such as Bible characters, an occupation, an activity, or where am I?
- Divide into teams.
- Take turns acting out something from the category. Do not use words or sound effects.
- Give each team a certain amount of time to guess what is being acted out.
- Each team should have the same amount of turns.
- Give a point each time a team guesses.
- The team with the most points wins.

592. ALPHABET GAME
C 1 HOUR 1

This is a fun game to play on a long car trip.

- As you are driving, look for the letters of the alphabet on signs, license plates, etc.
- The first person to spot all the letters of the alphabet starting with A is the winner.

593. SAMUEL AND ELI PUPPETS
C 1 HOUR 2

- Decorate and color 2 paper bags, one as the old priest Eli and the other as the young boy Samuel.
- Loosely tie a piece of yarn around the bags under the face to form a head and body.
- Cut a small hole on each side for your thumb and "pinkie" finger.
- Put your hand in the bag and your thumb and pinkie through the holes for arms. Put the middle fingers in the head.
- Act out the Bible story from 1 Samuel 3.

594. TALENT NIGHT
C 1 HOUR 5

- Invite over friends and neighbors to share their talents, such as playing a musical instrument or singing.

595. SPELLING BEE
C 1 HOUR 3

Hold a bee with your family or the neighborhood children!

- Make a list of words that would be the grade level of those participating.
- Give the list to those participating a few weeks before the bee will be held.
- One person will read a word and use it in a sentence and a

player will try to spell it.
- If the player spells it correctly he goes to the end of the line.
- If he spells it incorrectly he is out and the next player tries to spell it.
- Continue spelling until one person is left.
- The last person must spell correctly one more word to be the winner.

596. CHECKERS
$ 1 HOUR 2

- Cut a 16" x 16" sheet of white poster board.
- Cut thirty-two 2" x 2" squares of black construction paper.
- Cut thirty-two 2" x 2" squares of red construction paper.
- Glue the squares to the poster board in a checkerboard pattern starting with a red square in the upper left-hand corner.
- Cut 8 circles from red poster board and 8 circles from black poster board for checker pieces.
- Make these circles small enough to fit on a square of the checkerboard.
- Have fun playing the game!

597. PUMPKIN MATH GAME
C 1 HOUR 1

- Draw a pumpkin with a stem on a 5" x 5" piece of scrap paper.
- Cut out the pumpkin, then cut off the stem.
- Trace 15 pumpkins on a sheet of orange paper.
- Cut out 2 pumpkins at a time by placing a second sheet of orange paper behind the traced pumpkins. There will be 30 pumpkins.
- Trace 15 stems onto brown paper. Cut out 30 stems by placing a sheet of brown paper behind the traced stems.
- Draw curved lines on each pumpkin.
- Write an addition, subtraction, or multiplication problem on each pumpkin.
- Write the answer to each problem on a stem.
- Play the game by matching the problem with the correct answer stems in a set amount of time.
- Try to beat your own record.

598. FLAG FOOTBALL
C 1 HOUR 1

- Divide into teams.
- Mark the goals with sticks or rocks.
- Toss a coin to see which team will get the ball first.
- Give each player a strip of cloth to hook on a belt loop or pocket. Make sure the cloth or flag is loose so that it can be pulled off easily, and that the teams have different colors.
- Each team tries to score through their opponent's goal. The defense (the team without the ball) tries to stop the ball carrier by pulling off his or her "flag."
- A team that has 4 flags pulled from their players must give up the ball to the other team.

599. A WALK IN THE WOODS
C 1 HOUR 5

- Go for a walk in the woods and carry with you a notebook or journal.
- Divide several pages into categories such as Sight, Hearing, Smell, and Touch.
- Write things in each category. For example, under Touch, write rough bark or fuzzy leaf.
- See how many things you can write down.

600. MARBLE GAME
C 1 HOUR 2

- Cut strips of ½"–1"-wide lightweight cereal box cardboard.
- Draw a maze on the inside of a shoe box lid.
- Trace a few lines with glue.
- Place a strip of cardboard in the glue so the cardboard is standing up.
- Hold the strip in place until the glue dries enough for the strip to stand on its own.
- Continue tracing the maze lines with glue and standing up the cardboard.
- Let dry.

• Play the game by placing the marble at the starting point, holding the box in your hands, and trying to move the marble through the maze.

601. MARBLE CHUTE
C 1 HOUR 2

• Collect paper towel and toilet paper tubes and small boxes.
• Cut the tubes in half the long way.
• Cut holes in the boxes where needed.
• Tape tubes and boxes together to make one continuous chute.
• Roll marbles through the chutes and boxes from the top to the bottom.

602. BIG BOX MAZE
C 1 HOUR 3

• Collect large- and medium-sized boxes (from an appliance store).
• Duct-tape the boxes together to form a maze.
• Make dead-ends, windows, doors, and secret passages.
• When the maze is finished, invite friends over for a great time of crawling through the "secret passages."

603. AROUND-THE-WORLD GAME
$$ 1 HOUR 3

• Draw shipping lanes or lines on a world map across the oceans from South America to Antarctica to South Africa, etc.
• Place small Avery dots as evenly as possible along the shipping lines and on cities all around the world.
• Let each player choose a starting port.
• Use buttons for markers or markers from another game.
• Roll a die to see who goes first.
• To play, a player rolls a die and moves from his home port the number on the die.

• The first player to visit all seven continents and return to his home port wins.

604. BOWLING
$ 1 HOUR 2

• Clean off the paper labels from ten 8 oz. water bottles.
• Pour 2 colors of tempera paint into each bottle and gently turn to coat the inside of the bottle. Pour the colors down different sides of the bottle.
• Use the same colors in each bottle or make each bottle a different color.
• Let dry.
• Pour a little clean sand in the bottom of each bottle and cap it closed.
• Set the bottles up like bowling pins.
• Knock down the pins with a tennis ball.

605. FLIP CUP GAME
C 1 HOUR 3

• Poke a hole in the side of a paper or Styrofoam cup near the bottom.
• Tape the bottom of the cup to the end of a paper towel roll.
• Cover the roll and cup with 3 layers of newspaper strips dipped in a mixture of wallpaper paste and water. Do not cover the hole in the cup.
• Let dry.
• Paint with acrylic paint.
• Spray with a clear sealer.
• Cut a piece of yarn or string about 14" long.
• From the outside of the cup, put one end of the string through the hole and knot the end so it doesn't slip back through the hole.
• Tie or tape a small toy figurine or ball to the other end of the string.
• Try to flip the toy into the cup.

606. NOAH'S ARK CARD GAME
$$ 2 HOURS 2

These types of round cards are from India.

- Cut a 2" x 2" square of scrap paper.
- Cut off the corners of the square to make a circle.
- Trace the circle onto lightweight cardboard 56 times.
- Cut out all the circles.
- Divide the cards into 7 piles of 8 cards each.
- Paint each set of 8 cards with a different color of acrylic paint.
- With a marker, draw a different color border around each set of cards.
- Decide on 7 simple animal stick drawings.
- With a marker, draw one animal on each card of each set. For example, the red cards might have a lion and the yellow cards might have an elephant.
- Write numbers 1–7 on each set of cards.
- Seal each card with a spray sealer or varnish.
- To play, deal out all the cards.
- Each player turns over a card.
- The player who turns over the highest number takes the cards.
- If the numbers are the same, each player rolls a die. The player with the highest number takes the cards.
- The person with the most cards wins the game.

607. GOLIATH
$ 2 HOURS 4

Read about Goliath in 1 Samuel 17.

- Find one or two large cardboard boxes that will fit over your head and cover down to the knee.
- Cut off the flaps that close the box.
- If 2 boxes are needed cut the bottom off one and tape the 2 together to form a longer column.
- Put on the box and mark where your hands are when your arms are straight at your sides. Also mark where your eyes are.
- Cut a handhold on each side.
- Draw a rectangle at the eye area, mark it, and cut it out.

- Draw a helmet at the top, a mean face, ears, a neck, and a body.
- Draw armor on the body.
- Draw arms on the sides.
- Draw a spear on one side under the handhold.
- Draw a javelin on the back of the box in the middle.
- Try on the box and mark where your shoulders are.
- Poke 2 holes in the front and back.
- Paint the box with tempera paint.
- Put 2 dowels through the shoulder holes from the front to the back. This will help the box rest on your shoulders and give it some stability.
- Have an adult put a nail through each end of the dowels so they will not slip out of the holes.
- Act out the story of Goliath.

608. BIG BOX STORE FRONT
C 2 HOURS 5

You could also use this box for your own puppet theater!

- Draw a big square on the front of a refrigerator box to create a window. Make the window low enough for the height of the child.
- Cut out the window.
- Cut a door in the back of the box.
- Make a shelf by cutting a piece of cardboard ¼" shorter than the width of the window and 18" wide.
- Draw a line about 8" from the edge of the shelf down the length.
- Score the line.
- Fold along the scored line.
- Glue or tape the 8" folded part to the inside front so it forms a shelf over the edge of the window.
- Glue cardboard supports from the bottom of the shelf to the outside of the store front just under the window.
- Make a sign for the store with a piece of poster board and markers.
- To hang the sign, poke 2 holes in either end at the top and thread with yarn, then tie a knot at the ends of the yarn.

- Push a thumbtack into the box and hang the sign.
- Decorate the outside of the box with tempera paint.

609. BACKYARD CAMP OUT
C OVERNIGHT 4

- Pitch a tent in the backyard or sleep out under the stars.
- Invite a few friends. Have them bring their favorite game, a snack, and a flashlight.
- Play games by flashlight and enjoy the snacks.
- Make finger shadow puppets on the tent wall by holding a flashlight in front of your hand.

610. LICENSE PLATE GAME
C ONGOING 1

- While on a trip or just driving around town make a list of the different state license plates you see.
- Write down a detail about each state plate, such as the color or picture on the plate.
- See how long it takes to list every state.

611. LISTEN TO YOUR WORLD
C ONGOING 1

- Write down everything you hear for a whole day. You may be surprised how many different sounds you list and how you will become more aware of your surroundings.

ACTIVITIES FOR MIDDLER CHILDREN
EDUCATIONAL PROJECTS

612. SUGAR CUBE MATH
$ 15 MIN. 1

- Arrange 12 sugar cubes in groups that make 12. For example, one group of 12, one group of 2 x 6, and a group of 3 x 4.
- This can be done with other numbers, such as 15, 24, and 40.

613. CAR FIRST AID KIT
$$ 30 MIN. 3

- Gather items for the kit, such as a flashlight, tweezers, Band Aids, a blanket, antibacterial cream, a small bottle of water, rubber gloves, etc.
- Place the items in a box or duffel bag.
- Keep the kit in the trunk.

614. FLAT SUZY
C 30 MIN. 2

Children love receiving mail.
Here's an exciting way for them to get it.
You will be amazed at the items your child might receive in return:
Texas-sized jelly beans, clay from South Carolina,
a cactus needle from Arizona, a postcard from Pennsylvania.

- Draw a person on a piece of white paper. Trace and cut out several more.
- Using markers, watercolor paints, crayons, or colored pencils, add details to the paper doll, such as hair, eyes, and clothes to make the doll look like your self.
- Mail Flat (child's name) to friends and relatives all across the country or the world.
- Enclose a letter written by the child asking for information about that state or country.
- Sample letter: "Dear Aunt Martha, Hi, I'm mailing myself all over the country (world) to learn more about different states (countries). Please send me something from your part of the world. It could be anything from a dried plant to what you like to eat. Thank You, Flat (child's name)."

615. TYPEWRITER FUN
C 30 MIN. 2

- Put a piece of paper in an old manual or electric typewriter, or use a computer.
- Practice typing words. This will help you get to know where

the keys are.
- Type a thank-you note or a letter to your Sunday school teacher, friend, or grandparent.

616. ECO CREEK COLLECTION
C 30 MIN. 3

- Fill a big glass jar with water from a local creek.
- Use a magnifying glass to examine any creatures in the water.
- If you find a crayfish or frog, put some rocks in the jar so it is above the level of the water.
- Catch flies for the frog.
- Add more creek water everyday.
- Keep the jar out of the sun.
- Return the water and creatures to the creek after a few days.
- Write down the types of insects you find in the water.

617. TOOTHPICK FLAGS
C 30 MIN. 1

- Cut 1" x 1" rectangles of construction paper.
- Decorate the rectangle as the flag of a country with crayons or small pieces of construction paper.
- Glue the flag to the toothpick by laying a strip of glue along the left edge of the flag and placing the toothpick in the glue and rolling the edge around the toothpick.
- Use the flags to decorate a table place setting, a bulletin board border, or a castle.

618. BALANCE
$ 45 MIN. 4

- Make 3 holes around the top of 2 containers the same size. For example, yogurt cups, small milk cartons, or boxes. Make the holes in the same spot on each container.
- Cut six 6" lengths of string.
- Knot one end of the string, and thread through the holes.
- Knot the 3 strings of each container together at the top.

- Make sure the containers hang evenly.
- Hang the containers on paper clips.
- Tie a 6" length of string to each paper clip then to a piece of PVC pipe or a stick.
- Tie a string to the PVC pipe or stick.
- Hang the balance.
- If the containers are not even, try taping something light, like a paper clip or a penny, to the bottom.
- Weigh different things, such as a ½ cup flour and ½ cup sugar. Which one is heavier?
- Write the findings in a journal.
- Take the balance outside and weigh things from nature.

619. VOWEL CHART
C 45 MIN. 3

- Divide a 12" x 18" sheet of construction paper into 5 sections.
- At the top of each section, write a vowel. For example, "Long A, E, I, O, U."
- Cut out pictures from catalogs, old magazines, and newspapers that have the vowel sound, and glue them in the right section. For example, under long A, glue a picture of an ape. For long E, glue a picture of money.
- Write the word under each picture.

620. CHALK MONET GARDEN
C 45 MIN. 2

- Check out a book from the library about the French painter Claude Monet.
- Explore his famous painting style.
- Brush some water over a 9" x 12" sheet of white paper.
- Place the wet paper on a sheet of newspaper.
- Draw trees, flowers, and a pond on the paper with chalk. Follow a picture of one of Monet's paintings as an example.
- Fill in the whole paper with chalk.
- Let dry.
- Spray with hair spray to make the chalk adhere.

621. LEAF SCAVENGER HUNT
C 1 HOUR 3

- While on a day trip, vacation, or right in your own neighborhood, go on a hunt for leaves.
- Find as many different types of leaves as possible.
- Glue the leaves into a notebook.
- Label each leaf.

622. FAMILY INTERVIEW
$ 1 HOUR 2

- Make a list of questions to ask family members, such as great-grandparents.
- Include questions about what historical events happened in their childhood, where they were born, what their parents did, what pets they had, etc.
- Record their answers with a tape recorder.

623. SPAN AND CUBIT MEASUREMENTS
C 1 HOUR 2

- Measure the length of various objects around your home. A span is equal to 9" and a cubit is 18".
- Measure how tall you are. Find out how far it is to your mailbox.
- Study passages in the Bible about spans and cubits. For example, in 1 Samuel 17:4, Goliath was 6 cubits and a span tall!

624. FAMILY CREST
C 1 HOUR 2

- Research books from the library about family crests.
- See if you can find your family crest or design your own.
- Draw your crest on a 9" x 12" sheet of paper.
- Color or paint the crest.
- Cut out the crest and hang.

625. FOOD SURVEY BAR GRAPH
C 1 HOUR 1

- Ask 25 people what their favorite food is.
- Write down the person's name and his answer.
- On a piece of graph paper, trace over a line 3 squares in from the left side. Use a ruler and a marker or colored pencil. Stop the line 5 lines from the bottom.
- Trace over a line 5 squares from the bottom. Start the line where the first vertical stopped, and trace to the edge of the right side of the paper.
- Number each line on the left side. Start with #1 on the sixth line from the bottom.
- Write the name of the food vertically at the bottom. One food in each row.
- Fill in the bar graph by coloring the correct number of squares for each food category. For example: If five people said their favorite food was "pizza," color five squares on up to the #5 in the pizza column.
- Fill in all the food categories.
- Now, make some observations. For example, which food had the most number of people and which had the least? Were there any tie scores?

626. WEIGHT GRAPH
C 1 HOUR 1

Not only does this project help you learn about bar graphs and sequence, but it's a lot of fun trying to get a pet weighed!

- Weigh the people in your family, your pets, and any other object—anything can be weighed!
- As you weigh each person or object, write down the weight.
- On a piece of graph paper, starting at the bottom left, write one person or object in one row then skip a row and write the next object.
- On the left side, write a weight starting at the bottom with 1 lb. Write 5 lbs. on the second line going up. Skip 5 lbs. every line.
- Color in each row up to the weight of that person or object.

627. CLOTHESPIN MATH
$ 1 HOUR 2

- Paint at least 25 clothespins with acrylic paint.
- Write one number on each clothespin, 1–22, with a marker.
- Write a plus, minus, and multiplication sign on separate clothespins.
- String a clothesline between two chairs.
- Practice math facts by putting math problems on the line with the clothespins.

628. CHILDREN OF THE WORLD
C 1 HOUR 1

- Fold a 9" x 12" sheet of white construction paper in half.
- Fold the top down to the bottom.
- Fold the left side to the right side.
- Draw a boy or girl on the folded paper, making sure the arms are stretched out and the hands touch the folds.
- Cut out. There will be 2 sets of 4 figures..
- Color and decorate each doll as a child from another country.
- Place a dot of glue on the far right hand and the far left hand to join the dolls together. There will be 8 dolls side to side.
- Using a crayon or marker, write the phrase from Mark 10:14 NIV, "Let the little children come to me." A few words will fit on each doll.

629. WATER CONSERVATION QUILT POSTER
C 1 HOUR 1

- Cut 6 squares of 5" x 5" white paper.
- On each square, draw and color a different way to conserve water. For example, "Don't let the water run when brushing your teeth," "Don't be a drip," and "Don't overwater."
- Write a conservation saying on each square in marker or crayon.
- Arrange the squares on a sheet of 12" x 18" blue construction paper, leaving room at the bottom or top for the title, "WATER CONSERVATION."

• Write and color the title.

630. LINCOLN'S LOG CABIN
$ 1 HOUR 2

• Tape shut the opening of a half-pint milk carton.
• Cut cinnamon sticks to length and glue to the sides and top.
• Cut small black rectangles for windows and a door.
• Glue them to the logs.
• Paint a short cinnamon stick black and glue it to the roof for a chimney.
• Glue a small piece of cotton to the chimney for smoke.

631. MISSIONARY NOTEBOOK
C 1 HOUR 1

• Staple together ten 9" x 12" sheets of construction paper.
• Write on the front, "My Missionary Notebook."
• Decorate the front by gluing on pictures of people from different countries.
• On each page mount a missionary's card and write the name of the country he or she ministers in.
• Draw a small map of his or her country.
• When the missionaries visit your church have them autograph their page and write their favorite verse.

632. BOWLING BALL EARTH
$ 1 HOUR 3

• Sand an old blue bowling ball.
• Wipe clean.
• Cut out the continents from a small world map. Or draw the outlines on paper and label each one.
• Arrange the continents by taping them to the ball.
• Glue the continents to the ball.
• Label map details, such as oceans.

633. IMPRESSIONISTIC GARDEN SCENE
$ 1 HOUR 2

*Jesus and His disciples spent time in
the Garden of Gethsemane to be alone and pray.
It was in this garden that Jesus and His disciples sang hymns,
and where Judas betrayed Jesus (John 18:1–8).*

- Study the garden scenes of the French painter Claude Monet. Notice his short, quick brush strokes.
- Lightly draw a garden scene with pencil. Include trees, flowers, grasses, small birds, and maybe a ground squirrel.
- Fill in the drawing with short, quick strokes of pastel pencils or chalk.
- Spray with hair spray to make the chalk adhere.
- Sing the hymn, "In the Garden."

634. CIVIL WAR SOLDIER
$ 1 HOUR 1

- Cut a length of butcher paper 12" longer than the height of an adult.
- Have an adult lie down on the paper.
- Trace around the adult with a pencil.
- Look at books from the library about Civil War uniforms.
- Add uniform details with a pencil. For example, a hat, gun, buttons, etc.
- Paint the figure with tempera paint.
- Cut out the soldier and tape or staple to a wall.

635. HISTORY COLLAGE
$$$ 1 HOUR. 4

- Collect memorabilia from the family members interviewed in Project #622, as well as from their friends and family.
- Memorabilia could include a wedding invitation, photographs, newspaper clippings, dried corsages, etc. Arrange the items in a keepsake box frame.
- Glue, tape, and tack pieces in place. Use acid-free adhesives if possible.

- Slide on the glass.
- Give the keepsake to the family members.

636. 3-D PLANET POSTER
$$ 2 HOURS 4

- Purchase 10 Styrofoam balls, each a different size.
- Cut each ball in half with a knife.
- Paint the largest half yellow for the sun.
- Paint one half of each ball a different color using acrylic paint.
- Check out a book about planets from the library to refer to the color and size of the planets.
- On a table, arrange the balls from smallest to largest.
- Make a label for each planet from a small piece of white paper.
- Put the label to the smallest half ball starting with Pluto (the smallest planet). The next smallest planet is Mercury, then Mars, Venus, Earth, Neptune, Uranus, Saturn, and Jupiter.
- Glue the sun and planets in order to a black piece of poster board, starting with the sun at the far left of the board.
- Draw a curved line from the top to the bottom of the poster board going through each planet.
- To make rings for a few planets, cut thin strips of construction paper, long enough to go around the planet. Glue the ends of the ring to board on each side of the planet.
- Make the ring stand away from the planet by sticking a straight pin through the ring into the planet.
- Hang the poster.

637. YOUR LAND, MY LAND
C 2 HOURS 2

- Draw the outline of the United States on a 12" x 18" sheet of white construction paper. Leave a 2" border.
- Use the words from the song "This Land Is Your Land" to mark elements on the map. For example, write, "New York Island," draw and color a picture of "Redwood forests" in Northern California, and draw Highway 80 from Chicago to San Francisco and label it "ribbon of highway."

- Across the top in bubble or block letters, write "This Land Is Your Land."
- Across the bottom, write "This Land Is My Land."
- Fill in the letters with stripes and stars.
- Fill in the letters with red and blue markers, crayons, or colored pencils.

638. STATE FLOAT
$ 2 HOURS 2

- Choose a state to study.
- Decorate a large flat box as a float from that state.
- Cut out or draw pictures of the state bird, flower, agriculture, sports, etc. For example, use basketball figurines, a cardinal, cornstalks and Indianapolis 500 cars for a float from Indiana.
- To decorate around the bottom of the float, wrap tissue squares around the eraser end of a pencil and glue them to the box.

639. MUSEUM MODEL
$$ 2 HOURS 2

- Purchase an inexpensive plastic model of a military aircraft or vehicle.
- Assemble the model.
- Write a brief history of the aircraft or vehicle, from the model box or history books.
- Print the history on a card, and set up with the model to create a museum-like display.

640. SEASON POSTER
$ ONGOING 1

- Divide a sheet of poster board into 4 equal sections with a ruler.
- Write a season title on each section.
- During each season, glue objects or pictures to the section. For example, apple blossoms or seeds in the spring and a snowman or pinecone in the winter.
- Add as many objects to each season as possible.

641. SHADOW MEASUREMENT
C ONGOING 1

• Work with a partner and measure each other's shadow with a tape measure for one week at three different times of the day. Your partner could be a friend, neighbor, brother, or sister.
• Each time the measurement is taken, write down what the weather was like. For example, sunny, partially sunny, no sun, etc.
• Write your measurements and the weather in a chart form in the record keeping notebook from Project #212.
• Write down any observations. For example: Did the weather affect the length of the shadow? Did the sun have to be showing to have a shadow?

642. WORLD GEOGRAPHY
$$ ONGOING 1

• Purchase or obtain a world map and hang it on the wall.
• Collect stamps from different countries (check with relatives, church missionaries, post office, etc.).
• Mount stamps on the map for the respective country using a push pin or piece of tape.
• To learn more about a country, check out a book from your local library. Try to find out more about the artist who designed the stamp.

643. POSTCARD GEOGRAPHY
$$ ONGOING 3

This is a fun and very visual way to learn about the states and capitals. It will also make you want to travel!

• Tape or staple a blank outline of the United States to a wall or bulletin board. Make sure there is a lot of space around the map.
• Collect postcards from each state.
• Tape or thumbtack the postcards around the map.

- When you get a postcard, write the name of the state and its capital on the correct spot on the map.
- Write to the state capitals to get lots of great information.

644. NEW WORDS
C ONGOING 2

Learning the definition of a new word can be fun, especially when an adult doesn't know the word.

- Look through a page of the dictionary and pick out a word that is unusual.
- Write the word and its definition on an index card.
- See how many times during the week you can use the word.
- Ask adults what the word means—sometimes you'll be able to stump them!

ACTIVITIES FOR MIDDLER CHILDREN
FOOD PROJECTS

645. CANDY KISS FLOWERS
$ 15 MIN. 4

- Glue together the bottoms of 2 Hershey's Kisses.
- Wrap the Kisses in colored plastic wrap or cellophane wrap, leaving a short tail of wrap at one pointed end of the Kiss.
- Push a small dowel or skewer into the plastic tail.
- Wrap the plastic tail and the stick tightly with green floral tape.

- Secure several silk leaves under the flower Kiss with floral tape.
- Make several flowers to use as a bouquet or party favors.

646. BREAKFAST DRINK
$ 15 MIN. 3

- Chill one glass per person in the freezer.
- Place 1 cup of orange juice per person in a blender.
- Add one-quarter of a banana, 2 strawberries, a few drops of lemon juice, 1 large spoonful of Cool Whip, and 1–2 ice cubes per person to the orange juice.
- Blend.
- Pour into chilled glasses and serve.

647. SNOW ICE CREAM
C 15 MIN. 3

- Gather a large bowl of clean snow.
- Mix in a little sugar and cocoa powder to taste.
- Dish the ice cream into pretty dishes and enjoy.

648. CORNUCOPIA TREATS
$ 15 MIN. 1

- Ingredients: Bugle Snacks, Trix Cereal, tube of green frosting.
- Squeeze frosting into the opening of a Bugle Snack. Gently press 3 or 4 different Trix Cereal fruit shapes onto the frosting to resemble fruit in a cornucopia.

649. YOGURT SMOOTHIE
$ 15 MIN. 3

- Place one small container of yogurt, fresh cubed fruit, orange juice, and a few ice cubes in a blender.
- Put the lid on the blender and blend.
- Pour into a glass and enjoy.

650. GEOMETRIC CANDY FORMS
$ 30 MIN. 1

• Insert whole or half toothpicks into gumdrop candies to make a large form that stands by itself.

651. VELVEETA CARVING
$ 45 MIN. 3

• Carve a block of Velveeta with a table knife and spoon.
• Carve a word like LOVE with the L and O on top of the V and E.
• Place on a fancy plate and garnish with parsley.
• Use as a table centerpiece.

652. POPCORN BALLS
$ 1 HOUR 4

• Pop enough popcorn to make about 16 cups.
• In a large pan, mix together 1 cup packed brown sugar, 1 cup corn syrup, ½ cup margarine or butter, and 1 teaspoon salt.
• Heat the mixture on the stove, stirring constantly.
• Pour the mixture over the popcorn.
• Add M & M's or nuts.
• Let cool slightly.
• Form into balls.
• Wrap the balls in plastic wrap.
• Tie with a pretty ribbon.

653. LEMONADE AND COOKIE STAND
$$ 1 HOUR 4

• Make lemonade and cookies.
• Set up a table and chair in your yard.
• Make a sign advertising your goodies and their cost.
• Sell the goodies.

654. PLAN AND FIX A MEAL
$$ 2 HOURS 5

- Decide what you'd like to have for a meal.
- Look up the recipes.
- Make a list of the ingredients you need.
- Check the cupboard to see what ingredients you already have and cross these off your list.
- Go shopping with a parent to purchase the needed items.
- Fix, serve, and enjoy your special meal!

ACTIVITIES FOR MIDDLER CHILDREN
HOLIDAY PROJECTS

VALENTINE'S DAY

655. VALENTINE'S STATIONERY
$ 30 MIN. 1

- Cut sheets of 6" x 9" white paper.
- Draw a wavy line around the edge of each sheet of paper with a red marker.
- With a pink marker, draw a second wavy line around the edge, overlapping and curling around the first line.
- Draw tiny red and pink hearts around the wavy lines.

- Make red and pink dots throughout the lines and hearts.
- Write a special note to someone you love.

656. HEART PUZZLE
C 45 MIN. 1

- Fold a 9" x 12" piece of red construction paper in half.
- Starting and ending on the fold, draw a half of a heart. The heart should come to a point at the bottom and curve at the top and come down to the fold.
- Cut out the heart.
- Glue the heart to a thin piece of cardboard.
- Cut out the heart.
- Draw lines on the red heart to divide into puzzle-shaped areas.
- In each area, write a love characteristic from 1 Corinthians 13, such as, "Love is patient, love is kind and is not jealous; love does not brag and is not arrogant. . . . (NASB)"
- Write "1 Corinthians 13" in one space.
- Cut the heart into puzzle pieces.
- Place in a box or envelope.
- Give to a friend on Valentine's Day.

657. VALENTINE BINGO
$ 1 HOUR 3

- Place a 9" x 12" sheet of red or pink construction paper horizontally.
- In block letters, write, "VALENTINE" down the left side and "BINGO" down the right side.
- In the center, with a ruler, draw 25 squares in 5 rows of 5 squares. Line up each horizontal row with one of the letters in the word BINGO.
- In the center square draw a heart and write, "Free space" inside the heart.
- Draw little pictures or words in each square. For example, Kiss, Hugs, Red, Have a Heart, Be Mine, Love, February 14, Candy, etc.
- Photocopy the paper for the number of players.

- Cut the squares from the copies and glue to 9" x 12" sheets of construction paper in a different order than the original so each player will have a different Bingo card.
- Glue VALENTINE and BINGO on the sides of each card.
- Write each square and a letter from the word Bingo 5 times on small slips of paper (For example, B–Red, I–Red, etc.).
- Place the slips in a bag or small box.
- To play, have one person draw a slip and call out what is written on it. For example, N—Party.
- If a player has the square that is called he places a marker, like a candy heart, on that square.
- The first person to mark 5 in a row wins.

PRESIDENT'S DAY

658. PRESIDENTIAL BOOKMARKS
C 45 MIN. 1

- Cut a 1" x 6" piece of felt.
- Glue a penny or quarter to one end, with the face up.
- Cut small pieces of felt into shapes that remind you of these presidents, such as a hat, hatchet, cherries, etc.
- Glue the shapes to the bookmark.

659. PRESIDENTIAL POSTER
$ 1 HOUR 2

- Trace a Lincoln and a Washington silhouette from a book.
- Cut out the tracings.
- Trace onto red and blue construction paper.
- Cut out the silhouettes.
- Glue the silhouettes side by side on a white piece of poster board. The size of the board will depend on the size of the silhouettes.
- Glue pennies, nickels, and American flag stickers and stars around the edge as a border.
- Hang on a wall or the refrigerator.

EASTER

660. EGG ORNAMENTS
C 30 MIN. 1

- Poke a small hole in each end of an egg.
- Blow out the inside of the egg.
- Rinse and dry the egg.
- Glue each end of a short ribbon to the top of the egg for a hanger.
- Cover a small section of the egg with a thick layer of glue.
- Sprinkle birdseed onto the glue.
- Cover entire egg with seed, and let dry.
- Hang up to display.

661. PAPER EGG SLIPCOVERS
C 45 MIN. 3

- Cut a strip of thin cardboard about 2" wide and long enough to fit around a hard-boiled egg. Make it long enough to overlap the ends.
- Cut 3 small crosses from white poster board.
- Color 2 crosses brown and one red.
- Color the strip of cardboard green.
- Glue the crosses to the cardboard egg stand, with the red cross in the middle. Do not glue down the top of the red cross.
- Overlap the ends of the strip and staple.
- Cut a small square of construction paper.
- Punch 2 holes, one at each end of the paper.
- Write "He is not dead, He is risen!" on the paper.
- Thread a short piece of yarn through the holes and knot.
- Hang the sign on the red cross.

662. FLOWER POT EASTER EGG HOLDER
$ 1 HOUR 2

- Clean and dry a small flower pot.
- Paint the pot with several coats of acrylic paint.
- With a marker, write "He Is Risen!" near the rim.
- Place a colored hard-boiled egg in a flower pot at each person's place on Easter morning.

663. EASTER SIGN
$ 1 HOUR 3

- On an 8" x 11" sheet of scrap paper, write in block letters, "HE IS RISEN!", in a vertical row with HE on top, IS in the middle, and RISEN on the bottom. The letters should touch.
- Cut 3 different colors of tissue paper in 1" squares.
- Tape the pattern to a work surface.
- Cover the word design with a sheet of plastic wrap and tape it down.
- Fill in the word HE with a layer of glue.
- Arrange one color of tissue paper in the glue of the word HE. The tissue can overlap.
- Cover the other words with different colors of tissue.
- Let dry.
- Carefully peel the sign from the plastic wrap. The glue will cause the tissue to be shiny.
- Trim the edges and tape to a window.

664. MILK CARTON DONKEY PUPPET
C 1 HOUR 3

- Draw a pencil line around the middle of a one-pint milk carton.
- Cut the carton on the line on 3 sides, leaving the back uncut.
- Open the 2 halves until they meet in the back.
- To work the puppet, put your thumb in the bottom and fingers in the top.
- Mix some dish soap with brown tempera paint.

- Paint the carton.
- Glue on construction paper eyes, ears, tongue, teeth, and nostrils.
- Use the puppet in a Christmas or Easter play or skit.

665. EGGSHELL EASTER SCENE
C 1 HOUR 1

- Crush clean eggshells into pieces.
- Draw a stone, a tomb, flowers, and grass for a resurrection scene on a sheet of thin cardboard. Do not draw tiny details.
- Spread a small amount of glue over one section and lay crushed eggshells in the glue.
- Let dry.
- Paint with watered down tempera paints.

666. EASTER BONNET
$$ 1 HOUR 5

- Glue silk or dried flowers to a straw or fabric hat with a hot glue gun.
- Or sew on fresh flowers.
- Try to use colors that coordinate with your Easter dress.

667. STAINED GLASS CROSS PUZZLE
C 1 HOUR 1

- Draw a cross on a hill on a 6" x 9" piece of lightweight cardboard.
- With a pencil, divide the sky, cross, and hill into 9–12 different puzzle shapes.
- Trace over the pencil lines with a black marker.
- Fill in each shape with different shades of color. For example, use shades of blue for the sky, red for the cross, and brown for the hill.
- Carefully cut the picture on the black lines.

• Put the pieces in an envelope or decorated box and give as an Easter present.

668. STAINED GLASS EASTER CARD
C 1 HOUR 5

• Fold two 9" x 12" sheets of purple construction paper in half.
• Draw a heart in the middle of the front of one folded sheet.
• Cut out the heart.
• Draw a cross on the inside right of the second sheet.
• Cut out the cross.
• Cut four 6" x 9" pieces of wax paper.
• Place 2 pieces of wax paper side by side on a layer of newspaper.
• Sharpen old crayons onto both pieces of wax paper with a pencil sharpener.
• Place the other 2 pieces of wax paper on top.
• Place a piece of newspaper on top of the wax paper.
• Iron until the shavings melt.
• Trim one melted crayon paper to fit behind the heart.
• Glue it on the inside left, behind the heart.
• Trim the other melted crayon paper to fit behind the cross.
• Glue it behind the cross cutout.
• Glue the 2 pieces of purple paper together so the heart is the front of the card and the cross is on the inside right of the card.
• Write "Happy Easter" on the front and a verse on the inside.

669. TISSUE CROSS CARD
$ 1 HOUR 2

• Fold a 6" x 9" sheet of white construction paper in half.
• Draw a cross on the front.
• Cut 1" x 1" squares of brown tissue paper.
• Spread a layer of glue on the cross.
• Place the eraser end of a pencil in the center of a tissue square and wrap it around the pencil.
• Place the tissue in the glue and lift out the pencil.

- Cover the whole cross.
- Write an Easter message inside the card.

MOTHER'S DAY, FATHER'S DAY, GRANDPARENTS' DAY

670. MOTHER'S DAY COUPONS
C 30 MIN. 1

- Cut 2" x 4" strips of paper.
- Decorate each strip with a border.
- On each coupon, write a special thing you can do for your mother. For example, one hour of housecleaning, one big hug, one special dinner cooked, or a lovely breakfast served in bed.
- Give to Mom on Mother's Day.

671. FATHER'S DAY COUPONS
C 30 MIN. 2

- Cut 2" x 4" strips of paper.
- Decorate each strip with a border.
- On each coupon, write a special thing you can do for your father. For example, one free car wash, one big hug, one favorite meal cooked, or one favorite dessert baked.
- Give to Dad on Father's Day.

672. FATHER'S DAY SUNCATCHER
C 30 MIN. 3

- Holding 2 pieces of 12" x 12" wax paper together, cut out a heart, square, or triangle shape.
- Write a message on a piece of construction paper and place it in the middle of one sheet of wax paper.

- Arrange flowers, leaves, ferns, etc., around the message.
- Place the other sheet of wax paper on top.
- Cover with a sheet of newspaper.
- Iron with a low heat setting.
- Punch a hole at the top and thread with yarn.
- Hang in a window.

673. FATHER'S DAY TIE
$ 45 MIN. 3

- Buy a plain tie or use one you already have.
- Paint designs on the tie with fabric paint.
- Think of a design that might describe your dad. For example, tennis balls if he plays tennis.
- Let dry.
- Wrap and give to Dad on Father's Day!

674. GRANDPARENTS' DAY PRESENT
C 1 HOUR 4

Grandparents' Day is the first Sunday after Labor Day.
Your grandparents will love to receive this special gift.

- Place a picture of yourself inside an aluminum pie tin and trace around it with a pencil.
- Remove the picture and draw around the inside of the traced line about ⅛".
- Cut out the tin on the inside line to make the opening a little smaller than the picture.
- Place the tin on thick cardboard or on a layer of newspaper.
- Draw a design, such as hearts, around the cutout area.
- With a hammer and nail, punch holes around the drawn design. Space the holes evenly.
- Tape the picture to the back of the pie tin so your face shows through the cutout.
- Punch a hole through the rim at the top of the tin.
- Thread with a short piece of yarn and tie the ends together for a hanger.
- Give to your grandparents.

THANKSGIVING

675. WIGWAM INDIAN VILLAGE
C 30 MIN. 1

*The Indians were a great help to the Pilgrims many years ago.
Include them in your Thanksgiving decorating.*

• Turn a cone-shaped paper cup upside down and decorate it
   with Indian symbols.
• Cut a small slit for the door and fold it back.
• Poke 2 small sticks through the pointed top of the wigwam
   for poles.
• Make enough wigwams to create a village.
• Arrange on the table at Thanksgiving time.

676. THANKSGIVING NECKLACE
$ 30 MIN. 2

• Slice oranges and apples and place them on a wax paper-lined
   cookie sheet.
• Turn the slices every day for one to two weeks, until they have
   dried.
• Break off the kernels of a piece of Indian corn and soak them
   in a bowl of water for one day until softened.
• Thread a needle with heavy thread or fishing line. Knot the
   end. The thread should be long enough to fit over your
   head when the ends are tied together.
• Push the needle through several kernels of corn, then through
   an apple slice, through more corn, an orange slice, and more
   corn until the string is full.
• Tie the two ends of the thread together to form a necklace.

677. PILGRIM PEOPLE
C 45 MIN. 1

• Cover toilet paper rolls with construction paper to make
  Pilgrims and Indians. (For tall Pilgrims and Indians use
  paper towel rolls.)
• Cover the rolls with white or tan for the faces and brown or
  black for clothes on the bodies.
• Add an Indian headdress or Pilgrim hat.
• Hair can be made with yarn or fringed construction paper.
• Draw on facial features and other details.

678. PUMPKIN CARVING
$ 45 MIN. 4

• Cut a lid from the top of a pumpkin.
• Clean out the inside of the pumpkin.
• Draw 2 or 3 crosses on the sides of the pumpkin, depending
  on its size.
• Cut out the crosses.
• Place a candle inside the pumpkin and light.

679. PUMPKIN TURKEY
$ 45 MIN. 4

• Draw a turkey and feathers on the side of a pumpkin with a
  pencil.
• Paint the turkey with tempera paint.
• Poke holes with a small nail and hammer around the top of
  the painted feathers.
• Stick a lollipop in each hole.

680. PAPER BAG INDIAN
C 45 MIN. 3

• Cut a tan circle of construction paper large enough to cover
  the bottom of a lunch bag. The bag needs to be folded flat.

- Trim the circle into the shape of a face with a chin.
- Lay the face on a sheet of black construction paper and draw an upside down double U around the face for hair.
- Cut out the hair and glue it to the face.
- Cut two ¼" x ½" strips of brown construction paper. Fringe each strip for eyelashes.
- Glue the lashes near the hairline.
- Cut out eyes and glue to the face.
- Cut 2 small black circles and glue them to the center of each eye.
- Draw a round nose under the eyes.
- Cut a mouth from red construction paper and glue it to the face.
- Glue the face to the bottom of the bag.
- Make an Indian headband by cutting a strip of yellow construction paper 1" wide and long enough to fit across the head, over the hair.
- Glue on the headband.
- Decorate the headband with circles and strips of construction paper.
- Draw and cut out 2 or 3 feathers from orange and yellow construction paper.
- Draw veins on the feathers.
- Glue the feathers to the back of the hair making sure the veins face outward.
- For the Indian costume, cut a 2" x 5" strip of brown paper and fringe.
- Glue the fringe to the bottom of the bag so it hangs off the edge.
- Cut more fringe to form a V neck and shirt front and glue it to the bag.

681. THANKSGIVING SCROLLS
$ 1 HOUR 1

- Cut a ¾" x 4"-long strip of yellow, green, or orange construction paper.
- Write a verse about being thankful on the paper.
- Roll up the verse paper like a scroll and tie it with a small piece of ribbon.

- Paint the outside of an empty matchbox with tempera or acrylic paint.
- Put a fall or Thanksgiving sticker on the top of the box.
- Place the scroll inside the box.
- Place a matchbox at each seat for the Thanksgiving meal.
- Have each person read the verse in his or her matchbox.

682. THANKSGIVING PLACE CARD
$ 1 HOUR 5

- Fold a 9" x 12" sheet of white paper in half.
- Cut paper in half along the fold crease.
- Fold the 2 pieces in half again and cut.
- Fold all 4 pieces in half for the place card.
- Cut a 2" x 4 " piece of lightweight cardboard.
- Hold the cardboard horizontally.
- Using a crayon, draw an outline of a turkey or Pilgrim, or the word "Thanksgiving" on the cardboard. Make the drawing simple and apply the crayon in a thick layer.
- Note: If you use a word, make sure you write it backwards so it will read correctly after it's transferred.
- Place the drawing on a layer of newspaper.
- Place the front of a place card on the drawing. Cover with a sheet of newspaper.
- Press with a heated iron, being careful not to move the place card or cardboard.
- Gently lift one corner of the place card to check if the crayon has melted enough to transfer to the paper.
- Repeat pressing with the warm iron if necessary.
- Neatly print a name at the bottom of each place card.

683. THANKSGIVING BANNER
C 1 HOUR 2

- Cut a piece of white or brown butcher paper about 1½ yards long (54").
- Lightly print "Happy Thanksgiving" in large letters on the paper.

- Place different colors of tempera or acrylic paint on separate paper plates.
- Press a cattail into the paint and dab off any excess paint on a sheet of newspaper.
- Press the paint-loaded cattail onto a letter.
- Paint a small rock to use for printing a round or curved letter.
- Print the whole phrase.
- Press leaves and feathers into the paint and then print around the edge of the banner for a border.
- Let dry.
- Trace around each letter with a marker.
- Hang on a wall, window, or the garage door.

CHRISTMAS

684. MARBLED CHRISTMAS ORNAMENTS
$ 15 MIN. 2

- Pour 2 or 3 colors of acrylic paint onto a round, clear ornament. Try to pour the colors next to each other.
- Slowly turn the ornament so the paint swirls and covers the outside.
- Let dry.
- Hang on the Christmas tree.

685. CHRISTMAS BULB NECKLACE
$ 30 MIN. 2

- Cut a length of thin red, green, or gold ribbon long enough to fit over your head when the ends are tied together.
- Find the center of the ribbon by putting the ends together.
- Tie a colored Christmas bulb at the center.
- Tie the ends of the ribbon together.
- Paint line designs or squiggles on the bulb with puff paint.
- Hang to dry.

686. COUNT-DOWN-TO-CHRISTMAS CHAIN
C 30 MIN. 1

- Cut construction paper into 1" x 6" strips.
- To make the first loop, glue together the ends of a strip.
- Put a strip through the loop and glue the ends together.
- Continue gluing on a loop until you have a chain of 25 alternating colors.
- Hang the chain.
- Starting December 1, take off one loop each day until Christmas.
- Each day after a loop has been removed do something special, like pray for a friend, mail a Christmas card, or sing a carol.

687. CHRISTMAS PLACE MAT
C 45 MIN. 1

- Tear out hills from brown construction paper.
- Tear out 3 or 4 shepherds from construction paper.
- Use tan or white for the heads, different colors for their robes, sashes, sandals, and shepherds' crooks. Add facial details with crayons.
- Tear out lambs.
- Across the top of a 12" x 18" sheet of black construction paper in white crayon, write "Glory to God in the Highest!"
- Glue torn-out objects to the black construction paper beginning with the hills.
- Tear out an angel and glue in the sky.
- Add stars with construction paper or white and yellow crayon.
- Cover with clear contact paper.

688. PETAL-COVERED ORNAMENTS
$ 45 MIN. 1

- Cover a small section of a Styrofoam ball with tacky glue.
- Lay dried flower petals in the glue.
- Continue overlapping the petals until the whole ball is covered.
- Make several balls and display them in a pretty glass bowl, on a holiday plate, or on a mantel.

689. NATURE CHRISTMAS CARD
C 45 MIN. 3

- Place a 5" x 8" piece of wax paper on top of a large piece of newspaper.
- Sprinkle crayon shavings onto the wax paper. Shavings can be made by shaving an old crayon with a knife, or by sharpening the crayon with a hand-held sharpener. One or several colors of crayon can be used.
- Place a leaf, pine needles, holly leaf, or ivy on top of the crayon shavings.
- Top with another sheet of 5" x 8" wax paper.
- Place a sheet of newspaper on top of wax paper.
- Carefully rub a warm iron over the newspaper to melt the crayon shavings.
- Let cool.
- Center the wax paper collage and glue to the front of a 9" x 12" folded piece of construction paper.
- Write a message inside.

690. CINNAMON STICK CENTERPIECE
$$ 45 MIN. 4

- Tie together a large bunch of long cinnamon sticks with thin wire.
- Cut a long length of wide Christmas ribbon and wrap around the bunch, tying a bow on top.
- Using a glue gun, glue pinecones, red berries, and baby's breath on the top around the bow.

691. CHRISTMAS GIFT WRAP
$ 1 HOUR 2

- Partially unroll a tube of white or brown butcher paper and weigh down the corners.
- Cut a potato in half and draw a bell on the cut side with a pencil.
- Cut away the potato on the outside of the line.
- Place small amount of gold or silver acrylic paint on a paper plate.

- Dip the bell stamp into the paint, being careful not to get too much paint. Practice stamping on a piece of newspaper.
- Press stamp on the paper.
- Reload the stamp with paint and stamp until the paper is filled.
- Unroll the paper to the next section, and continue stamping until the whole roll has been stamped.
- Wrap the gift.

692. SNOWMAN ANGEL
C 1 HOUR 4

- Mix together 2 cups flour and 1 cup salt. Stir in 1 cup water.
- Knead for approximately 7 minutes.
- Form the snowman by rolling 3 different sizes of a ball of dough.
- Stack the 3 balls with the largest ball on the bottom, then the middle-sized ball, then the small ball on the top. Use a little water to help the pieces stick together.
- Form a small piece of dough into a carrot nose, button eyes, scarf, and mittens.
- Attach to the snowman figure.
- Make a pair of wings from the dough. Place the wings on a cookie sheet about 2" from the snowman. (The wings will be glued to the snowman later.)
- Bake at 325° for 30–40 minutes. If a piece is browning too fast, cover it with foil. Prick any part that bubbles.
- Let cool.
- Paint the snowman and the wings with acrylic paint.
- Glue the wings to the back of the snowman.
- Spray with a clear sealer.

693. CHRISTMAS STAINED GLASS WINDOW
C 1 HOUR 5

- Place two 6" x 9" sheets of construction paper together and fold in half.
- Draw half the shape of a Christmas tree, bell, or star, starting and ending on the fold.

- Cut out the shape.
- Cut two 6" x 9" sheets of wax paper.
- Place one sheet of wax paper on a layer of newspaper.
- Sharpen old crayons with a pencil sharpener over the wax paper.
- Top with the second sheet of wax paper.
- Top with a sheet of newspaper.
- Iron until the shavings melt.
- Place a strip of glue around the edge of one shape frame and place the wax paper shavings on top.
- Place a strip of glue around the edge of the wax paper and top with the second frame.
- Hang in the window or on the Christmas tree.

694. GOOD NEWS NATIVITY SCENE
C 1 HOUR 1

- Cut out pictures from a coloring book or old Christmas cards that could be included in a nativity scene. For example, baby Jesus, Mary, Joseph, sheep, angels, etc.
- Trace the cutout pictures onto a sheet of newspaper that has words only, like the classified section.
- Cut out the newspaper shapes.
- Arrange the shapes on a sheet of red or green construction paper, leaving room at the top for a title. The size of the paper will depend on the size of the shapes.
- Cut out the words "Good News" and an exclamation point from newspaper print.
- Glue the title at the top of the construction paper.
- Glue on the shapes.
- Add details to the shapes with a black marker.

695. CHRISTMAS STOCKING
C 1 HOUR 1

- Draw a stocking on a 12" x 18" sheet of construction paper.
- Cut out the stocking.
- Decorate the stocking with crayons, markers, glitter, etc.

- Lay the stocking on a second 12" x 18" sheet of construction paper and trace.
- Cut out the second stocking.
- Lay one stocking on a 9" x 12" sheet of white construction paper.
- Trace the top and 4" down each side of the stocking.
- Draw a line on the white paper from one end of the 4" side to the end of the other 4" line.
- Cut out the white cuff.
- Glue the cuff to the top of one stocking.
- Glue the 2 stockings together by laying a strip of glue around the edge. Do not glue the top closed.
- Fold a 1" x 5" strip of construction paper in half.
- Glue together the ends.
- Glue to the back top right corner for a hanger.
- Hang the stocking on the refrigerator or mantel, or thumb-tack on a wall.

696. CHRISTMAS TREE SCENE
C 1 HOUR 2

- Draw a Christmas tree on a 9" x 12" sheet of white paper.
- Cut out the tree.
- Trace the tree on another 9" x 12" sheet of white paper and cut out.
- Lay one tree on several layers of newspaper.
- Place a small amount of green tempera or acrylic paint on a paper plate.
- Wad up a sheet of plastic wrap and dip it in the paint.
- Print over the entire tree by pressing the paint-loaded plastic onto the paper.
- Let dry.
- Repeat with another color of paint such as red or gold.
- In the center of the second tree draw and color a manger scene.
- Add details like small pieces of straw in the manger and a scrap of fabric for the swaddling clothes.
- Cut a horizontal and vertical slit in the center of the printed tree by folding in half and cutting a slit. Do not fold enough to make a crease.

• Glue around the edge of the manger scene tree.
• Place the printed tree on top.
• Fold back the flaps on the printed tree and glue them down so the manger scene is showing.

697. POPCORN AND CRANBERRY GARLAND
$ 1 HOUR 2

• Thread a needle with a double strand of thread. Knot the end of the thread.
• Push the needle through several pieces of popcorn, then through a cranberry or two.
• Continue alternating popcorn and cranberries until the string is full.
• Several strands can be tied together to complete a long garland.
• Hang on the Christmas tree or doorway.
• After Christmas, hang outside for the birds!

698. HAND WREATH
C 1 HOUR 2

• Trace your hand at least 12 times onto green construction paper.
• Cut out the hands.
• Draw a circle on a 12" x 12" square of lightweight cardboard.
• Draw another circle in the center.
• Cut out the center circle.
• Cut around the outside circle.
• Glue the hands in an overlapping pattern to the wreath.
• Cut small circles of red construction paper.
• Glue in groups of 3 around the wreath.
• Draw and color a bow.
• Cut out the bow and glue it to the wreath.
• Curl the fingers of each hand by wrapping them around a pencil.
• Hang on a door.

699. STYROFOAM-PRINT CHRISTMAS CARDS
C 1 HOUR 2

• Trim off the edges of a Styrofoam tray.
• On a piece of paper, draw a Christmas design such as baby
    Jesus in a manger, stars, wise men, or bells. Make sure the
    drawing is fairly large and simple.
• Place the drawing on top of the piece of Styrofoam and trace
    over it with a ball point pen.
• Remove the pattern.
• Re-draw the lines in the tray to make them deeper.
• Cut a piece of white paper twice the size of the tray and fold
    in half.
• Paint the tray with acrylic or tempera paint. The paint should
    not go into the lines of the traced design.
• Place the card carefully on top of the paint, making sure you
    have the right side of the paper so the design will be on the
    front of the card.
• Rub the paper with your hand or the back of a spoon to trans-
    fer the paint to the card.
• Peel the card from the Styrofoam.
• Let dry
• Write a message inside the card.

700. CHRISTMAS STORY PICTURE
C 1 HOUR 1

This project is a version of traditional African art.

• On brightly colored pieces of construction paper, lightly draw
    simple shapes from the Christmas story. For example, a star,
    the manger, Jesus, Mary, Joseph, animals, shepherds, sheep,
    and Magi.
• Cut out the various shapes.
• Cut 2 strips each of 1" x 12" and 1" x 18" yellow construction
    paper.
• Glue the strips around the edge of a 12" x 18" sheet of black
    construction paper.
• Arrange the shapes on the black paper.
• Glue down the shapes.

701. CHRISTMAS PAPIER-MÂCHÉ
$$ 1 HOUR 3

- Purchase an angel or reindeer papier-mâché form from a craft supply store.
- Paint the form with 2 to 3 coats of acrylic paint.
- Spray with glitter spray.
- Seal with a clear sealer.

702. CHRISTMAS-AROUND-THE-WORLD POSTER
$ 1 HOUR 2

- Cut a large sheet of white butcher paper or use a sheet of poster board.
- Decorate the edges with markers, crayons, or red and green construction paper. Make a scalloped-, wavy-, or triangle-shaped border.
- Look up information about Christmas in another country, such as Italy.
- Decorate the poster with the flag of the country, drawings of special native Christmas foods, a recipe, pictures of Christmas costumes, the name of the country in big letters cut from construction paper, and pictures or descriptions of special traditions.

703. TISSUE WREATH AND VERSE
$ 1 HOUR 2

- Fold a 12" x 18" sheet of red construction paper in half.
- Open the paper and draw a large wreath on one side. Do not go over the crease.
- Glue small squares of green tissue paper to the wreath. Cover the whole wreath.
- Glue a few red circles of tissue paper to the wreath for holly berries.
- Glue a red tissue paper bow to the top of the wreath.
- Write Isaiah 9:6 on an 8" x 11" sheet of white paper in nice lettering.
- Glue the verse to the red paper beside the wreath.

704. STRAW AND STAR GARLAND
$ 1 HOUR 2

- Cut a long piece of yarn and knot one end.
- Draw a star on a scrap piece of paper and cut it out.
- Trace the star on different colors of construction paper.
- Cut out lots of stars.
- Cut the straws into 2" lengths.
- Thread the yarn through a straw, then through 3 stars, then another straw, and then 3 more stars.
- Continue adding straws and stars until the yarn is used.
- Knot the end.
- Hang on the Christmas tree or doorway.

705. CHILDREN-OF-THE-WORLD GARLAND
C 1 HOUR 1

- On a 3" x 3" piece of scrap paper, draw a simple outline of a boy and a girl.
- Cut out the paper dolls.
- Trace the dolls onto white paper.
- Decorate each paper doll as a child from a different country.
- Cut out the dolls.
- Glue them to a sheet of construction paper.
- Cut out the dolls from the construction paper.
- Hole-punch a hole through the construction paper at the top of the head.
- String the dolls on a ribbon, thread, or cord.
- Hang on the Christmas tree, mantel, or doorway.

706. GROCERY BAG MANGER SCENE
C 1 HOUR 1

- Decorate the blank side of a grocery bag with a manger scene. Draw baby Jesus in a manger with straw, animals, an angel, a star, etc.
- Leave about 2" at the top.
- Color the scene.
- For more detail, glue on fabric, hay, fur, and glitter.

- Stuff the bag with wadded-up newspaper.
- Fold down the top of the bag to the top of the scene and staple it shut.
- Place under the Christmas tree or on a shelf.

707. CHRISTMAS-AROUND-THE-WORLD PLAY
C 1 HOUR 3

- Write a short play about the traditions of the country you researched in Project #702.
- Draw the people in the play on white paper. The people could include a family on the way to a Christmas Eve service, a church building, and baby Jesus.
- Color and cut out the figures.
- Glue the figures to Popsicle sticks.
- Use the figures in the play performance.

708. CHRISTMAS-AROUND-THE-WORLD FEAST
$$$ 2 HOURS 4

- Make Christmas food from the country you chose in Project #702.
- Decorate the dining area with the poster from Project #702 and with other festive decorations.
- Serve the food at a special Christmas meal.

709. CHRISTMAS DOOR DECORATION
$ 2 HOURS 2

- Cut 2 lengths of white or brown butcher paper to cover a door.
- Tape the 2 sheets together to fit the width of the door.
- Draw a large manger scene on the paper.
- Color the drawing using tempera paint, crayons, and markers.
- Tape it to the door.
- Cut a hole for the doorknob.

710. MAGI
$ 2 HOURS 3

- Stack, upside down, 3 different sizes of terra-cotta pots.
- Put the largest pot on the bottom, the medium-sized pot in the middle, and the smallest pot on the top. This last one will be the head.
- The terra-cotta "Magi" can be smaller to display on a shelf or larger to put on the porch near the front door.
- Glue the 3 pots together.
- Paint the stack with acrylics to look like the Magi, with the small pot as the head.
- Add 3-dimensional objects, like jewels, pearls, buttons, and fabric.
- Spray with a clear sealer.
- Make several Magi to display at Christmas.

ACTIVITIES FOR MIDDLER CHILDREN

MISCELLANEOUS PROJECTS

711. RUBBER EGG
C 15 MIN. 2

- Place an unshelled, hard-boiled egg in a plastic container with a lid, making sure the egg has room to expand.
- Fill the container with vinegar, leaving about ¼" to ½" space at the top.

- Loosely place the lid on top of the container, but do not seal.
- Leave the egg in the vinegar, at room temperature, for 3 to 4 days.
- Write down anything you notice about the changes in the egg.

712. SNOW WRITING
C 15 MIN. 1

- Fill a plastic dish soap bottle with colored water made by adding a few drops of food coloring to the water.
- Write a message in the snow for your mom or dad to read when he or she returns from work or running errands. For example, "We love you, Dad!" or "God loves you!"

713. FACE PAINTING
$ 15 MIN. 2

- Paint each other's face using face paint.
- Become a cat, rabbit, cowboy, football player, or your favorite cartoon or Bible character. Use your imagination!

714. POCKET NAPKIN
C 15 MIN. 1

- Fold a cloth napkin in half.
- Fold the top of the top layer down to meet the bottom.
- Turn the napkin over.
- Fold each side into the center.
- Fold one side to meet the other.
- Turn napkin over and fill the pocket with a candy cane, fall leaves, a flower, a verse written on pretty paper, or anything else to dress up the table!

715. NAIL CHIMES
$ 30 MIN. 2

- Hang different sizes of nails from a piece of driftwood or a stick.

- Hold or hang the chime so the nails move freely, and strike each nail to get a different tone. Strike the nails with another large nail.
- Try to play a favorite chorus or hymn.

716. SONG WRITING
C 30 MIN. 1

- Pick a verse from the Book of Psalms.
- Make up your own tune for the verse.
- If you know a little about playing the piano, pick out the tune on the piano.
- Write down the notes of the new tune.

717. THE PHARISEE AND THE TAX GATHERER
C 30 MIN. 2

- Read Luke 18:9–14.
- Write out a short script for the Pharisee and the Tax Gatherer.
- Find a few items, like a bathrobe, hats, and sandals to dress as the different characters.
- Act out the skit.
- At the end of the skit read the definition of humble: having an awareness of your defects or shortcomings.
- Also read Galatians 6:3.

718. ACTION SONGS
C 30 MIN. 2

- Make up actions for a hymn or chorus. For example, in "His Name Is Wonderful," Jesus could be shown by pointing to the palm of both hands.
- Books about sign language from the library might help with actions to show words.
- Perform the song for friends and family.

719. GRAPH-PAPER HYMNS
C 30 MIN. 1

• Play a tape or CD of your favorite Christian artist or your
   favorite hymns.
• Starting at the bottom of a sheet of graph paper, draw a line
   going up when the music goes up.
• Draw a line going down when the music goes down.
• If the music is on the same note, draw a line going across the
   paper.
• Draw several hymns or songs on the same sheet of graph
   paper using a different color of ink or pencil.
• Label each song.

720. CLOUD WATCHING
C 30 MIN. 1

• On a cloudy day, sit outside or lie on the grass and see if you
   can find different shapes in the clouds. For example, a
   mountain, a face, or an animal.
• List the various shapes you see in a notebook, such as the one
   from Project #789.

721. ICE SCULPTURE
$ 30 MIN. 2

• Partially fill a half-gallon or pint ice cream carton with leaves,
   cranberries, and shelled nuts. Tape objects up the side of the
   carton.
• Tape an empty plastic cup inside the carton so the top of the
   cup is even with the top of the carton.
• Fill the carton with water and place in the freezer.
• When frozen, place the carton in hot water to melt some of
   the ice. Peel away the carton.
• Trim off any tape that might be showing.
• Place a candle in the cup.
• Put the sculpture outside or in a bowl as a centerpiece and
   light the candle.
• Several sculptures can be used to light a front porch or
   walkway.

722. LEGO MAZE
C 30 MIN. 1

• Arrange Lego pieces into a maze on a large Lego plate.
• Try to move a marble through the maze by holding and tilting the maze.

723. PRACTICE SESSION
C 30 MIN. 1

To be really good at something—
like singing or playing a sport—
you need to practice a lot.
Here's a way to practice and have fun, too!

• Hit a tennis ball against a wall as many times as you can without missing.
• Or make as many free throws in a row as you can.
• If you want to practice singing, see how many songs on your favorite tape or CD you can sing along with in a row.
• Try to beat your record or play with a friend and try to beat each other's record.
• Be creative as you make up your own special practice session!

724. FIND THE CENTER
C 45 MIN. 1

• Make a list of objects that you could find the center of. For example, the center of the Bible or another book, the center of a room, a driveway, a town, or your yard.
• To find the center of some things you will need a tape measure.
• Keep adding to your list as you think of them.

725. JESUS SPEECH
C 45 MIN. 3

• Study the sermons of Peter in Acts 2:14–40 and of Stephen in Acts 7:2–53.

- Write down a few main points. What were they trying to say or get across to their audience? For example, at the end of his sermon, Peter, in Acts 2:38, asks his audience to repent.
- Write a short speech about Jesus.
- Memorize it.
- Give the speech to your family and to your Sunday school class.

726. PAUL'S DEFENSE
C 45 MIN. 3

- Read about Paul's life and his conversion in Acts 8–9.
- Write a short speech telling the audience why you, Paul, should be accepted by the Christians in Jerusalem.
- Include some of his background. For example, "Yes I, Paul, was a very wicked man and I was glad that Stephen was stoned, but one day as I was on the way to Damascus. . . ."
- Dress up in an old robe and a sash and sandals.
- Give the speech to your family and to your Sunday school class.

727. IDENTIFICATION CARD
$$ 45 MIN. 3

*These cards can be used to help children feel
more secure when away from home.
They can also be used to help identify a lost person or pet.*

- Take a picture of someone or something important to you—a child, parent, grandparent, or pet. When taking the picture, stand far enough away to get a small picture so it will fit on the card.
- Have film developed.
- Trim picture and glue on thin cardboard or poster board. Cut the card a size that's easy to carry.
- Place your thumb on an ink pad then stamp it on the card.
- Add personal information to card, such as name, address, color of eyes, etc.

• Cover card with clear contact paper. Carry in purse, wallet, or backpack.

Name: _____

Address: _____

Phone Number: _____

Parents: _____

Parents' Work/Other Phone: _____

Child description: Ht. _____ Wt. _____

Eyes: _____ Hair: _____

Medical Info: _____

728. FLANNELGRAPH PICTURES
$ 45 MIN. 2

• Cut pictures from magazines or catalogs that illustrate the flannelgraph verse in Project #731. For example, for a verse from Psalm 23, you could use a picture of a shepherd; sheep; a big, green field; or still water, like a lake.
• Glue scraps of felt to the back of each picture.

729. RECORDED NOISES
$ 1 HOUR 1

• Record different sounds. For example, the noise of a wall heater, chopping food, rain, or a truck going by. The possibilities are endless.
• Make a list of the sounds as they are recorded.
• Make up your own sound effects, like blowing and popping a bubble.
• Send your recording to a friend to listen to and try to guess the sounds.

730. SECRET CODE ENCOURAGEMENT VERSE
C 1 HOUR 1

- Draw a picture for each letter of the alphabet. For example, an egg for the letter E.
- On a 9" x 12" piece of paper, write "Isaiah 41:10," using a picture for each letter and number. Make sure to leave a space between each word.
- Mail the alphabet code and the coded verse to a friend, relative, or pastor.

731. FLANNELGRAPH VERSE
$ 1 HOUR 2

- Pick out a favorite verse.
- Print the verse on a piece of construction paper.
- Cut the verse apart.
- Glue scraps of felt to the back of each word.
- Cover a large, thick piece of cardboard with felt.
- Place the verse on the cardboard, then have one person take away a word and see if the other players can guess the word. Say the verse each time a word is taken away. Keep taking words away until all of them are off the board.
- Scramble the verse and place the words on the board. Place the words in the right order.

732. BLACK AND WHITE PHOTOS
$$ 1 HOUR 4

- Gather old hats, jewelry, men's jackets, clothes, and women's purses.
- Set up a few lamps without the shades for lighting, or take the pictures outside in a sunny spot. Avoid taking pictures with shadows in them.
- If taking indoor shots, hang a sheet for the background.
- Take turns dressing up in the clothes.
- Take black and white photos.
- Have the film developed.
- Frame your favorite shot.

• Send out with Christmas cards for an old-fashioned, nostalgic look.

733. LETTER PHOTOGRAPHY
$$ 2 HOURS 4

*This project will really help you
begin to see things in a different way!*

• Take pictures of things that form a letter shape. For example, a curved slide for the letter S or the legs of a swing set for the letter V.
• Have the pictures developed.
• Use the pictures to spell out words.

734. CAR WASH
C 2 HOURS 4

Here's a fun way to earn a little summer spending money!

• Make signs advertising a car wash and the cost—whatever the going rate might be.
• Place the signs by the street and the corner.
• Gather rags, towels, and a hose.
• Wash the neighborhood cars!

735. "MY CITY" PHOTO ALBUM
$$ 2 HOURS 5

• Take pictures of interesting buildings, statues, land features, your church, school, etc., in your town or city and its surrounding area.
• Have the pictures developed.
• Cut pieces of construction paper 1" larger than the size of the pictures. Cut enough for a front and back cover and two pictures on each page.
• Stack the paper.

- Staple on the left.
- Glue the pictures in the paper album or use photo mounting corners.
- Label each picture.
- Write "My City Photo Album" on the front cover.
- Color the cover.

736. PATTERNS AND DETAILS
$$ 2 HOURS 3

*God has created beautiful patterns and detail in nature.
This project will help you
take time to see and enjoy His handiwork.*

- Take your camera on a walk and take close-up pictures of things that have a pattern or design. For example, the bark of different kinds of trees, the inside of a flower, or a pebbled beach.
- Mount the pictures in a book, such as the one from Project #631.

737. IGLOO
C 3 HOURS 2

- Fill a plastic shoe box with snow to form a snow brick. Pack it tightly for a solid brick.
- Turn over the box and slip out the brick. Begin stacking to form walls. This will take a lot of bricks.
- Leave a space in one wall for the door.
- When the walls are high enough, place a large board or several "2 x 4s" across the top.
- Add more snow bricks on top of the board roof.
- Don't add so many bricks on top that the boards sag. Snow gets very heavy.
- Have fun playing in your igloo!

ACTIVITIES FOR OLDER CHILDREN
PAPER PROJECTS

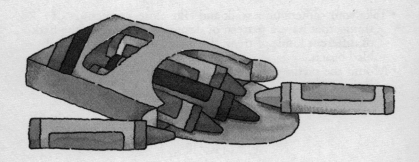

738. ADD-A-CHARACTER STORY
C 15 MIN. 1

- Make up the beginning of a story.
- Write one or two paragraphs.
- Send this short beginning to a friend or grandparent asking him or her to add to the story and mail it back.
- When the story is returned, add a few more paragraphs and send it back to your friend or grandparent.
- Continue adding to the story until you decide to finish it.

739. ENVELOPE
C 15 MIN. 2

- Cut a 7" x 10" sheet of white paper.
- At each corner, cut off a 1" x 3" rectangle. Measure the 3" length from the top and bottom and the 1" width from the sides.
- Round off each corner.
- Fold in the sides, then the bottom and top.
- Put a small amount of glue on each side and fold up the bottom.
- To seal, use a sticker or a small amount of glue.

740. BOUNCING GREETING CARD
C 30 MIN. 1

- Fold a 9" x 12" sheet of white construction paper in half.
- Draw and color a scene on the front.
- Write a message on another piece of construction paper.
- Accordion-fold 2 narrow strips of paper 4 or more times.
- Glue the strips to the inside of the card and to the back of the message.

741. BOOK COVER
C 30 MIN. 2

When you examine a butterfly or caterpillar
you will see that God decorated these insects
with colors, shapes, and patterns.
Here's a fun way to decorate a book cover with a unique pattern.

- Cut an oversized sheet of white paper 2" wider and longer than the open book that you want to cover.
- Cover the book. First, center the book within the paper, then fold the edges to form a complete covering. Cut off extra paper as needed.
- Take the cover off the book and draw a shape or a word, such as "Math" if covering a Math book, on the front and center of the cover.

- Draw around this shape until the edge of the cover is reached.
- Using markers, fill in some shapes with a pattern, such as hearts, dots, lines, X's, O's,or stars.
- Color in some shapes with a solid color.
- Trace the outline of each shape with a black marker.
- Re-cover the book.

742. MOVING PICTURES
C 30 MIN. 1

- On a 9" x 12" sheet of light blue construction paper draw a scene of children flying kites.
- Re-create the kites and several objects from the picture on another piece of paper. Cut these objects out.
- Accordion-fold narrow strips of paper 4 or more times.
- Glue one end of a folded strip to the big picture and the other end to the construction-paper kites and other objects. The kites and other objects will bounce above the picture.

743. FAMILY WORD SEARCH
C 30 MIN. 3

- Make a list of all the names of the people in your family. Include parents, grandparents, uncles, aunts, cousins, etc.
- Arrange the names in columns and rows of letters with unused letters around them.
- Names could be arranged backwards, forwards, diagonally, up, and down.
- Make copies.
- Hand out at a family get together.
- See who can find all the names first!

744. CRAYON AND NATURE
NOTEBOOK COVER
C 30 MIN. 3

- Cut 2 pieces of wax paper slightly smaller than a notebook you want to cover.
- Place a sheet of wax paper on top of several layers of newspaper.
- Arrange leaves and grass on the wax paper.
- Sprinkle crayon shavings on the wax paper.
- Top with second sheet of wax paper.
- Cover with a sheet of newspaper
- Rub a warm iron over the wax paper until the crayon shavings melt.
- When cool, glue the design to the cover of your notebook.

745. POINTILLISM SUNSET
C 45 MIN. 1

*Pointillism is a fun artistic process of applying
small strokes or dots of color to a surface
so that from a distance they look like they all blend together!*

- Lightly draw hills or mountains on the bottom third of a 9" x 12" sheet of paper.
- In the center, draw a setting sun and clouds.
- Fill in the scene with small dashes using crayons or markers. Preserve the tip of the crayon or marker by making a dash instead of a dot by placing the crayon or marker on the paper and pulling it slightly so you have a small dot with a little tail.
- When filling in an area, use different shades of a color.
- Hang it up so everyone can admire your pointillism sunset!

746. SIMPLE SHADING
$ 45 MIN. 3

Here's another exercise in learning to see.

- Set up a still life by placing a simple object like a vase near a table lamp.
- Turn on the lamp.
- Lightly draw the vase on a sheet of white paper.
- Draw in the table line.
- Notice which part of the vase is lighter and which is darker.
- Shade in the vase with a soft-leaded pencil like a B or B2.
- Shade lighter where the light shines the most on the vase, and darker where there is less light.
- If the vase casts a shadow, shade it in on the paper.

747. GRAPH PICTURE
C 45 MIN. 1

- Color or write in the squares of a sheet of graph paper to create a design. For example, a Bible verse, a name, a sign, flowers, or geometric shapes.
- Each square could be a solid color or shaded light-to-dark from one side of the square to the other.

748. THE LAUGH BOOK
C 45 MIN. 2

This funny book would be a great gift for a friend in the hospital or for someone who needs a good laugh!

- Collect funny cartoons from newspapers and magazines.
- Fold several 8" x 11" pieces of construction paper in half.
- Staple on the folded side.
- Glue in cartoons.
- Decorate cover by gluing on a cartoon. Write the title or cut out letters from a magazine.
- Write at the bottom of the booklet, "Compiled by. . .(your name)."

749. CREATION MURAL—
DAY 1: NIGHT AND DAY
$ 45 MIN. 2

Creation of the world by God was an awesome event.
Though Exodus 20 is usually thought of as
the listing of the Ten Commandments,
it also talks about creation. Read Genesis 1–3 and Exodus 20.
When Projects 749–755 have been completed,
hang the plaques together to make a mural.

• Draw a double, wavy line on a piece of lightweight cardboard.
• Cut out the wavy line and glue it down the center of a 9" x 12" sheet of heavy cardboard.
• Cover with a piece of heavy-duty foil, folding the foil over the edges of the cardboard.
• Tape the foil to the back of the cardboard.
• Gently trace around the edges of the wavy line with a cotton swab.
• Paint one side with white tempera paint.
• Coat the other side with black india ink.
• Rub off the ink with a soft cloth or paper towel. Do not rub off all the ink.
• With a black marker, write "DAY 1: Night and Day," in the upper left-hand corner.

750. CREATION MURAL—
DAY 2: SEPARATE WATER AND SKY
$ 45 MIN. 2

• Cut waves from lightweight cardboard.
• Glue the waves to the bottom half of a 9" x 12" sheet of heavy cardboard.
• Cover with a piece of heavy-duty foil, folding the foil over the edges of the cardboard.
• Tape the foil to the back of the cardboard.
• Gently trace around the edges of the waves with a cotton swab.
• Paint the top with light blue tempera paint.

- Coat the bottom with india ink.
- Rub off the ink with a soft cloth or paper towel. Do not rub off all the ink.
- With a black marker, write "DAY 2: Separate Water and Sky," in the upper left-hand corner.

751. CREATION MURAL—
DAY 3: DRY LAND AND VEGETATION
$ 45 MIN. 2

- Cut mountain, tree, and flower shapes from lightweight cardboard.
- Glue the shapes to a 9" x 12" sheet of heavy cardboard.
- Cover with a piece of heavy-duty foil, folding the foil over the edges of the cardboard.
- Tape the foil to the back of the cardboard.
- Gently trace around the edges of the shapes with a cotton swab.
- Coat the design with india ink.
- Rub off the ink with a soft cloth or paper towel. Do not rub off all the ink.
- With a black marker, write "DAY 3: Dry Land and Vegetation," in the upper left-hand corner.

752. CREATION MURAL—
DAY 4: SUN, MOON, AND STARS
$ 45 MIN. 2

- Cut sun, moon, and star shapes from lightweight cardboard.
- Glue the shapes to a 9" x 12" sheet of heavy cardboard.
- Cover with a piece of heavy-duty foil, folding the foil over the edges of the cardboard.
- Tape the foil to the back of the cardboard.
- Gently trace around each shape with a cotton swab.
- Coat the design with india ink.
- Rub off the ink with a soft cloth or paper towel. Do not rub off all the ink.
- With a black marker, write "DAY 4: Sun, Moon, and Stars," in the upper left-hand corner.

753. CREATION MURAL—
DAY 5: FISH AND BIRDS
$ 45 MIN. 2

- Cut fish and bird shapes from lightweight cardboard.
- Glue the shapes to a 9" x 12" sheet of heavy cardboard.
- Cover with a piece of heavy-duty foil, folding the foil over the edges of the cardboard.
- Tape the foil to the back of the cardboard.
- Gently trace around each shape with a cotton swab.
- Coat the design with india ink.
- Rub off the ink with a soft cloth or paper towel. Do not rub off all the ink.
- With a black marker, write "DAY 5: Fish and Birds," in the upper left-hand corner.

754. CREATION MURAL—
DAY 6: MAN AND ANIMALS
$ 45 MIN. 2

- Cut cattle, creeping things, a man, and a woman from lightweight cardboard.
- Glue the shapes to a 9" x 12" sheet of heavy cardboard.
- Cover with a piece of heavy-duty foil, folding the foil over the edges of the cardboard.
- Tape the foil to the back of the cardboard.
- Gently trace around each shape with a cotton swab.
- Coat the design with india ink.
- Rub off the ink with a soft cloth or paper towel. Do not rub off all the ink.
- With a black marker, write "DAY 6: Man and Animals," in the upper left-hand corner.

755. CREATION MURAL—
DAY 7: GOD RESTED
$ 45 MIN. 2

- Cut 2 eyes and a smile from lightweight cardboard.
- Glue the shapes to a 9" x 12" sheet of heavy cardboard.
- Cover with a piece of heavy-duty foil, folding the foil over the edges of the cardboard.
- Tape the foil to the back of the cardboard.
- Gently trace around each shape with a cotton swab.
- Coat the design with india ink.
- Rub off the ink with a soft cloth or paper towel. Do not rub off all the ink.
- With a black marker, write "DAY 7: God Rested," in the upper left-hand corner.

756. PAPER BEADS
C 45 MIN. 2

- Make a small rectangle and triangle pattern from scrap paper.
- Trace the pattern on old magazine pictures.
- Cut out the shapes.
- Starting at the large end of a triangle or the short side of a rectangle, tightly roll the paper around a toothpick.
- Secure with a small dot of glue.
- Remove the toothpick.
- String the beads on a thin piece of elastic or thread for a necklace.

757. ILLUSTRATE A VERSE
C 45 MIN. 2

- Cut out pictures from catalogs or old magazines to illustrate a verse. For example, Isaiah 40:31 could be illustrated with a picture of an eagle, a mountain scene, and a person running.
- Cut out the words of the verse and its reference from the text of a catalog, magazine, or newspaper. Each word might be

in a different type style, size, and color.
- Glue the pictures on a piece of colored construction paper.
- Glue the words around the edge of the paper.
- Hang on the refrigerator or a wall.

758. NAME DESIGN
C 45 MIN. 1

*We are all important to God
and we each have our own special name.*

- Draw the first letter of your first, middle, and last names in block or fancy letter shapes on three, 2" x 3" pieces of white paper.
- Cut out each letter.
- Trace the letters onto 3 different colors of construction paper and cut out. Cut out at least 15 letters. Pick colors that you like together or that match your room.
- Arrange the letters on a 12" x 18" sheet of construction paper. This background piece should be a different color than the letters.
- Arrange or play with the letters several times until you get a design you like. Letters may be placed backwards, upside down, or right side up.
- Glue the letters to the background paper.
- Outline the letters with a black marker.
- Hang on your bedroom door or wall.

759. POCKET PROMISE ACCORDION BOOK
C 45 MIN. 1

*You can keep God's promises close by with this nifty little resource!
Choose your own favorites,
or use the promises from Hebrews 13:5,
John 14:2–3, Psalm 37:4, and Proverbs 3:5–6.*

- Cut a 3" x 18" piece of white construction or butcher paper.
- With a ruler and pencil, mark a line every 3".
- Fold the left end up to the second 3" line.

• Turn the paper over and fold the same end up to the next line.
• Continue turning and folding until finished.
• Cut two 3" x 3" squares of colored construction paper.
• Write "God's Promises" on one square and decorate with dots,
   stripes, stars, or hearts.
• Decorate the back cover.
• Glue the front cover to the first "page" of the accordion book.
   The first fold should be on the left.
• Fold the book and glue on the back cover.
• Unfold the book and write a promise on each 3" x 3" section.

760. OPTICAL ILLUSION PICTURE
C 45 MIN. 1

• Cut any picture into ½"–1" strips. As each strip is cut, lay it in
   order on the work area.
• Using the far left strip, glue to a piece of construction paper.
   The construction paper should be bigger than the picture
   before you cut it apart.
• Leave a space of ¼"–½" between strips. Glue the next strip
   about ¼" higher than the first strip.
• Glue the third strip about ½" lower than the second strip.
• Continue gluing on strips, alternating the height.

761. QUILL WRITING
$$ 45 MIN. 2

Can you imagine copying an entire book of the Bible?
Scribes made copies of some of the Old Testament books
to read in the Temple.

• Cut off the tip of a feather quill at a 45-degree angle.
• Practice writing on a piece of paper, dipping the tip of the
   quill in the thinned tempera paint or ink.
• Choose a short Psalm or Bible verse to copy.

762. SAUL VS. PAUL
C 1 HOUR 4

• Read about Saul or Paul in the Book of Acts. The Bible dictionary or concordance in the back of your Bible will help you find specific references.
• At the top left of lined paper, or in your Daily Quiet Time Journal from Project #771, write "Saul" and "Paul" toward the right to form 2 columns.
• Write descriptions of Saul in the left column and of Paul in the right. For example, under Saul write "persecuted Christians," and under Paul write "a missionary to the Gentiles."
• See what a difference Christ can make in a person's life.

763. MATTHEW 4:19 LETTER COLLÉ
$ 1 HOUR 1

Collé' is a process where scraps of paper are pasted to a surface, such as a canvas or other background, to provide texture to a scene.

• Look up Matthew 4:19, and, from old catalogs or magazines, cut out the letters of the verse.
• Cut out letters that could be used to form a fisherman and another man. For example, O's for the head and upper body, an S for the lower body, capital I's for the upper legs and L's for the lower legs and feet. I's also work for arms.
• From brown paper tear out hills and glue toward the top of a 12" x 18" piece of blue construction paper.
• Tear out grass from green construction paper and glue, overlapping the bottom of the hills.
• Tear out a lake from blue paper, making sure to cover the rest of the background.
• Glue down the shapes.
• Arrange the letters into a man standing on the shore of the lake.
• Arrange the letters of the verse at the bottom of the paper.
• Glue down the verse.
• Arrange the letters for the second man in the blue of the lake.
• Make a fishing pole from letters and place in the hand of

the man on the shore.
- Arrange letters as the fishing line with a J at the end of the hook. The hook should be catching the man in the water. The letters of the fishing line could spell out a phrase such as, "He will save you."
- Glue down all the letters.
- Sing the hymn, "Love Lifted Me."

764. ACROSTIC NAME CHART
C 1 HOUR 1

- Write the letters of your name down the left side of a 9" x 12" sheet of white paper.
- Space out the letters evenly, and write each letter in block or bubble style.
- Beside each letter, write a characteristic of yourself. For example, for the name Pat: P—Patient, A—Always on time, T—Terrific.
- Write the words in bubble- or block-style lettering.
- Fill in and color each letter with a different pattern such as stars, stripes or hearts, using crayons or markers.
- Fill in the background with one pattern.
- Trace around each letter with a dark marker or crayon.
- Mount on a larger sheet of construction paper. Choose a color that goes well with the design.

765. MELTED CRAYON BOAT SCENE
C 1 HOUR 5

*The Scriptures mention Jesus' using
boat transportation several times during His ministry.
Here's a fun project that will result in
an impressionistic style "painting."
Use caution, as a candle flame will be needed.*

- Draw a scene of boats, water, and land on a 9" x 12" sheet of white paper. Do not get too detailed. A paper with a smooth surface will give a different effect than a rough surface.

- Remove the paper from the crayon to be used and melt the tip of the crayon over the flame of a candle. When the crayon softens, apply it to the boat scene. White and yellow crayons will carbon more than other colors so they should not be held to the flame very long.
- Several different colors layered on top of each other will create interesting textures.
- Use more than one shade of color for the water, land, and boat hulls.
- Cover the entire scene with melted crayon.
- Mount the picture on a larger piece of black construction paper.

766. STAFF OF MOSES
C 1 HOUR 2

- Draw a staff on a 6" x 18" sheet of brown paper.
- Cut out and trace on a second sheet of paper.
- Draw 11 squares on one staff.
- Lay the staff on an old magazine or a layer of newspaper.
- Cut each square on the sides and bottom lines with an X-Acto knife, leaving the top of each square uncut.
- Fold up each square like a flap.
- Place the second staff underneath and trace each square.
- Starting at the top, write a plague in a traced square. Blood, frogs, lice, flies, cattle, disease, boils, hail, locusts, darkness, slaying of the firstborn.
- Glue the staff with the flaps onto the staff listing the plagues.
- Write "The Staff of Moses" and "Exodus 7–12" on the front.

767. LINCOLN'S STOVEPIPE HAT
C 45 MIN. 5

- Measure around your head with a tape measure.
- Cut a piece of black poster board 8" wide and 2" longer than the measurement of your head.
- Bend the paper into a tube and staple each end.
- Stand the poster board tube upright in the middle of a second piece of black poster board.

- Trace around the bottom of the tube.
- Draw another circle about 4" outside the traced circle.
- Draw a circle 1½" inside the traced tube circle.
- Cut out the outside circle.
- Cut out the inside circle.
- Cut slits from the inside circle to ¼" past the traced tube circle.
- Fold the slits up.
- Place the black poster board circle on your head to check for fit. If the hole is too small, cut the slits longer and fold up the slits again.
- Place the black circle on top of the tube.
- Fold the tabs down into the tube and tape down. If the tube does not fit correctly, take out the staples and form the tube around the slits and restaple.
- Turn the hat over and place on your head!

768. MYSTERY WRITER
C 1 HOUR 1

- Write a mystery story in a blank book or spiral-bound note-book.
- Draw and color pictures to illustrate your story, or cut out pictures from old magazines or newspapers.

769. "CLIMB EVERY MOUNTAIN" SCENE
C 1 HOUR 1

- Cut out pictures of mountains, a river, pine trees, and an eagle from catalogs and old magazines.
- Arrange the pictures on a 9" x 12" sheet of white or light blue construction paper. Overlap the pictures to give them depth.
- Glue down the pictures.
- Cut out pictures of climbers.
- Glue the climbers to the scene.
- Cut out faces of family and friends from old photographs and glue them to the body of each climber. Don't forget to

include your own face!
- Cut out a small conversation bubble for each climber.
- Write parts of Habakkuk 3:19 on each bubble.
- Glue a bubble near the mouth of each climber so it seems like he or she is saying part of the verse.

770. STANDING LETTERS
C 1 HOUR 2

- Cut 1" x 5" strips of construction paper.
- On a 12" x 18" sheet of construction paper or poster board, print a favorite verse and reference in block letters.
- Trace the first letter on a 1" x 5" strip of construction paper and cut to length.
- Trace over the letter with a line of glue.
- Place a strip of paper on the first letter so that it is standing up. Hold until glue dries a bit and the strip stays standing in place.
- Repeat for all the words and numbers in the verse and reference.

771. QUIET TIME JOURNAL
$ 1 HOUR 4

A special place all your own to record what you're learning about God's Word!

- Fold eight 9" x 12" pieces of white paper in half.
- Cut paper in half along the fold.
- Fold each 6" x 9" paper in half.
- Cut 2 pieces of 4½" x 6" thin cardboard.
- Cut one piece of 1" x 6" thin cardboard.
- Lay all 3 pieces of cardboard on a piece of 7" x 12" construction paper with the 1" x 6" piece between the 4½" x 6" pieces. Allow ¼" between the 3 pieces.
- Glue the cardboard to the construction paper.
- Let dry.
- Fold the construction paper over the edges of the cardboard and glue down.

- Fold the cover so there is a crease on both sides of the 1" x 6" piece of cardboard. Matching the front cover edge with the back cover edge.
- Stack all 16 pieces of the folded 4½" x 6" white paper.
- Glue the pages together by gluing the back of the first folded sheet to the front of the second folded sheet. Then glue together the back of the second folded sheet to the front of the third folded sheet.
- Continue gluing until all folded sheets have been glued.
- Glue the front of the first folded sheet to the back of the front cardboard cover, making sure that everything is lined up.
- Glue the back of the last folded sheet to the back cover. This will give the front and back inside covers a finished look.
- When you close your book, the stacked pages should neatly rest against the 1" x 6" center strip of cardboard.
- Write "Quiet Time Journal" on the front cover.
- Decorate the front and back covers with markers.
- On each page write, "Date:" and "Passage:".
- Now, write your thoughts about the Bible passages you have studied!

772. ROOM SIGN
$ 1 HOUR 4

Your bedroom is your special space.
Here's a project to decorate your door.

- Practice printing your name backwards on a scrap piece of paper. Not only should the name be backwards, but the letters also.
- Some letters like the A and I do not have to be backwards.
- Also, write the word, "ROOM."
- Hold the backwards name up to a mirror to see if you can read it forward okay.
- On a large piece of sandpaper, write your name and the word "room" backwards with crayon.
- Refer to the practice sheet for the way the letters should be written.
- Trace the letters on the sandpaper with heavy crayon, making the lines thick.
- If there is any room left on the sandpaper, fill in with a few

simple designs. For example, a soccer ball or flowers.
- Lay a piece of white paper, cut to the same size as the sandpaper, on top of the crayon design.
- Top with a newspaper
- Rub a warm iron over paper to melt the crayon.
- Let cool.
- Trim with special-edged scissors.
- Cut a piece of black construction paper a little bigger than design.
- Glue the sandpaper print to the black paper and mount on your door.

773. COMMEMORATIVE PLATE
C 1 HOUR 3

- Decide which biblical character to commemorate.
- Make a silhouette by taping a 9" x 12" piece of white paper to the wall and have a boy or girl sit on a chair in front of the paper. Then, set up a light so the person's shadow is cast on the paper. Make sure the shadow is small enough to fit on a large paper plate.
- Trace the shadow.
- Cut out the silhouette and trace it onto black paper.
- Cut out the black silhouette.
- Glue the silhouette to a large paper plate.
- Write the Bible character's name under the silhouette.
- Around the edge of the plate, write short statements that tell about the character and his accomplishments. For example, for "Luke," the border might read, "A doctor," "Wrote two New Testament books, Luke and Acts," etc.
- Hole-punch 2 holes on both sides at the top of the silhouette.
- Thread with yarn, tie the ends, and hang.

774. BIBLE VERSE FLIP CHART
$ 1 HOUR 1

- Punch a hole in the top left and right corners of index cards. (Make sure the left and right holes are in the same position on each card.)

- Write a Scripture verse on each side of the card.
- Group the verses according to themes. For example, God's love, God's promises, or the "Romans Road."
- Cut two 3" x 5" pieces of lightweight cardboard.
- Punch a hole in the top left and right corners of the cardboard pieces. These will be the front and back covers.
- Decorate and color the front of one piece and the back of the other cardboard piece.
- String the front cover, the verse cards, and the back cover on metal rings.
- Memorize the verses.

775. THE ROMANS ROAD
C 1 HOUR 3

- Lay a 12" x 18" sheet of white construction paper horizontally.
- Write the title, "The Romans Road," across the top of the paper.
- Draw a wavy double line around the edges.
- Draw a broken line in the middle of the wavy line, to resemble a road.
- Color the road lightly with a black crayon, and the lines white or yellow.
- In the center, draw 5 2½" x 2½" squares in a horizontal row, ¼" apart.
- Cut out each square with an X-Acto knife.
- Cut a 3½" x 14" strip of red construction paper.
- Place the red paper behind the 12" x 18" sheet of white construction paper.
- Trace each square onto the red paper.
- In the first square, write the words and reference of Romans 3:23.
- Write Romans 6:23 in the second square.
- Write Romans 5:8 in the third square.
- Write Romans 10:9–10 in the fourth square.
- Write Romans 10:13 along the road at the bottom of the paper.
- Decorate the front of the white construction paper with hearts.
- Turn the white paper over, put a strip of glue around each square, and place the red paper on top. The verses should

show through the cutouts.
• Use the Romans Road to show someone how to become a Christian.

776. FAVORITE-OBJECT STILL LIFE
$ 1 HOUR 2

• Pick out 3 things that are your favorite possessions. For example, a baseball glove, stuffed animal, or book.
• Arrange the objects on a table. Place the objects close together with one in front of the others; this will give the still life depth.
• Lay a 9" x 12" sheet of white paper vertically.
• Draw a line across the paper about 3" from the bottom. This will form the table.
• Lightly draw an outline of the 3 objects. Do not worry if your drawing is not perfect.
• Study the still life. Notice which parts are light and dark.
• Shade in the objects with the side of the pencil lead.
• Shade in the table.
• Hang on your wall.

777. "NO OTHER GODS" COMIC STRIP
C 1 HOUR 2

Read about the golden calf and Israel's sin in Exodus 32.

• Place a 9" x 12" sheet of white paper horizontally and divide the paper into 9 rectangles with a ruler.
• Trace each line with a black marker.
• Draw one scene per box. For example, in box one, draw Moses on the mountain talking with God, and in box two, draw the people saying to Aaron, "Where's Moses?"
• Color each scene with colored pencils.

778. SCRIPTURE POCKET
C 1 HOUR 1

- Cut a paper plate in half.
- Draw and color a Bible on the back.
- Place the half of the paper plate, back side up, on another whole paper plate.
- Staple around the edge to make the pocket.
- Write in block letters, "HOLY BIBLE," around the top curved edge of the whole paper plate.
- Color the letters.
- Color the edges of the plate and pocket.
- Draw an open Bible on a 3" x 3" square of white construction paper.
- Cut out the Bible and trace it onto 6 more 3" x 3" squares of paper.
- Cut out the Bibles.
- Look up verses that mention the Bible and write one on each paper Bible. For example, 2 Timothy 3:15–17.
- Tuck the Bibles in the pocket and hang.

779. FAVORITE VERSE BOX
C 1 HOUR 1

This project would also make a great gift.

- Decorate a shoe box, a wooden box, or a papier-mâché box with magazine pictures, stickers, beads, and paint.
- Decorate the borders of index cards with tiny stickers, or draw a border and fill in with marker.
- Write some of your favorite verses on the cards.
- Place the cards, a special pen or pencil, and blank cards inside the box.
- Whenever you read a verse or hear one at church that you like, add it to your collection.
- Read through your verse collection when you need some extra encouragement.

780. PAPIER-MÂCHÉ BRACELET
$ 1 HOUR 2

- From cereal box cardboard, cut a strip 9" long and ½"–1½" wide. The width will depend on how wide you want the bracelet to be.
- Bend the strip of cardboard into a circle, overlapping the ends about ½". Tape the ends together.
- Make sure the bracelet will easily fit over your hand. (Keep in mind that when the papier-mâché is applied, the bracelet opening will be smaller.)
- Fold a sheet of newspaper several times into a long length and wrap around the cardboard bracelet and tape in place.
- Continue adding newspaper until you get the thickness you want.
- Tear strips of newspaper into lengths of about 1" x 6". (Newspaper does have a grain so it will tear easier one way.)
- Make a paste of wallpaper paste and water. The paste should have the consistency of Cream of Wheat cereal. If the paste is runny, add more wallpaper paste.
- Dip a strip of newspaper into the paste. Wipe off any excess paste by pulling the strip carefully between two fingers.
- Apply the strip to the bracelet.
- Apply 3 or 4 layers of overlapping strips.
- Apply one layer of nonprinted paper, such as newsprint, to the bracelet. This layer will keep the print from the newspaper from showing through.
- Let it dry overnight in a warm area.
- Paint the bracelet with acrylic paints.
- Decorate with stars, moons, stripes, X's and O's, lambs, dots, hearts, sequins, puff paints, or plastic jewels. Use your imagination!

781. SPIRAL CARD
C 1 HOUR 3

- Fold a 9" x 12" sheet of construction paper in half. Pick a color you like or a color to go with the season or holiday.
- Lightly draw a circle in the center of the front of the card, leaving a 1" border.

- Cut out the circle.
- Fold a 9" x 12" sheet of white paper in half.
- Place the colored paper on top of the white paper and lightly trace the circle.
- Inside the circle on the white paper, write a verse to go with the occasion you are sending the card for. For example, write the words of Matthew 1:21 for a Christmas card.
- Glue the colored paper to the white paper so the verse shows through the cutout circle.
- Decorate and write a message on the white inside.
- Draw a circle that is about ½" larger than the circle cut out of the card. Make sure this circle fits on the card.
- Draw a spiral on this circle and cut out.
- Glue the largest of the spirals to the card so it covers the cutout.
- Let dry.
- On the front of the card, write "Pull the spiral to see the message underneath."
- Send or give the card to someone.

782. GOD'S WORD
C 1 HOUR 2

- Draw an open Bible on a 9" x 12" sheet of black construction paper.
- Cut out the Bible.
- For pages, trace the Bible onto a 9" x 12" sheet of white construction paper.
- Cut ¼" inside the line so the pages will be smaller than the black Bible cover.
- Draw a line down the center of the page with a black marker.
- Place the white page on a cutting board, or on a stack of newspapers or magazines.
- Place a brightly colored flower near the edge of the white page and cover it with plastic wrap.
- Tap the plastic-covered flowers with a hammer.
- Remove the plastic wrap and any flower residue.
- Repeat all the way around the edge of the white Bible page.
- Write " 'The grass withers and the flowers fall, but the word of the Lord stands forever,' 1 Peter 1:24–25 NIV."

783. NEWSPAPER ARTICLE
C 1 HOUR 3

- Read Acts 7:54–60 and Acts 9:1–31.
- Write a newsbreaking article about Paul's conversion.
- Include the "who, what, when, where, why, and how."

784. COMIC-STYLE BIBLE STORY
C 1 HOUR 2

- Select a favorite story from the Bible.
- Divide the story into scenes.
- Divide a 12" x 18" sheet of white paper into as many square and rectangle spaces as needed for the story.
- Draw a scene in each space.
- Add speech bubbles and write in them what the people said.
- Add captions along the bottom.

785. POSITIVE/NEGATIVE CROSS DESIGN
C 1 HOUR 4

- Cut four 3" x 3" squares of red and black construction paper.
- Stack 2 black pieces of paper together.
- Draw one-half of a cross on the top black paper on the right side.
- Cut out the cross, keeping both pieces together.
- Repeat with the other 2 black pieces.
- Stack 2 pieces of red paper together and draw one-half of a heart on the top red piece on the right side.
- Cut out the heart.
- Repeat with the other 2 red pieces.
- Lay a 9" x 12" sheet of purple construction paper vertically.
- Arrange the positive and negative pieces on the purple sheet so the black negative cross is in the top left corner and the black positive cross beside it. A positive piece is the shape itself and a negative piece is the paper it was cut from.
- Then, arrange a red negative and positive heart. This will complete the top row.
- Glue down the top row.

- The second row should start on the left with a red negative heart, then a positive heart, a black negative cross and a positive cross.
- Lay out the next 2 rows.
- Glue all the pieces down one at a time.
- Do not worry if the pieces do not line up exactly.

786. NAME OF JESUS COLLAGE
C 1 HOUR 1

- Trim off one inch on one 18" side and on one 12" side of a 12" x 18" sheet of light blue construction paper.
- Center the trimmed sheet on top of a 12" x 18" sheet of black construction paper.
- Glue the blue paper to the black paper.
- Write the names of Jesus on a white piece of paper about 2" apart with a black marker or colored pencil: Revelation 21:6—Alpha and Omega; John 10:9—Door; Luke 1:17—Dayspring; John 8:58—I Am; Isaiah 7:14—Immanuel; Revelation 19:16—King of Kings; Revelation 5:5—Lion of Judah; John 1:38—Master; Isaiah 9:6—Mighty God and Prince of Peace; John 15:1—True Vine.
- Draw a shadow around each name.
- Color in the shadow with marker or colored pencil.
- Cut around each name leaving a border of about ½".
- Arrange the names on the background paper. Do not overlap.
- Glue down the names with rubber cement.
- Hang the collage.

787. MELTED CRAYON FLAG
C 1 HOUR 5

- Cut a 6" x 7" piece of blue construction paper.
- Draw 4 or 5 different-sized stars on the paper.
- Lay the paper on several layers of newspaper or an old magazine.
- Cut out the stars with an X-Acto knife.
- Lay the paper in the top left corner of a 12" x 18" sheet of white construction paper and trace the stars.

- Cut out the white stars with an X-Acto knife.
- Cut 2 sheets of wax paper 19" long.
- Place one sheet of wax paper on a layer of newspaper.
- Sharpen a lot of red crayons onto the wax paper.
- Place the second sheet of wax paper on top, then a sheet of newspaper.
- Iron until the crayon melts.
- Cut the melted crayon paper into 7 stripes about 1" wide.
- Place the blue paper at the upper left corner of the white paper and trace the bottom and side.
- Glue the red stripes to the white construction paper flag background starting at the top with a red stripe. Then, skipping about 1" for a white stripe, glue on another red stripe. Trim the red stripes to stop at the blue field.
- Continue gluing on red stripes until there are 7 red and 6 white stripes. The fourth white stripe should be right under the blue field.
- Cut two 6" x 7" sheets of wax paper.
- Lay one sheet on a layer of newspaper and sharpen white crayons over it.
- Top with wax paper and a sheet of newspaper and iron until the shavings melt.
- Place the white melted crayon paper in the upper left corner of the white construction paper and glue down.
- Glue the blue construction paper on top of the white wax paper.
- Hang in a window or on a sliding glass door.

788. FINGERPRINT AUTOGRAPHS
C 1 HOUR 3

- Cut two 3" x 3" squares of construction paper.
- Cut seven 3" x 3" squares of dark-colored paper.
- Cut seven 3" x 3" squares of white construction paper.
- Place the 14 dark and white squares between the first squares and staple on the left side.
- Collect fingerprints of people who are important to you. For example, parents, Sunday school teachers, club leaders, brothers, and sisters.
- To lift a fingerprint, have the person put his print on a flat,

dark surface. Smooth glass and metal show fingerprints the best.
- Sprinkle a small amount of talcum powder on the surface.
- Gently brush the powder around with a very soft brush or feather.
- The talcum will stick to the fingerprint.
- (If the surface that the fingerprint is on is light, use graphite powder by sanding a pencil over the print.)
- Place a piece of Scotch tape over the exposed fingerprint. The tape will "lift" the print.
- Place the piece of tape on a page in your booklet.
- If you have a talcum print, place the tape on a dark page. If you have a graphite print, place the tape on a white page.
- If you can, have the people write their names under their fingerprints.
- There are three common types of fingerprint classifications: loop, whorl, and arch. Find out more information about each type, then examine each print to see their differences.

789. MARBLED NEWS REPORTER NOTEBOOK
$ 1 HOUR 5

*Hang this notebook around your neck
and you'll be ready to write a newsbreaking story!*

- Decide what colors you want the outside of your notebook to be.
- Place a small amount of artist's oil paint in a tin pie pan and dilute with a little paint thinner.
- Thin each color chosen in separate tins.
- Fill a pan or tub with water.
- Cut two 4" x 6" sheets of white paper.
- Place drops of each color from the pie tin on the surface of the water with a paintbrush.
- Stir the water gently with the end of the brush.
- Put on a pair of rubber gloves.
- Lay the paper on the surface of the water.
- Lift off the paper quickly. Make sure the paper remains flat and not tipped so the pattern of oil paint doesn't run.
- Lay the paper aside to dry.

- Repeat with another sheet of paper.
- Cut 2 pieces of 3" x 5" lightweight cardboard.
- Cover the cardboard pieces with the marbled paper overlapping the edges.
- Cut ten 3" x 5" sheets of white paper.
- Cut a piece of yarn long enough to fit over your head and hang down a little when the ends are tied together.
- Stack the 3" x 5" papers on top of the marbled cardboard with the marbled side down. The top is the 3" side.
- Place the yarn across the 3" side so the center of the yarn is on the paper.
- Top with the second piece of cardboard with the marbled side facing up.
- Staple across the top making sure to catch the yarn.
- Tie the ends of the yarn together.
- Hang around your neck.

790. BIBLE SUMMARY BOOK
$ 1 HOUR 2

- Fold a 9" x 12" sheet of black construction paper in half. This will be the cover.
- Write "Bible Summary Book" on the front with a yellow crayon.
- Trace around each letter with a white crayon.
- Cut 6" x 9" sheets of construction paper: 5 red, 12 yellow, 6 blue, 12 green, 4 brown, 4 purple, 1 tan, 21 blue, and 1 pink.
- Place, in order, inside the folded black paper and staple down the left side.
- Write the categories at the top of the page indicated: LAW—5, HISTORICAL—12, POETICAL—6; PROPHETICAL: MINOR—12, MAJOR—4; GOSPELS—4, HISTORY—1, EPISTLES—21, PROPHECY—1.
- Number the pages.
- Cut pieces of lined paper to size and glue them to the front of each page.
- At the top of each page write the corresponding book of the Bible.
- On each page write one of your favorite verses from that

book, or, when you hear a sermon from that book write the main points on the page.

791. WATER MOBILE
$ 1 HOUR 3

- Punch a hole 1" in from the edge of a paper plate.
- Punch a second hole in the opposite edge.
- Cut 6"–10" strips of several shades of blue tissue paper.
- Glue one end of each strip to the back of the paper plate. The longer strips will hang over the edge of the plate.
- Glue on a lot of strips so the plate is full.
- Draw 5 dots on the back of a second paper plate. One dot in the center and the other 4 dots in a circle around the center dot.
- Poke small holes through the dots.
- Thread, from the front of the plate to the back, a 12" length of blue yarn through each hole and knot the ends near the hole.
- On a piece of scrap paper, draw and cut out a big raindrop.
- Trace 15 raindrops onto blue paper.
- Cut out 30 raindrops by placing another sheet of blue paper behind the traced drops and cutting out 2 at a time.
- Punch a hole through the top and bottom of each drop with a hole punch. Be careful not to get too close to the edge. Do not put a hole in the bottom of 5 of the drops. These will be the last drops in the mobile.
- Write Psalm 23:2 NASB, "He leads me beside quiet waters," on 6 raindrops.
- Put a strip of glue around the edge of each drop.
- Sprinkle blue or silver glitter in the glue. Let dry.
- Knock off the excess glitter onto a sheet of newspaper.
- Decorate the back of each drop with some glitter.
- Staple together the paper plates so the tissue is on the top and the yarn strings hang down at the bottom.
- Thread some raindrops through each piece of yarn and knot. Space the drops evenly.
- String together the verse drops on the center length of yarn.
- Leave the drops with no hole at the bottom for the last drop on each string.
- Hang the water mobile.

792. LOVE POSTER
C 1 HOUR 2

- Draw a leaf on a 2" x 2" piece of scrap paper.
- Cut out the leaf.
- Trace the leaf onto green construction paper and cut out about 19 leaves. Hold several pieces of paper together and cut out several leaves at one time.
- Draw veins on each leaf with a green crayon.
- Draw a heart about the size of the leaf on a piece of scrap paper.
- Cut out the heart.
- Trace the heart onto red construction paper and cut out about 10 hearts.
- Write " 'Nothing can separate me from the love of God!' Romans 8:39," in the middle of a 12" x 18" sheet of white construction paper. Make sure to leave room around the edges for the border.
- Arrange the leaves and hearts around the edges for a border. Turn the leaves and hearts in different directions.
- Glue down the heart and leaf border.
- Draw vines between the hearts and leaves.
- Draw 2 or 3 hearts in the empty white space around the verse.
- Poke a hole in the center of each heart and cut it out.
- Glue red, pink, or purple tissue or construction paper behind each heart cutout.
- Hang the poster.

793. ACCORDION HEART BOOK
$ 1 HOUR 3

- Fold a 4" x 4" piece of scrap paper in half.
- Draw one-half of a heart starting and ending on the fold.
- Cut out the heart.
- Trace the heart twice onto a piece of thin cardboard.
- Cut out the hearts.
- Cover the hearts with heavy-duty foil.
- Glue small pieces of red tissue paper to the front of the foil-covered hearts, overlapping the edges to the back.
- Let dry.

- Cut the edges off paper doilies and glue to the back of each heart so they overlap the edge and form a border around the hearts.
- Cut 2 foil hearts a little smaller than the cardboard heart and glue to the back of each heart to give it a finished look.
- Fold over one end of a 3" x 12" strip of red construction paper 3".
- Turn over and fold accordion style.
- Draw a heart on the folded paper so the sides touch the left and right folds.
- Cut out the heart, leaving about ½" on each fold uncut.
- With the hearts folded, glue the front of the first heart to the back of a foil-covered heart.
- Glue the back of the last heart to the back of the second foil heart.
- Let dry.
- On each heart, write a reason you like the person you are giving the book to. For example, "I love you because you're helpful. You're Great!"
- Write a reference about God's love on the remaining hearts.
- Give as a gift.

794. STAINED GLASS TRIPTYCH
$ 1 HOUR 3

- On a 9" x 12" sheet of black construction paper draw a window with a point at the top with thick chalk lines. Then cut out.
- Trace and cut out 2 more windows.
- On the back and in the middle of each black window, draw a shape with thick chalk lines. For Christmas, the shape could be a bell, star, or manger. Draw on the back so the white lines won't show when the window is turned over.
- Starting from the center figure, draw different shapes to the outside white line edge.
- Lay the window on a layer of thick newspaper.
- Cut out all the black spaces with an X-Acto knife. Cut only on the outside of each chalk line. This will create the lead of a stained glass window.
- Decide what color tissue paper you want for each center shape.

- Place the black window frame on top of the colored tissue paper and trace the shape.
- Cut out the tissue shape, staying ⅛" outside the line. This will make the tissue shape a little bigger than the hole in the black frame.
- Put a very thin line of glue around the middle shape on the back of the black frame.
- Lay the tissue shape carefully down on the black frame and the glue.
- Continue tracing each shape onto the different tissue colors, cutting, then gluing each tissue shape in place.
- If the tissue shape is too big, trim the edges.
- Turn over the window to see how the front looks.
- Finish all 3 windows.
- Lay the windows beside each other so the sides are touching.
- Cut 4 strips of ½" x 1" black paper.
- Fold in half.
- Glue 2 strips to the back right of the first window and the back left of the second window for hinges. Do the same thing to the back right of the second window and the back left of the third window.
- Stand up the triptych to display.
- Votive candles can be lit behind each window to shine through the "stained glass." Be careful that the candle is not too close.

795. FAMILY SCREEN
$ 1 HOUR 4

- On the back of a 22" x 28" piece of poster board, draw a line every 4", and carefully score with a knife. Do not cut or score all the way through the poster board.
- Accordion-fold the poster board by folding one end up to the second line, then turning over and folding to the next line.
- Continue to turn and fold to the end.
- Cut pieces of construction paper and glue them to the board in a checkerboard pattern. The construction paper can be the same color or different colors.
- Tape white paper to a blank wall.

- Have a member of your family or a friend sit in a chair near the paper on the wall.
- Shine a light from behind the person.
- Trace the person's shadow onto the white paper.
- Cut out the silhouette.
- Place silhouette on colored construction paper and trace.
- Cut out the color silhouette.
- Glue a silhouette on each square. The color of the silhouette should be a different color than the square.
- Or, glue a silhouette on a square and write about the person in the next square.
- Stand the screen in a special place.

796. PYRAMID STORY
C 1 HOUR 2

Read the story of Joseph, from Genesis 39–47, before doing this activity!

- Draw a pyramid on a 9" x 12" sheet of light brown construction paper.
- Lightly draw lines on the pyramid to depict the stone blocks.
- Lay drawn pyramid on several layers of newspaper.
- Cut 3 sides of several stone blocks and fold back on the fourth side to create a door.
- Trace and cut out a second pyramid.
- Lay the plain pyramid behind the drawn one.
- Open a door and trace the opening with a pencil.
- Draw and color a scene from Joseph's life behind each door. Scenes could include Joseph wearing his coat of many colors; the stars, moons, and wheat sheaves from his dream; Joseph being sold into slavery; Joseph in prison; Joseph as second in command; and Joseph seeing his brothers in Egypt.
- Place a small strip of glue around the edge of the pyramid with the scenes on it.
- Place the other pyramid carefully on top.
- To view a scene, open a door.

797. FRIENDSHIP NUT
C 1 HOUR 3

- Carefully crack a walnut in half.
- Dig out the meat.
- Accordion-fold a 1" x 11" strip of white paper.
- Round off the corners with scissors, making sure to leave some of the fold on each side.
- Fit the folded strip into the walnut. Trim smaller if necessary.
- Cut 2 pieces of gift wrap and glue to the front and back of the folded strip.
- Open the strip and write a Bible verse or a line from a poem about friendship on each section. Verses could include parts of Ruth 1:16–17, Proverbs 17:17, and John 15:13.
- Draw a tiny picture on each section.
- Color the picture with sharp colored pencils.
- Glue the back of the folded book into one half of the walnut shell.
- Place the shells together and tie with a thin ribbon.
- Give as a gift to a special friend or parent.

798. BIRTHDAY TABLE RUNNER
$ 1 HOUR 2

- Pick 3 colors of construction paper that go with the birthday decorations.
- Fold 2 sheets of 12" x 18" construction paper in half.
- Cutting from the fold, cut 1" strips across the paper to ½" from the edge of the paper.
- Unfold each cut paper and lay end to end, overlapping about ½".
- Glue the overlapping end to make one long piece.
- Cut 1" wide strips of 2 different colors of construction paper.
- Weave one strip under and over through the long runner. Push it to one end of the runner.
- Glue both ends of the strips.
- Continue weaving alternating colors and the under/over pattern.
- Place the runner on the table.

799. CARTON VILLAGE
C 2 HOURS 1

- Cover half-pint and pint-sized milk cartons with construction paper.
- Tape the openings shut.
- Decorate each carton as a different building in an American village. For example, Union Bank, Post Office, Gas Station, Corner Drug Store, etc.
- Draw and color windows, doors, signs, flower boxes, dogs, and people. Or, cut out pictures from catalogs and magazines and glue them on the cartons.

800. LIFE OF JOSEPH TIMELINE
C 2 HOURS 2

- Read about Joseph in Genesis 37–50.
- Make a timeline on a 12" x 18" or larger sheet of paper. Several pieces of paper can be taped together.
- Draw a line through the center of the paper from end to end.
- Starting on the left end, with the birth of Joseph, write different events on the timeline in chronological order.
- Draw and color pictures to illustrate Joseph's life.
- Cut out the pictures and glue them in the correct spot on the timeline.
- Pictures could include a well, camel, his family, Potiphar, a jail, etc.

801. PAPIER-MÂCHÉ TORTOISE
$ 2 HOURS 4

*Many animals are mentioned in the Bible—
and Adam got to name them all!
Some of those animals are
fish, lambs, donkeys, leopards, mice, and whales.
Go to the library and check out a book on tortoises
and begin an animal collection of your own.*

- Place a plastic bowl upside down on a newspaper-covered work area.
- Make papier-mâché paste from wallpaper paste mixed with water.
- Tear newspaper sheets into strips.
- Dip a strip of newspaper into the paste. Wipe off excess paste by running the strip gently between two fingers.
- Cover the bowl with several layers of newspaper dipped in the paste. Try to make an edge like a tortoise shell and dip in the edge on one side to create space for a neck and head.
- Let dry.
- Carefully remove the shell from the bowl.
- To make the legs, cut 2 toilet paper rolls in half.
- Attach the 4 legs to the shell with masking tape.
- Stand up the body. (If the body is not balanced, wad up newspaper and tape it to the end of a leg near the shell.)
- For the head and neck, cut a paper towel roll in half. Wad up a piece of newspaper to form a head and tape it to the end of the paper towel roll. The end of the head should be pointed.
- Tape the end of the neck to the underside of the tortoise shell in the dip.
- Cover the legs, neck, and head with strips of newspaper dipped in wallpaper paste.
- Let dry.
- Paint tortoise with acrylic paints. Add details like eyes and toenails.

ACTIVITIES FOR
OLDER CHILDREN
PAINT PROJECTS

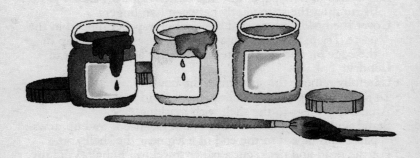

802. ROCK OF AGES
C 30 MIN. 1

- Using a small paintbrush and acrylic paint, paint the words of 2 Samuel 22:2–4, or Isaiah 26:4 on a clean rock. Or, use a bottle of fabric paint that has writing tips.
- Spray with a clear sealer.
- Place the rock where you will be reminded Who your strength is.

803. COTTON SWAB PAINTING
C 1 HOUR 1

• Draw a horizontal and vertical line in the top left corner of a 9" x 12" sheet of white construction paper to form the blue field of the United States flag.
• Draw a small star on a piece of scrap paper and cut it out.
• Draw 12 evenly spaced lines to form the 13 stripes of the flag.
• Trace 13 stars in a circle inside the blue field area.
• This is the United States flag from 1777.
• With a cotton swab, paint in the blue field and red stripes. Paint the top stripe red, then skip a white stripe and paint another red stripe. Continue painting to the last red stripe. Use watercolor or tempera paints.

804. FRUIT AND VEGETABLE NOTECARDS
$ 1 HOUR 1

• Fold several sheets of white paper in half.
• Cut an orange, an apple, a carrot, a green pepper, an artichoke, and a pear in half. Corn does not need to be cut in half.
• Cover the work surface with newspaper.
• Paint the fruit or vegetable with tempera, acrylic, or watercolor paint.
• Practice printing on a piece of newspaper.
• Paint the fruit or vegetables again.
• Print by pressing it onto the front of the notecard.
• Prints can go off the edge of the paper.
• Print several cards.
• Add details like seeds or carrot tops with a paintbrush.

805. HARVEST MONO PRINT
$ 1 HOUR 4

• Make a template by drawing a shape like a pumpkin, Indian corn, Pilgrim, Indian, or gourd on a 6" x 7" piece of thin cardboard.

- Cut out the shape.
- Draw highlights, like lines, for kernels of corn, or curved lines on a pumpkin.
- Make these lines deeper with an ink pen. Or cut out the highlights. For example, cut out a few kernels of corn or the buckle on the Pilgrim.
- Anything cut out or scored on the template will be white.
- Ink a small ink roller with black, brown, yellow, or orange paint.
- Place the template on a layer of newspaper and ink.
- Place the template ink side down on a 9" x 12" sheet of white paper.
- Gently rub the back of the template, being careful not to move it.
- Lift the template off and place on another part of the paper.
- Gently rub.
- Lift off.
- Re-ink the template.
- Lay ink side down, overlapping the 2 prints.
- Gently rub.
- Lift off the template.
- Re-inking the template once in a while will make light and dark prints, giving the picture depth.
- Let dry.
- Mount the mono print on a 10" x 13" sheet of construction paper the same color as the print.

806. BATIK CAMEL
$ 1 HOUR 2

Camels are mentioned many times in the Bible.
They were used for transportation and were a sign of wealth.

- Draw a simple, large camel on a 12" x 18" sheet of white construction paper with thick chalk lines.
- Add details using thick chalk lines, like mountains in the background, a sun in the sky, and palm trees in the desert.
- Paint inside the chalk lines with tempera paint. Do not use black paint or paint over the lines.
- Let dry.
- Wipe off the chalk lines with paper towel.

- Brush black india ink over the entire scene, being careful not to overlap the brush strokes.
- Let the ink dry for at least 30 minutes.
- Hold the scene under cool water and gently rub off the ink. Not all the ink will come off.
- Let the scene dry.

807. SCRATCH ART TREES
$ 1 HOUR 3

- Cut a 7" x 12" piece of cardboard.
- Cut a piece of heavy-duty foil bigger than the cardboard.
- Place the cardboard on the dull side of the foil.
- Fold the foil over the edges and tape to the cardboard.
- Place the cardboard foil side up on several layers of newspaper.
- Brush on several coats of india ink, letting each coat dry before applying the next one.
- Lay the board horizontally.
- Divide the cardboard into 2 sections by carefully scratching a line down the center with an open paper clip or nail.
- On one side scratch out what you think the Tree of Life would look like, being careful not to rip the foil.
- On the second side draw a different type of tree for the Tree of Knowledge of Good and Evil.
- Scratch out the title of each tree.

808. PRINTED ANIMAL BANDANA
$ 1 HOUR 3

- Wash, dry, and iron a large men's white handkerchief.
- Cut off the end of a large carrot.
- With a pencil, draw a triangle on the fat end of the carrot.
- Cut away the carrot on the outside of the drawn line.
- Cover the work area with newspaper.
- Tape the handkerchief down.
- Place a small circle of fabric paint on a paper plate.
- Dip the carrot in the paint, then practice printing the shape

on a piece of scrap paper.
- Print the shape onto the handkerchief, starting in the center and printing toward the edges. Be careful not to use too much paint.
- Move the handkerchief to a clean newspaper to dry.
- Tie around the neck of your pet.

809. FREE-FORM VERSE DESIGNS
$ 1 HOUR 1

- Fold two or three 9" x 12" sheets of white paper in half.
- Open the paper and place blobs of red, white, and blue tempera paint on one side of the fold.
- Fold the paper and rub gently to smear the paint.
- Unfold the paper and let dry.
- With a pencil, write the words and reference from John 8:32 in bubble or block letters, on the dried painted sheets.
- Cut out the letters.
- Glue to a 12" x 18" sheet of white construction paper.
- Trace around the letters with a black, red, or blue marker.

810. STAFF OF MOSES
C 1 HOUR 1

Read about Moses' staff in the Book of Exodus.

- Smooth the surface of a long stick or branch with sandpaper.
- Paint it with acrylic paint.
- Decorate by painting on designs such as stripes; waves to symbolize the Red Sea; frogs for one of the twelve plagues in Egypt; the words of one of the Ten Commandments, such as "Honor your father and mother. . . ."
- After the paint has dried, coat the staff with a clear sealer.

811. PLASTER BLOCK PRINTING
$ 1 HOUR 4

- Find a small cardboard box lid.
- Check to make sure there are no holes in the lid. Tape up any holes.
- Cover the inside of the lid with Vaseline.
- Mix 1 cup plaster of paris and ⅔ cup water in a disposable bowl—don't let any plaster of paris go down the sink.
- Pour plaster into the lid "mold."
- Plaster should be 1"–2" thick. If more is needed mix another small batch.
- Let plaster harden. This will take at least one hour.
- Carefully tear off the cardboard lid.
- Cut a piece of white paper the size of the plaster block.
- Draw a simple design on the paper such as 3 crosses and hills for an Easter card or a snowman and falling flakes for a winter scene.
- Place a sheet of carbon paper, carbon side down on the plaster block.
- Place drawing on top of the carbon paper.
- Trace over all the lines of the drawing with a pen.
- Remove design and carbon paper.
- Carve out the lines of the drawing with a nail. When the card is printed, these scratched-out lines will be white.
- Coat plaster block with varnish.
- Let dry.
- Roll a small ink roller in paint covering the whole roller.
- Roll the paint-loaded small ink roller over the plaster block, completely coating it with paint.
- Place a sheet of white paper over the block and carefully rub the surface with one hand, being sure that the block and paper do not move.
- Lift paper off.
- Repaint block and repeat for another print.
- For cards, place one side of a folded piece of white paper on the painted block and rub.

812. CLOTHESPIN MEMORIZATION
$$ 2 HOURS 3

*This is a great project to help you memorize
the books of the Bible, verses,
or just about anything you want to memorize.*

• Paint the flat edge of 66 clothespins with different colors of
  acrylic paint.
• Write the name of a book of the Bible on each clothespin
  with a marker or puff paint. If the book name is long,
  abbreviate it.
• Let dry.
• Seal by brushing on Mod Podge or glue thinned with water.
• Let dry.
• Put the clothespins in the wrong order on an outside clothes-
  line or on a string hung in the house.
• See if you can put the pins in the right order.
• Take a few off the line and try to say the books in order.
• Or put the pins on the line in groups and memorize those and
  then add more.
• Put the pins in order and have one person take some off the
  line, then try to guess which ones are missing.

ACTIVITIES FOR OLDER CHILDREN
CRAFT PROJECTS

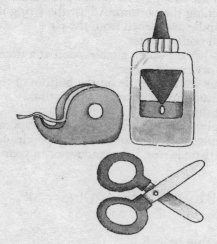

813. CONSTRUCTION STRAWS
$ 30 MIN. 2

- Cut drinking straws into different lengths.
- Cut construction paper into different shapes like circles, squares, triangles.
- Slit both ends of the straws so they can be connected to the construction-paper shapes.
- Build cars, animals, or buildings by connecting straws and shapes.

814. BRIGHT CANDLE
$ 30 MIN. 3

Even children can let their lights shine.
Read Matthew 5:16 and discuss with your child
how he or she can shine the love of Jesus in many ways—
by being kind, inviting non-churched friends to church
or youth group, or by helping a neighbor rake leaves.

- Form a pipecleaner into the shape of a candle with a flame on top.
- Tie one end of a string to the flame of the candle and the other end to a pencil.
- Drop the candle into a wide-mouthed glass jar and lay the pencil across the mouth. The candle should hang in the jar without touching the bottom. Adjust the string if necessary.
- Remove the candle and pencil from the jar.
- Fill the jar with boiling water.
- Mix borax into heated water, a tablespoon at a time. Mix in 3 tablespoons per cup of water.
- When the borax starts to settle on the bottom of the jar, stir in food coloring until you create a dark tint.
- Put the candle into the jar.
- Set aside overnight. As the water cools and evaporates, the borax molecules will form around the pipe-cleaner candle.
- Hang on a Christmas tree, in a window, or in your room.

815. HOMEMADE SPEAR
C 30 MIN. 5

- Choose a long thin branch.
- Whittle one end into a dull point with a knife.
- Use the spear to pretend you are David and Jonathan on a hunting trip or fighting the enemies of Israel.

816. EGGSHELL GARDEN
C 30 MIN. 1

- Poke a small hole in each end of an egg.
- Blow out the inside of the egg.

- Carefully tear away some of the eggshell to create a bigger opening.
- Rinse out the egg.
- Fill the egg with potting soil.
- Poke a few seeds down into the soil and cover. Do not put the seeds in too deep.
- Place eggshell garden in the egg carton and water.
- Place in a sunny spot.
- Watch the seeds sprout and grow.
- After the seeds have sprouted, plant the eggshell and the young plant in the outside garden.

817. ORANGE VOTIVE CANDLE
C 30 MIN. 2

- Cut a thin slice off the bottom of an orange so it will sit upright.
- Cut off the top of the orange.
- On the outside skin of the orange, carve out simple designs. For example, stripes, hearts, and circles.
- Scoop the inside of the orange out.
- To secure the votive candle, drip some wax into the bottom of the orange and place the candle in the wax.
- Light the candle and use as a centerpiece, or make one for each place setting!

818. BUTTON FLOWER PINS & MAGNETS
C 30 MIN. 2

- Lay a large button on a piece of poster board and trace around it.
- Draw 4 to 6 flower petals around the traced circle.
- Place the button on the center of the flower and mark the holes with a needle.
- Poke small holes through the needle marks.
- Cut out the flower.
- Thread a needle and sew the button to the cardboard flower.
- Glue a pin back to the back of the cardboard flower.
- Or glue a magnet to the back.

819. WOLF PAPERWEIGHT
$ 45 MIN. 3

Wolves are mentioned in the Bible in Isaiah 11:6.

• Form a hunk of clay into a ball about the size of your palm.
• Form the ball into the shape of a wolf lying down. Use a picture of a wolf as a guide.
• From the body, pull out some clay to form a head and nose.
• With a pencil, poke in eyes and scratch lines for the fur.
• Dry or bake according to the package instructions.
• Paint with acrylic paint or according to package instructions.

820. RUBBER BAND SIGNATURE STAMP
C 45 MIN. 2

• Write your name on a 3" x 4" piece of lightweight cardboard.
• Trace over the writing with glue.
• Lay pieces of rubber bands in the glue following your signature. Do not overlap the bands.
• Let dry.
• Press band side down on an ink pad.
• Print onto a piece of paper.

821. OPEN BIBLE CARVING
C 45 MIN. 4

• Carve a line down the center of a large bar of soap.
• Trim off the ends at an angle to create a beveled edge.
• On the ends, carve several tiered lines for pages.
• Cut a thin ribbon the width of the soap and glue to the soap down the middle.
• Carve the word "Holy" to the left of the center line and "Bible" to the right of the center line.

822. POTATO CARVING
C 45 MIN. 4

- Peel a large potato.
- Mark out different facial features and shoulders.
- With a small paring knife, carve the potato into a bust of a boy or girl. A bust is a sculpture showing the head, shoulders, and upper chest of a person.

823. VERSE RECORDING
$ 45 MIN. 1

- Make a list of your family's favorite Bible verses.
- Practice reading the verses out loud.
- Put a blank cassette tape in a tape recorder.
- Tape yourself reading the verses and stating their references.
- Try playing soft music in the background while you are taping.
- Play the verse cassette at home, in the car, or when exercising —anytime and anywhere!
- This makes a thoughtful and helpful gift.

824. RIBBON AND FELT BOOKMARK
$ 45 MIN. 2

- Choose ribbon and felt colors that coordinate.
- Cut a piece of felt 1¼" x 8".
- Cut a piece of ¾"-wide ribbon 7½" long.
- Cut 3 pieces of very thin ribbon 6" long.
- Pin the thin ribbon to one end of the felt.
- Pin the wide ribbon on top of the length of felt.
- Hand- or machine-stitch around the edges of the ¾" ribbon.
- Put a small knot in the end of each thin ribbon.

825. EGG VERSE
C 45 MIN. 2

Making a project like this will help you memorize God's Word.

- Poke small holes in the ends of 4 eggs and blow out the

insides of the eggs.
- Rinse the eggs with water and let dry.
- Write parts of Proverbs 16:32 on each egg with markers. Handle the eggs gently.
- Egg 1: "He who is slow to anger" Egg 2: "is better than the mighty." Egg 3: "And he who rules his spirit" Egg 4: "than he who captures a city. Proverbs 16:32."
- Use different colors of markers to highlight certain words. For example, red for the word "anger" and purple for the word "mighty."
- Decorate the eggs with designs colored in with markers.

826. STRING OF GARLIC
$$ 45 MIN. 2

After the children of Israel walked out of Egypt,
they began grumbling about not having food
like meat and garlic that they had while in slavery.
They were rejecting the Lord's constant care of them
as He led them to true freedom.
Make this project so you can be reminded
every time you look at it not to complain.

- Tie clusters of garlic onto 3 lengths of raffia.
- Tie the 3 strands together at the top.
- Twist the strands together and tie at the bottom.
- Make a bow from raffia and tie to the top.
- Hang the garlic in the kitchen.

827. SOAP INSTRUMENT
C 1 HOUR 4

- With a pencil, draw an outline of a musical instrument on a large piece of soap.
- Carve out the instrument with a table knife.
- Tear old sheet music into small pieces and glue to the soap, covering the whole instrument.
- Seal with a coat of glue or clear nail polish.

828. FAT ON THE BONES
C 1 HOUR 1

The Bible is full of amusing phrases.
Here's a fun project using one of them!

- Lay a 9" x 12" sheet of black paper horizontally.
- On the left half of the paper arrange cotton swabs into a skeleton. The swabs can be cut into different lengths.
- Glue down the swabs.
- Write, "Good news puts fat on the bones! Proverbs 15:30" in block or bubble letters on a sheet of classified newspaper.
- Cut out the letters and arrange on the right side of the black paper.
- Glue down the words.
- Trace the letters with a black marker.

829. CROSS BUTTONS
$$ 1 HOUR 3

- Pick a blouse or shirt that the buttons can be changed on.
- Make a square of paper small enough to fit through the button holes. This will be the button pattern.
- Roll out a small piece of Fimo clay (available from many craft suppliers). Choose a color that goes with the shirt.
- Place the paper pattern on the Fimo and trace around it with a toothpick.
- Trace as many buttons as needed.
- Cut out the buttons.
- Smooth the edges of the buttons.
- Roll out another color of Fimo.
- Cut out small crosses and place one on top of each button.
- Poke 2 small holes side by side in each button with a toothpick.
- Make sure the holes are big enough for a needle to pass through.
- Bake according to package instructions.
- Sew the buttons on your shirt.

830. 3-D SCENE
$ 1 HOUR 1

- Tear jagged rocks from brown, tan, and black construction paper.
- Glue the rocks to the lower left corner of a 22" x 28" piece of blue poster board. Overlap the rocks to form a cliff. Save one rock for later.
- Draw and color a lighthouse on a 5" x 11" piece of white construction paper.
- Cut out the lighthouse and glue it on top of the rocks.
- Write in large block letters on the right side: Jesus said, "I am the light of the world."
- Lay several lines of glue from the light at the top of the lighthouse like rays of sun.
- Lay yellow yarn in each line of glue.
- Trace one letter at a time with a line of glue and lay a piece of yellow or orange yarn in the glue to form yarn letters.
- Glue the last rock overlapping the bottom of the lighthouse.

831. HEART SUNCATCHER
C 1 HOUR 4

- Cut two 9" x 12" sheets of wax paper.
- Lay one sheet of wax paper on a layer of newspaper.
- Sharpen red, pink, and white crayons over the wax paper with a pencil sharpener.
- Lay the second sheet of wax paper on top of the shavings.
- Top the wax paper with a layer of newspaper.
- Iron the newspaper.
- Carefully lift off the newspaper to check the crayon shavings. If the shavings are not melted, replace the newspaper and iron again.
- Let cool.
- Draw a large heart on the wax paper design.
- Cut out the heart.
- Place the crayon heart on a 12" x 18" sheet of red construction paper and trace.
- Draw another heart, ½" inside the traced heart.
- Poke a hole in the center and cut out the smaller heart. This

will create a heart frame.
- Place a strip of glue around the inside edge of the heart frame.
- Lay the melted crayon heart face down on the glue.
- Cut up paper doilies and glue to the edge of the back so that when the heart is turned over the doily frames the heart.
- Hang in a window or give as a Valentine.

832. TWIG WEAVING
$ 1 HOUR 2

- Wrap yarn around a twig that is in the shape of a Y. Use one or more colors.
- Secure the yarn by gluing the ends.
- Tie 3 or more short pieces of yarn from one side of the Y to the other.
- Cut a long piece of yarn and tie one end to one center piece of yarn.
- Weave the yarn under/over, over/under, through the center yarn until covered.
- Hang the weaving.

833. SOAP SCULPTURE
C 1 HOUR 5

- Carefully carve a large bar of soap into a shape such as a fish, book, cross, flower, or car.
- For tools, use a table knife, nail, paring knife, and nail file.

834. FLOWER CARDS
C 1 HOUR 2

- Fold a 9" x 12" sheet of white paper in half.
- Place the folded sheet on a cutting board, several newspapers, or magazines.
- Place a brightly colored flower on the paper.
- Cover it with plastic wrap.
- Tap the plastic-covered flower with a hammer.

- Remove the plastic wrap and any flower residue.
- Repeat with more flowers and leaves until the design is complete.
- Write a message inside.
- Give to a friend.

835. SAND CANDLE
$ 1 HOUR 5

Psalm 119:105 states that the Word is a lamp to light our way. Here's a fun project to remind you of this promise.

- Put clean, damp sand in a box or bucket.
- Hollow out some sand with your hand or a tool like a plastic bath toy. The hollow can be oval, round, or shaped like a star.
- Arrange small seashells around the sides of the hollowed-out area.
- Tie a small rock to the end of a length of candle wicking.
- Place the rock inside the hollow and measure the wick to the top. Tie to a stick and lay across the top of the sand. The wick should be straight between the weight and the stick, and in the center of the hollow or mold.
- Melt wax in a tin can in an electric skillet filled with water. Do not get the wax too hot; its flash point is about 400°. If the wax starts to burn, turn off the heat and cover with a lid or douse with baking soda.
- For color, add old crayons to the melting wax.
- Pour the melted wax into the sand hollow.
- Let wax cool and set.
- Take the candle out of the box or bucket and wipe off excess sand.
- Place candle outside to light the path to the front door or on a patio.

836. TISSUE-COVERED CAN
$ 1 HOUR 1

- Cut several squares, 1" x 1", of tissue paper.
- Cover a clean, label-free tin can with tissue by placing the

eraser end of a pencil in the center of a square and twisting around the pencil.
- Cover a small section of the can with glue.
- Touch the tissue-covered pencil onto the glue and lift the pencil out.
- Tissue can be one color or different colors laid in a pattern on the can.
- Use the can to hold pencils, pennies, or treasures.

837. TEXTURED ROOM PICTURE
C 1 HOUR 1

- Design a scene of a living room, a family room, or the Upper Room from Luke 22, using scraps of fabric, foil, plastic wrap, burlap, and wallpaper.
- Arrange the furniture, wallpaper, etc., on a 9" x 12" sheet of lightweight cardboard.
- Glue down the objects.

838. GINGERBREAD COOKIE FRAMES
$ 1 HOUR 4

- Make a batch of gingerbread dough.
- Use cookie cutters to cut out different shapes.
- Trace a small picture, like a school photo, on white paper.
- Cut out the pattern about ¼" inside the traced line.
- Place the pattern on each cookie and trace.
- Cut out.
- Bake the cookies.
- Decorate the cookies with tempera and puff paint.
- Seal with a clear sealer.
- Glue the picture to the back of the cookie.
- Glue a magnetic strip to the back of the cookie.
- Give to a relative or friend as a present.

839. FISH PLAQUE
$ 1 HOUR 4

- Draw a simple outline of a fish on a thick, 6" x 8" sheet of balsa wood.
- Leave about a 1" border around the fish.
- To make a raised design, carefully pound around the outside of the fish with a hammer. Or, pound the head of a screw into the wood to indent it around the fish.
- Indent the entire background.
- With a nail, scratch out scales, an eye, and fins.
- Brush on a coat of wood stain, making sure to stain the sides of the plaque.
- Wipe off the stain with a soft rag.

840. GIFT BAG FLOWER ARRANGEMENT
$ 1 HOUR 4

- Fill any type of gift bag with Sahara Dry Flo Brick.
- Cover the top of the brick by gluing on moss.
- Stick silk flowers, eucalyptus stems, baby's breath, dried flowers, and holiday picks into the foam.
- Secure several bunches of baby's breath to a floral pick with floral tape, then insert into the Styrofoam.
- Give as a gift.

841. CLAY POT
$$ 1 HOUR 3

- Roll out some non-baking clay with a rolling pin.
- Cut out a shape for the bottom of the pot. The pot could be circular, square, or star-shaped.
- Measure around the shape with a piece of string.
- Roll out 4 snakes of clay a little longer than the string.
- Place a little water around the edge of the bottom shape.
- Lay a clay roll around the edge of the shape, pushing gently so the roll sticks.
- Place a little water on the first roll and place the next roll of clay on top.

• Position all 4 rolls.
• Smooth out the bottom edge and the rolls into even sides.
• Let dry according to package instructions.
• Paint with acrylic paint.

842. DOORSTOP
$ 1 HOUR 5

• Take a picture of a pet or use a magazine picture of a favorite
  animal.
• Enlarge the picture to 8" x 10".
• Cut out the pet so there is no background.
• Glue the cutout to a piece of plywood.
• Cut out the picture with a jigsaw.
• Sand the edges of the plywood and cover the picture and
  edges with several coats of varnish. Let each coat dry.
• Coat with 2–3 coats of varnish. After each coat has dried,
  lightly sand and dust off the doorstop.
• Glue a brick to the back.

843. CORN HUSK RUTH DOLL
$ 1 HOUR 3

• Soak dried corn husks in warm water for about 15 minutes, or
  until soft.
• Pat off the excess water with a towel.
• Roll several husks into a ball for the head.
• Cover the ball with 2 wide husks. Fold the edges in around
  the head.
• Wrap thin florist's wire around the husks under the head.
• Roll several husks into an oval for the body.
• Wrap a husk around a pipe cleaner for the arms and secure
  with wire.
• Place the arms and body under the husk below the head.
• Tie at the waist with wire.
• Trim the bottom evenly.
• Cut a piece of fabric long enough and wide enough to cover
  the doll.
• Fold the fabric in half and cut a small hole for the head.

- Place the fabric over the head and tie with a long, thin piece of fabric for the sash.
- Cut a small piece of fabric for a head covering.
- Make a small bunch of grasses and weeds and tie with a strip of fabric.
- Bend the arms to hold the bunch of grass.
- Draw facial features with a marker.

844. PENCIL TOPPER
$ 1 HOUR 3

- Decide on the type of pencil topper. For example, a big fish for Jonah, a lion head for Daniel, or a heart for the love of Jesus.
- Draw a simple outline on a 2" x 2" piece of scrap paper.
- Cut out the shape and trace it onto a piece of felt.
- Cut out the felt shape and trace it onto another piece of felt. Cut out the second shape.
- Put a strip of glue down the center front of one felt shape.
- Lay the pencil in the glue so the eraser is about 1" above the shape.
- Cover the back side of the second felt shape with glue and lay it on top of the pencil, matching the edges to the first shape.
- Press the shapes together.
- Let dry.
- Thread a needle with 3 strands of embroidery thread.
- Blanket-stitch around the edge of the shape.
- Add any details, like eyes, by gluing on small pieces of felt.

845. DRIED FLOWER WREATH
C 1 HOUR 1

- Gather flowers and leaves from your yard, neighborhood field, and the woods.
- Put the flowers between a layer of paper towels.
- Put the flowers and paper towels between the pages of a heavy book. Stack other books on top.
- Press for about a week.

- Cut a large circle from a thin piece of cardboard, then cut out a smaller circle from the middle to make a wreath.
- Glue the dried pressed flowers and leaves to the cardboard. Overlap the petals so no cardboard is showing.
- Hang the wreath or use as a centerpiece with a candle in the middle for a special glow at dinner time.

846. SHOE BOX AQUARIUM
C 1 HOUR 1

This is a fun project to do after a trip to an aquarium.

- Draw a rectangle ½" inside the edge of a shoe box lid.
- Cut out the rectangle to make a window in the lid.
- Decorate the inside of the box with blue paint or cover with construction paper.
- Make fish, seaweed, starfish, and other sea creatures from construction paper.
- Stand the box on its side.
- Glue a few rocks to the inside of the box.
- Spread glue on the side of the box that will be the bottom of your aquarium scene.
- Sprinkle sand, salt, and/or brown sugar in the glue.
- Add the paper animals. Glue a starfish to a rock.
- Hang the fish from the top of the box with clear thread and glue some to the back wall.
- Add the seaweed.
- To make the figures stand up, glue a small strip of paper in the shape of a triangle to the back of the figure.
- Glue a piece of blue plastic wrap to the inside of the lid and place on the box.

847. PERSONALIZED PILLOWCASE
$ 1 HOUR 3

All kinds of fun pictures can be drawn on a pillowcase.
A favorite Bible verse, story book characters, or animals.

- Cut a piece of cardboard to slip inside a plain, clean pillow-

case. If it is new, wash it before decorating.
- With a pencil, draw designs on one or both sides of a white pillowcase. If a picture is dark enough, it can be slipped inside the case and traced.
- Fill in the designs with permanent markers or fabric paint.
- Follow the instructions on the fabric paint bottle.
- Outline the designs to make them stand out.

848. SCRIPTURE VERSE FLOWER POT
$ 1 HOUR 1

- Clean a terra-cotta flower pot.
- Paint the flower pot with 2 to 3 coats of acrylic paint as a base color.
- Plan where the Bible verse will go.
- Decorate the pot with designs.
- Write the verse with a marker, paintbrush, or writing tip bottle. Use Proverbs 3:18 (NASB), "[Wisdom] is a tree of life to those who take hold of her." Or, Matthew 7:17 (NIV), "Every good tree bears good fruit."
- Plant a pretty flower in the flower pot.

849. DOMINO BULLETIN BOARD
$$ 1 HOUR 4

- Cut a piece of plywood to fit the space where the bulletin board will be hung.
- Sand the edges of the board.
- Glue squares of cork to the front of the board.
- Attach 2 picture hangers on the back, 1"–2" from the top and 3" from the sides.
- Glue-gun or tacky-glue the dominoes, stacking and layering them all around the edge.
- Hang on a wall.

850. JELLY BEAN BULLETIN BOARD
$$ 1 HOUR 4

- Cut a piece of plywood to fit the space where the bulletin

board will be hung.
- Sand the edges of the board.
- Glue squares of cork to the front of the board.
- Attach 2 picture hangers on the back, 1"–2" from the top and 3" from the sides.
- Glue-gun or tacky-glue jelly beans, stacking and layering them all around the edge.
- Coat with several coats of varnish or polyurethane.
- Hang on a wall.

851. WIND CHIMES
$ 1 HOUR 5

In Luke 8:24, even the wind obeyed Jesus.

- Place a tin can upside down and make a hole in the center of the bottom with a hammer and nail.
- Make 2 more holes, spaced evenly, one on each side of the center hole.
- Cover the can with construction paper.
- With the can still upside down, write the message of James 1:6 around the rim of the can: "Ask in faith without doubting, for he who doubts is like the surf of the sea driven and tossed by the wind."
- Decorate with pictures of the ocean cut from catalogs or magazines.
- Using a drill, make holes in the top of 9–12 shells.
- Tie a knot in the middle of three 12" strings.
- String the first shell by pulling the top of the string through the hole in the shell.
- String the other shells from the bottom, tying a knot after each shell.
- The shells should touch each other.
- String 3 or 4 shells on each string.
- Put a string through each hole of the can.
- Pull the strings up evenly so the top shell on each string is partially inside the can. Knot the string.
- Tie the 3 ends together.
- Hang the chimes.

852. NAME LICENSE PLATE
$ 1 HOUR 1

- Cut a 6" x 12" sheet of heavy cardboard.
- At the top, print the state you live in.
- Cover the letters with a strip of glue.
- Lay one type of seed, rice, or popcorn in the glue. If there is room glue a double line of seed for each letter.
- Print your name in large block letters under the state.
- Cover the letters with a layer of glue.
- Lay another type of seed in the glue.
- Cover the remaining background with glue and different types of seeds.

853. 3-D WORD LAPEL PIN
$ 1 HOUR 3

- Think of words that describe God. For example, love, unchanging, peace, forgiveness, joy, truth, way, life, etc.
- Write a word on a lightweight piece of cardboard. The letters should connect.
- Cut out the word in one piece. Cut out any space between the letters with an X-Acto knife.
- Cover the word with 3 layers of small newspaper scraps dipped in a solution of glue mixed with a little water.
- Cover the word with one layer of plain newsprint paper.
- Let dry.
- Decorate the word with 2 coats of acrylic paint.
- Decorate each letter with a different pattern such as dots, X's, or hearts. Or, make the word one color and outline it with a contrasting color of acrylic paint.
- Glue a pin clasp or small safety pin to the back.

854. MAY DAY BASKET
$ 1½ HOURS 3

- Fold 14 sheets of tissue paper into long thin strips by folding the top to the bottom. Then fold the bottom half way up and crease. Fold the top half way down and crease. Repeat the

last step. For the last fold, fold the top down to the bottom.
- The strips will be about 1" wide and 20" long.
- Staple together the ends of one tissue strip to form a circle.
- Insert one end of another strip into the bottom and open edge of the circle and staple.
- Insert the other end into the opposite side of the circle and staple.
- Continue inserting and stapling strips until they are all the way around the circle. Make sure the strips are stapled close together.
- Use one strip to make a handle by stapling each end to opposite sides of the circle.
- Weave the remaining strips through the basket going under and over.
- Staple the ends.
- The weaving strips could be a different color of tissue.
- Fill the basket with flowers and verses from Project #257.

855. SAND CARVING
$$ 1 HOUR 5

- Mix together 3 cups sand, 1½ cups cornstarch, 1½ tablespoons powdered alum, and 1⅛ cups water in an old pan.
- Cook over low heat; stir constantly.
- Remove from heat when it has thickened.
- Let cool.
- Mold into a rectangular block.
- Let dry for several days, turning the block several times.
- Carve the sand block with a table knife. Work outside or on a newspaper-covered area.
- Carve a totem pole, the Tower of Babel, or an animal. Use your imagination!

856. COIN-CASTED PLAQUE
$$ 1 HOUR 4

- Cover 6–8 coins on both sides with a thin coat of Vaseline.
- Place the coins face side down around the inside of a pie tin.
- In a large tin can mix together some water and plaster of

paris. The mixture should be thin enough to pour, but not runny.

- Spoon some plaster of paris carefully over each coin and spread it so the coins are covered.
- Fill the pie tin about 2" deep with plaster of paris.
- Place a large paper clip in the plaster near the edge of the pie tin. This will be the hanger.
- Let the plaster dry overnight.
- Carefully remove the plaster plaque from the pie tin.
- In the center of the plaque write with a pencil, "Do not store up for yourselves treasures upon earth. . .but store up for yourselves treasures in heaven" Matthew 6:19–20 NIV.
- With a nail, scratch the letters deeply into the plaster.
- Paint the plaque with tempera paint, being careful not to push the paint into the etched letters.
- Lift the coins out of the plaster with a metal fingernail file.
- Or leave the coins in the plaque.
- Hang the plaque.

857. ICE SCULPTURE
C 1 HOUR 5

This is a fun project to try on a hot day!

- Fill a clean milk carton with water and freeze it. For colored water, add food coloring.
- Tear off the carton.
- Place the ice block on a towel to keep it from slipping.
- Carve the block into a car, statue, ball, etc., with a chisel and hammer.

858. TIN CAN LANTERNS
$ 1 HOUR 4

In John 8:12, Jesus said, "I am the light of the world."

- Cut a piece of white paper to fit around a tin can.
- Draw a cross and light ray designs on the paper.
- Tape the paper to the can.

• Tape the can to a table or sidewalk surface.
• Poke holes along the lines of the design, through the can, with a hammer and nail. Be careful to space each hole the same distance apart. Remove the paper design.
• Place a votive candle in the can.
• Have an adult light the candle with a long match.

859. SUN MIRROR
$$ 1 HOUR 5

• Purchase clay and a small flat mirror.
• Roll out the clay into an 8" x 8" square about 1" thick.
• Draw a sun and rays on an 8" x 8" square of scrap paper.
• Cut out the sun pattern.
• Press the sun pattern onto the clay and cut it out.
• Place the mirror on the clay and trace around it with a pencil.
• Carve out the mirror area making it a little bigger than the actual mirror.
• Poke a large paperclip into the top edge.
• Bake according to the clay instructions.
• After the sun has cooled, paint it with several coats of acrylic paint.
• Glue the mirror in the center.
• Paint the words from Psalm 65:8 NASB: "Thou dost make the dawn and the sunset shout for joy," on the rays of the sun.

860. CHARACTERISTIC PICTURE FRAME
C 1 HOUR 2

• Cut 2 pieces of 6" x 9" lightweight cardboard.
• In one piece, cut a hole a little bit smaller than the picture of the person or pet you want to frame. The hole does not have to be a rectangle; it could be a heart, oval, or other interesting shape.
• Spread glue over a small area of the frame.
• Lay small pieces of torn tissue paper in the glue, smoothing the piece down.
• Cover the entire front of the frame overlapping the outside edge and the edge of the hole.

- Let dry.
- Cover tissue with a final coat of water-thinned glue.
- Tape the picture in place.
- Tape the ends of a piece of ribbon to the back of the front cardboard frame, 1" in from each side.
- Tape a second piece of cardboard to the back.
- Cut out words from old catalogs or magazines that describe the person or pet framed. For example, Loving, Kind, Fun, and Playful.
- Glue the words to the front of the frame.
- Coat with thinned glue.
- Hang the picture.

861. GOURD BOWL
$ 1 HOUR 4

- Cut off the top of a gourd.
- Cut off a small part of the bottom so the gourd will sit straight and not wobble.
- Scoop out the inside.
- Place on a newspaper in a warm spot to dry. This could take several weeks.
- Scratch a design on the outside of the gourd with a nail.
- Place the bowl on newspaper.
- Wipe wood stain over the outside of the bowl with a rag.
- Wipe off the stain with a rag.
- The stain will darken the etched design.
- Use as a serving bowl or to hold your treasures.

862. BEAR SACHET
$ 1 HOUR 3

This sachet makes a great present.

- Fold a scrap of fabric in half with the right sides together.
- Draw a simple outline of a teddy bear.
- Sew small buttons on the right side of one of the pieces for eyes and vest buttons.
- Pin right sides together.

- Sew around the bear ¼"–½" in from the edge. Leave a 2" opening.
- Clip all the way around, being careful not to cut the stitching.
- Turn the bear so the right side is showing.
- Fill with potpourri.
- Sew the opening shut.
- Tie a ribbon around the neck.
- Place in a dresser drawer.

863. THE MORNING STAR
$ 1 HOUR 3

- Draw a 5-point star on a 12" x 12" square of medium-weight cardboard.
- Cut out the star.
- Poke 6 holes in the star using a pair of pointed scissors. One in the center and on each point.
- Cover one side of the cardboard with a thick coat of white acrylic paint.
- Sprinkle cornmeal onto the wet paint.
- Let dry.
- Cut 6 different lengths of 1"-wide ribbon.
- On one ribbon write "The Bright," and write "Morning Star" on another ribbon.
- Write "Revelation 22:16" on a third ribbon.
- Leave 1" at the bottom and top of each ribbon.
- On a sheet of 9" x 12" lightweight cardboard, draw 6 different sizes of stars.
- Cut out the stars.
- Poke a hole through one point of each star.
- Paint with white acrylic paint.
- Sprinkle cornmeal onto the wet paint.
- Let dry.
- Repeat on the back of each star.
- Decide how you want the stars to be positioned. For example, put the largest star in the middle.
- Thread the top end of each ribbon through the front of a hole in the large star and tape or glue on the back.
- Thread all 6 stars.
- Hang by taping or thumbtacking the large star to the ceiling.

864. ANIMAL WIND BLOCKER
$ 1 HOUR 5

- Draw an animal, like a rabbit, about 8" tall and 6" wide.
- Cut a piece of fabric 16" x 76".
- Put the ends of the fabric together so the right sides of the fabric are on the inside.
- Pin the fabric together.
- Place the pattern ½" from the left end of the fabric and trace around the top of the animal only.
- Continue moving the pattern down the strip and tracing it onto the fabric, leaving ½" at the opposite end.
- Cut around the top of each animal.
- Open the fabric and sew on buttons for eyes on the front strip.
- Stitch all the way around the strip, about ½" from the edge, leaving an opening at the bottom.
- Clip around the edge being careful not to clip through the stitching. This will make it easier to turn.
- Turn the wind blocker right side out.
- Stuff with batting or old panty hose.
- Sew the opening closed.
- Place at the bottom of a door.

865. TIN-PUNCHED MOBILE
$ 1 HOUR 4

- Cut a round circle of white paper to fit inside a canning jar lid.
- Draw a heart on the paper.
- Draw a cross in the center of the heart.
- Mark dots on the drawing about ¼" apart.
- Tape the paper to the lid.
- Place the lid on an old magazine and pound a small nail through each dot on the heart and cross design. Make sure the nail goes through the lid.
- With a larger nail, poke a hole through the top of the lid and make 3 holes about 1" apart along the bottom of the lid.
- Cut a 6" length of twine and thread it through the top hole for the hanger. Knot.
- Cut two 10" lengths of twine and one 14" length.

- Thread the middle hole with the 14" length and knot the end near the lid.
- Thread the other lengths and knot.
- Thread beads and bells in a pattern on each piece of twine, and knot in place.
- Knot the ends of each length of twine.
- Hang the mobile.

866. NOAH'S ARK BRACELET
$ 1 HOUR 4

- Roll out different colors of Fimo clay.
- Cut out tiny animals.
- Add details like eyes and stripes with Fimo.
- With a large needle, poke 2 holes through the body of the animal.
- Bake according to package instructions.
- Cut a length of wide, colored elastic to fit around your wrist. Make sure to allow a little extra for overlapping.
- Sew the animal buttons on the elastic.
- Sew the ends of the elastic together.

867. EAGLE'S NEST
$ 1 HOUR 3

There is security and safety in the Lord.
Under His wings we are secure, says Psalm 91:4.

- Cut off the top two-thirds of an oatmeal box.
- Spread glue on a section of the outside.
- Lay nest-building materials, such as small sticks, feathers, dryer lint, and Hiawatha green moss, in the glue.
- Cover the outside of the carton.
- Fill the carton with the same materials.
- Cut out a small picture of yourself.
- Mount the picture on heavy paper or lightweight cardboard and cut out.
- Place the picture in the nest.

- Draw and color an eagle a little bigger than your picture.
- Cut out the eagle and mount it on heavy paper or lightweight cardboard.
- Glue small feathers to the wings.
- Place the eagle over your picture in the nest.
- Write a verse on a small piece of paper and set it in the nest. For example, Psalm 17:8, Psalm 36:7, Psalm 57:1, Psalm 63:7, Psalm 91:4, or Deuteronomy 32:10, 11.

868. BUTTON BULLETIN BOARD
$$ 1 HOUR 4

- Cut a piece of plywood to fit the space where the bulletin board will be hung.
- Sand the edges of the board.
- Glue squares of cork to the front of the board.
- Attach 2 picture hangers on the back, 1"–2" from the top and 3" from the sides.
- Glue-gun or tacky-glue buttons, stacking and layering them all around the edge.
- Coat with several coats of varnish or polyurethane.
- Hang on a wall.

869. FALL PUMPKIN TRANSFER PICTURE
$$ 2 HOURS 4

- Find a magazine picture of a fall scene or of autumn leaves.
- Tape the picture face up on a sheet of wax paper.
- Paint the fall picture with 7 or 8 coats of clear polymer. Polymer is a painting medium for acrylic paint. Alternate the direction of each coat, allowing each layer to dry about 20 minutes.
- After all the coats have been applied, allow an hour to dry.
- Soak the print in warm, soapy water until the paper can be peeled off the back of the polymer. Some of the paper might have to be rubbed off.
- Do not tear or stretch the polymer layers.
- Let dry.
- Coat a pumpkin with a layer of polymer.

- Lay the print on the pumpkin smoothing it out as much as possible.
- Coat the pumpkin with another layer of polymer.

870. JOYFUL NOISE MOBILE
$ 2 HOURS 5

- Make a batch of salt dough (as described in Project #500).
- On a 9" x 12" piece of scrap paper, draw a trumpet.
- Cut out the trumpet.
- Roll out the dough to ½" thick.
- Lay the pattern on the dough and trace around it with a pencil.
- Take off the pattern and cut out the trumpet with a table knife.
- With a straw, poke 2 holes through each end of the trumpet. These will be holes for the hanger.
- Poke 6 holes along the body of the trumpet to hang notes from.
- Transfer the trumpet to a cookie sheet.
- Make 7 musical notes from the leftover dough. Make the body of each note about the size of a 50-cent piece.
- Use a little water to attach the stems of the notes.
- Poke a hole through the stem of each note.
- Place the notes on the cookie sheet.
- Check all the holes to make sure they are poked all the way through and large enough for yarn to be threaded through.
- Bake at 350° for 20 minutes. (Baking time may vary.)
- Let cool.
- Paint the trumpet with several coats of gold acrylic paint.
- Paint the notes with black paint.
- With white acrylic paint, paint one word of the phrase, "Make a joyful noise unto the Lord" on the body of each black note.
- Cut a 14" length of yarn, and thread each end through the top 2 holes of the trumpet. Knot on the back.
- Cut 6 different lengths of yarn for the notes.
- Thread one end of each length through the stem of a note and knot on the back.
- Thread the ends of the note yarn through the holes in the

bottom of the trumpet and knot on the back.
• Hang the mobile.

871. LEAPING LAME MAN
$ 2 HOURS 4

In Luke 5:17–26, we read about the lame man Jesus healed. Can you imagine his joy in being able to walk?

• On a piece of white paper, draw a body shape with the arms up and legs open. Make a V shape in the middle at the neck.
• Cut out the paper pattern and trace it onto 2 pieces of felt.
• Cut out the bodies.
• On a piece of white paper, draw a hand, with the fingers together, and a foot. Cut out.
• Trace the hand on 4 small pieces of light pink felt and cut out.
• Trace the foot on 4 small pieces of brown or black felt and cut out.
• Put the hands and feet together and sew around the edge leaving a small opening.
• Turn the hands and feet right side out.
• Stuff the hands and feet.
• Sew the openings closed.
• Lay one felt body down.
• Place the hands and feet on top of the felt so they face into the body.
• Place second body on top and pin together.
• Sew around the body, leaving a small opening. Be careful not to catch the toes of the feet and the fingers of the hands in the stitching.
• Turn body right side out.
• Stuff the body.
• Sew the opening closed.
• For the head, cut out 2 circles of pink felt. Make the circles big enough to fit in the V of the body.
• Sew 2 small buttons touching each other to the pink circle, about ½" from the top.
• Cut out a small circle of pink felt for the nose.
• Glue the nose right under the button eyes.

- Place second felt circle on top and pin the 2 circles together.
- Sew around the edge, leaving a small opening.
- Turn the head right side out and stuff.
- Sew the opening closed.
- Sew a piece of bound-edged lace to the bottom of the face then fold the lace and sew another layer of lace above the first layer. Sew several layers up to just below the nose to create a beard.
- Sew the head to the body.

872. 3-D PALM TREE
$ 2 HOURS 3

- Make several palm tree trunks by painting paper towel and toilet paper rolls with different shades of brown tempera paint. To make a lighter brown, mix a little white into the brown paint.
- Let dry.
- Draw bark lines on the rolls with a marker.
- Draw different sizes of palm branches on green paper.
- Cut out and glue to the top of the painted rolls. Glue some on the outside and the inside top.
- Glue on enough branches to make the tree look full.
- Mix up a batch of salt dough (as described in Project #500).
- On a large piece of heavy cardboard, form the salt dough into a landscape.
- Cover the whole cardboard with the salt dough.
- Arrange the palm trees in small groups at opposite corners of the cardboard.
- Place some glue around the bottom of each palm tree and press it into the salt dough.
- Build up the dough around the bottom of each tree for stability.
- With a toothpick or pencil, scratch some of the phrases from Psalm 92:12–15 into the dough. Make sure to use the phrase, "The righteous man shall flourish like the palm tree."
- Let the dough dry.
- Paint the dough with tempera paint.

873. BIRTHDAY FLOAT
$ 2 HOURS 2

• Decorate a large, flat box with items that would describe the birthday person. For example, a figurine depicting a sport he or she plays or enjoys, pictures of animals glued to a Popsicle stick and stood up by poking a hole in the box, a Matchbox car, etc.
• Decorate around the bottom of the box by twisting squares of tissue paper around the eraser end of a pencil and gluing to the box.
• Display at the birthday party.

874. RECYCLED BIRD FEEDER
$ 2 HOURS 4

• Draw a long oval shape on a small, clean dish soap bottle.
• Cut out the oval.
• Cut a 14" length of string.
• Double the string and knot the ends together.
• Put the string through the front of the bottle and up through the pour spout.
• Cover the bottle with several layers of newspaper strips dipped in a mixture of wallpaper paste and water. Let each layer dry before applying the next layer.
• Make sure to overlap the edge of the oval and around the string at the top.
• Cover with a layer of newsprint.
• Let dry.
• Poke a hole through the front of the bottle under the oval opening.
• Paint the feeder with several coats of acrylic paint. Let it dry between coats.
• Paint small birds on the feeder.
• Seal with several coats of spray sealer or varnish.
• Place a short stick in the hole for a perch.
• Hang outside and fill with a small amount of birdseed.

875. CARDBOARD WEAVING
C 2 HOURS 2

- Cut a 8" x 12" piece of heavy cardboard.
- Cut notches every ½" along the top and bottom.
- Make a knot in the end of the yarn and slip the yarn through the first notch at the bottom left corner.
- Thread the yarn to the top left notch, then the second notch at the top.
- Next, go to the second notch at the bottom then the third notch.
- Continue to the top third and fourth notch.
- Continue threading the yarn through each notch.
- Cut the yarn and knot the end.
- Tape the knots down on the back.
- Weave with different types of yarn, twine, ribbons, and raffia. Weaving under/over, over/under, alternating each row.
- After each row is woven, push the row close to the previous row.
- Carefully lift the weaving off the cardboard.
- Add more weaving material to each end if necessary.
- Hang from a dowel or yarn hanger.

876. TIE-DYED T-SHIRT
$$ 2 HOURS 5

Sewing the fabric will result in a more controlled design.

- Purchase a white T-shirt.
- Draw designs, like letters, flowers, or different shapes, on the shirt with a pencil.
- Thread a needle and knot one end.
- Sew a row of stitching around each design. Leave the end loose.
- Sew a second row of stitching around each design. Leave the end loose.
- Gather the fabric by pulling the loose threads and knot.
- To dye the shirt, follow the directions on the bottle of fabric dye. If using several colors of dye, start with the lightest color.

- Make sure the container used to dip the shirt in is large enough. If it is too small the shirt will not dye evenly.
- Remove the stitching when the shirt is dry.

877. SALT RELIEF MAP/PICTURE
$ 2 HOURS 4

- Mix together 3 cups flour and $\frac{1}{2}$ cup salt. Mix in $\frac{1}{2}$–$\frac{3}{4}$ cup of water to make a dough. It should not be sticky.
- Draw the outline of Palestine (Israel) on a 9" x 12" piece of heavy cardboard. Refer to a globe or to a map in the back of a Bible.
- Press out the salt dough on the cardboard to the borders of the map. Leave room on the left for the Mediterranean Sea. Do not cover this area with dough.
- Build up the dough in the mountainous areas.
- Carve out the Dead Sea and the Sea of Galilee.
- Let dry.
- Paint the seas and the Jordan River blue, the mountains brown, and Palestine tan.
- With a black marker, label important cities, areas, rivers, seas, and mountains.

878. LION BANNER
$ 2 HOURS 4

- Cut a 14" x 14" square of blue felt.
- Draw a face of a lion with a mane on a 12" x 12" piece of white paper. This will be the pattern.
- Cut the mane off the pattern.
- Place the mane pattern on a piece of dark brown felt and trace around it.
- Place the lion face on a piece of light brown felt and trace around it.
- Cut out the face and the mane.
- Arrange the mane and face on the blue square at least 2" from the top. Pin down.
- Sew around the mane and face with even stitches.

- Cut other details from black felt—eyes, nose, and whiskers.
- Pin to the lion appliqué.
- Sew around the details.
- Lay banner face down and fold down the top edge about 1" and pin.
- Sew along the edge of the folded-down top to form a tube.
- Slide a dowel through the tube.
- Tie each end of a cord or string to each end of the dowel for a hanger.

879. MINIATURE SPORTS FIGURINES
$ 2 HOURS 4

*Besides looking great on your shelf,
these action figures make nice gifts and memorable trophies.*

- Twist a white pipe cleaner into a head and arm figure.
- Bend another pipe cleaner in half, placing the middle around the neck, then twisting to form the body and legs.
- Bend the figures into different stances, like throwing a ball.
- Roll out self-hardening clay to 1" thick.
- Cut into small squares for the base of the figure. Make the base large enough to give balance to the figure.
- Push the legs into the clay base.
- Let the clay harden.
- Mix plaster of paris in a can with water.
- Dip the figure into the plaster so it is covered. Do not dip the base into the plaster.
- Shake off excess plaster and stand the figure to dry. Do this quickly; the plaster dries fast.
- Dip the figurine again.
- Let dry.
- Paint with acrylic paints.
- Seal with a clear sealer.
- Add small details, like a baseball or football formed from clay and painted.
- Glue to the base or the figure.

880. COMMANDMENT PLAQUE
$ 2 HOURS 5

- Check a narrow box lid for holes. Tape any holes on the outside of the lid.
- Cut a strip of thin cardboard, fold it in half, and tape it to the inside of the lid to form a pointed top. Make sure there are no gaps between the cardboard strip and the box lid.
- Coat the inside of the lid with Vaseline.
- Mix one cup plaster of paris and ⅔ cup water in a disposable bowl. Do not let any plaster of paris go down a sink.
- Pour the plaster of paris into the mold (the lid).
- Let it harden for at least an hour.
- Carefully tear off the cardboard lid.
- Write one or two of the Ten Commandments on the plaster with a pencil.
- Scratch the letters into the plaster with a nail.
- Sponge gray tempera paint onto the plaque to give it a stone texture.

881. PAPIER-MÂCHÉ GLOBE
$ 2 HOURS 4

- Tape a round, blown-up balloon to a plastic dish to make the balloon stand up.
- Tape a long string of yarn to the top of the balloon. This will be the hanger.
- Cover the balloon with 3 layers of newspaper strips dipped in a mixture of wallpaper paste and water, working around the string.
- Cover the balloon with 2 layers of plain newspaper print.
- Let dry overnight.
- Draw the basic shape of the seven continents on the globe with a pencil.
- Paint each continent with a different acrylic color.
- Paint the oceans with blue acrylic paint.
- Label each continent with a marker.
- Label the globe with names of your church's missionaries and their countries.
- Hang the globe.

882. PAINTED CANVAS RUG
$$ 3 HOURS 3

This type of rug is often called a "floor cloth."

- Fold over the edges of a square- or rectangle-shaped piece of non-treated canvas about 1" on each side.
- Miter the corners by cutting off a triangle-shaped piece of each corner.
- Glue down the folded edges with fabric glue. This will be the back side of the rug.
- Paint the front of the canvas with 3 to 4 coats of acrylic paint. Choose a color that goes with the room where the rug will be displayed.
- Cut a square of thin cardboard, 2" x 2".
- Trace the square around the edges of the rug in a double row.
- Paint every other square with acrylic paint to create a checkerboard pattern. Several coats will be needed depending on the background color chosen.
- With a pencil, write a saying in the middle of the rug. For example, "Love one another," or, "Be a doer of the word," or, "Consider it all joy."
- Draw designs on the rug with a pencil.
- Paint the designs and words with acrylic paint.
- Let dry.
- Seal with several coats of varnish. Lightly sand the cloth and dust it off between each coat. Use a very fine grit of sandpaper.

883. HOMEMADE TARP
$ 3 HOURS 3

- Weave twine through the holes of plastic soda 6-pack carriers to create a large tarp. This will take a lot of plastic carriers.
- Tie one edge of the tarp to a fence.
- Anchor the other end to the ground with sticks.
- Weave strips of fabric, thick leaves, or vines through the tarp.
- Have fun playing in the shelter!

ACTIVITIES FOR
OLDER CHILDREN
GAMES

884. PING-PONG RACE
$ 15 MIN. 1

- Divide into teams.
- Set up 2 obstacle courses that are exactly the same. Use chairs, paper towel tubes taped to the floor, etc.
- Mark the start and finish lines.
- Give each player a straw and each team a Ping-Pong ball.
- At the start signal, one player from each team must blow his Ping-Pong ball through the obstacle course.

- When the player crosses the finish line he picks up his Ping-Pong ball and runs back to his team, handing the ball to the next player.
- The first team to have every player blow his Ping-Pong ball through the course and return to the start line wins the race.

885. FIND-THE-WORDS GAME
C 15 MIN. 1

- See how many words you can make from one of the two longest names in the Bible:
- Jonathelemrechokim (found in the title of Psalm 56)
- Mahershalalhashbaz (found in Isaiah 8:1, 3)

886. RELATED WORDS GAME
C 15 MIN. 1

- One player chooses a story or character from the Bible. For example, Joseph.
- Set a time limit of 2 minutes.
- The other players write down as many words as they can think of about that story or character. For example, brother, son, pit, dreamer, Egypt, etc.
- The player with the most related words wins.

887. BIBLE CATEGORIES
C 15 MIN. 2

- Across the top of a lined sheet of paper write 4 Bible categories. For example, People, Places, Animals, and Miracles.
- Down the side, write the word, "Jericho," placing one letter on a line.
- To play, set a time limit of 3–5 minutes.
- Each player tries to fill in a category. For example, "J" and "People" could be answered with "Jesus."
- If the players are allowed to use their Bibles to find some answers, lengthen the time.
- At the end of the time, the player with the most answers wins.

888. CRACKER WHISTLE
C 15 MIN. 1

- Divide into teams and line up.
- Set stacks of 3–5 crackers on a table.
- The first person on each team runs to the table, eats all the crackers, and tries to whistle.
- When the player has whistled he runs back to his line and the next player goes.
- The first team to have all their players whistle wins the game!

889. FIVE-LETTER WORD GAME
C 15 MIN. 1

- Set a time limit like 3 minutes.
- Write down as many 5-letter words as you can think of.
- The person with the most words wins.

890. NAMES AND PLACES OF THE BIBLE
C 30 MIN. 1

- The first player says the name of a person or place found in the Bible. For example, Jerusalem.
- The next player names a person or place that begins with the last letter of the preceding name or place. For example, the last letter was "m" so the second player could say, Mary.
- If a player can't think of a name or place that hasn't been used, he is out.
- The last player left in the game wins.

891. BLIND MAN'S FIND
C 30 MIN. 2

- Mark a large circle or square with twine.
- Divide into teams.
- Have each team decide on an animal noise, like a moo, cluck, or neigh.
- Blindfold one person from each team.

- Place bean bags inside the twine boundary.
- Guide the blindfolded players into the boundary area.
- The blindfolded players try to find as many bags as they can.
- Team members may give help by making their animal sound when the player is getting close to a bean bag.
- Let every player have a turn.
- The team that finds the most bean bags wins.

892. WORD SEARCH
C 30 MIN. 1

- Make a list of famous characters from the Bible.
- Hide the names among other letters.
- Print the letters in columns. Words can be hidden backward, forward, vertically, and horizontally.
- Mail the word search to a friend.

893. GUESS-THE-BIBLE-CHARACTER GAME
C 30 MIN. 1

This is a fun game to play at a party.

- On small slips of paper, write the name of a Bible character. Make one for each guest.
- When your guests arrive, pin a name on their backs, but do not tell them the names.
- The guests are to guess the name on their back by asking the other guests up to 10 yes-or-no questions. For example, "Is my character from the Old Testament?"

894. FINISH THE STORY...
C 30 MIN. 1

- Pretend that you are living in a different time period, such as the Bible times.
- Make up a sentence, then finish it by writing a story. For example, "I was playing by the Nile when I saw a mother place a baby in a basket and put it in the river. Why did she

do that? Do you think. . . ?" or, "Today we went to hear Jesus talk and boy, was I getting hungry. We didn't bring any food. . . ."

895. RESURRECTION SUNDAY GAME
C 30 MIN. 1

- Cut eighteen 3" x 5" rectangles from different colors of construction paper.
- Write one letter from the words, "Resurrection Sunday" on each rectangle.
- Form new words from the letter cards. For example, "sand," "rest," "sun," "day."
- See how many words you can come up with!

896. CINQUAIN POEM
C 30 MIN. 1

- Write a cinquain poem about a character from the Bible.
- This type of poem has five lines. The first line has one word, a noun. The second line has two words describing the noun. The third line has three action words describing the noun. The fourth line has four words of feeling about the noun, and the fifth line has one synonym word that points back to the first word.
- For example: Mary/wonderful mother/provider, giver, comforter/love, joy, hope, happiness/companion

897. THREE DESCRIPTIVE CLUES GAME
C 30 MIN. 1

- One player thinks of a person, place, or thing from the Bible and gives three descriptive words as clues to the other players. For example, "roar, den, and ferocious" for lion, or "water, build, and sons" for Noah.
- The first player to shout out the correct answer is awarded 5 points.

- Let every player have 3 chances to give clues.
- The player with the most points wins.

898. CONVERSATIONS GAME
C 30 MIN. 1

- Two players decide on a character or story from the Bible, such as Cain.
- They start a conversation about the character. For example, one player may say, "I lived a long time ago." The second player might say, "I was one of the few men living on the earth."
- The other players try to guess the person or story.
- The player who correctly guesses the answer chooses another player and they start a new conversation.

899. BIBLE ASSOCIATION
C 30 MIN. 1

- One player starts by stating one or two words or concepts found in the Bible. For example, God's love.
- The next player responds with the first word that pops into his mind. For example, the cross.
- Continue with the first concept until everyone has had at least one chance to respond.
- Let each player have a turn starting the association.

900. LICENSE PLATE SCRABBLE
C 30 MIN. 1

- Write down the letters you see on license plates of passing vehicles and form words.
- The first person to make up 10 words wins.
- Or, assign a point value to the words. For example, 1–3-letter words are worth 2 points, 4–6-letter words are worth 4 points, and 7 or more letters are worth 6 points.
- The person with the most points wins.

901. LICENSE PLATE MATH
C 30 MIN. 1

- Players decide to add or multiply the numbers they see on a license plate.
- The first player to give the answer is awarded one point.
- The first player to reach 20 points wins.

902. JAPANESE HAIKU POEM
C 30 MIN. 1

- Write a haiku poem about an animal from the Bible.
- A haiku has three lines. There are five syllables in the first line, seven in the second, and five in the third. Haiku does not rhyme.
- For example: The donkey carried/my dear Lord through the city/they cried, Hosanna!

903. SPIN THE COIN
C 30 MIN. 1

- Stand a coin on its edge.
- Flick the coin with your thumb and index finger to make it spin.
- See whose coin will spin the longest.

904. LITTLE MAN SKIT
$ 30 MIN. 4

- Cover a table with a cloth to the floor.
- Have the person sitting put his arms through a pair of pants and his hands in a pair of shoes.
- Hang a sheet behind the seated person.
- Have a second person stand or kneel behind the sheet.
- Cut small holes in the sheet for person #2's arms.
- Have person #2 be the arms of person #1.
- Have person #2 feed person #1 a banana, brush his teeth,

comb his hair, wash his face, put on makeup, or shave.

905. BIBLE DRILL
C 30 MIN. 2

- Make a list of verses about a specific subject like prayer.
- Write each reference on a slip of paper.
- Have one person choose a slip, call out the reference and say, "Ready, set, go."
- The others race to see who can find the reference first.
- Whoever finds the passage first gets to read the verse and call out the next one.
- Or, divide into teams. The team who finds the most references wins.

906. HANGMAN
C 30 MIN. 1

- Draw a pole and rope.
- One player secretly chooses a word or phrase and draws one line per letter.
- The second player guesses a letter that may be in the phrase or word.
- If the letter is in the puzzle, player #1 writes it on the correct line.
- If the letter is not in the puzzle, player #1 draws a head, then another body part for each missed letter.
- To win, player #2 has to guess the word or phrase before all the body parts are drawn and he is hanged.

907. "WHAT IF?" GAME
C 30 MIN. 1

- Start with the phrase "What if. . .?"
- Finish the phrase with something that seems unlikely. For example, "What if there were no stairs?" Or, "What if we could run as fast as a car?" Or, "What if one day gravity didn't work?"

• Discuss the question and its ramifications, or write several paragraphs to answer the question.

908. CREATE AN INVENTION
C 30 MIN. 2

• Pick 3 random, unrelated items, like a shovel, light bulb, and coat hanger.
• Try to think of something you could invent with them.

909. GUESS-THE-DEFINITION GAME
C 30 MIN. 1

• Decide how many words will be used.
• One player chooses an unusual word from the dictionary and writes its definition on a slip of paper.
• The remaining players write down what they think the word means on a slip of paper. All players should use the same color pen or pencil.
• The player who chose the word collects the slips, mixes them up, and lays them on the table for the other players to see.
• Each player chooses the definition he believes to be the correct one.
• Give a point to the player that picks the right answer.
• The player with most points wins the game.
• Let each player choose a word and write its definition.

910. BIBLE ASSOCIATION GAME
C 30 MIN. 2

• One player starts by saying the name of a biblical character, such as David.
• The next player adds on a person, place, or thing that was associated with David, such as Jonathan or Saul.
• Keep adding to the association until a player is stumped.
• Start with another name, such as Esther. . . .

911. ADD-ON GAME
C 30 MIN. 1

- One player starts the game by saying, "I went on a trip with my dad, and in his suitcase he packed _____." Fill in the blank with a packable item, like socks.
- The next player says the sentence with the socks plus another item.
- Continue the game until one player can't remember all the items in order.

912. PAINT BAG BIBLE QUIZ
$ 30 MIN. 3

- Squeeze acrylic paint into a Ziploc-style plastic bag.
- Squeeze out the air and close the bag.
- Spread out the paint evenly in the bag.
- Each person on the team needs a paint bag.
- Divide into teams.
- One person asks questions. For example, "Is the book of Galatians in the Old or New Testament?"
- Team members write the answer on their paint bags with their fingers.
- Erase the answer by smoothing out the bag.
- Award a point for each correct answer.
- The team with the most points wins!

913. GUESS-THE-BOOK GAME
C 30 MIN. 1

- One player chooses a verse and writes the book of the Bible the verse is from on a slip of paper.
- The remaining players write down the book they think the verse comes from. All players should use the same color pen or pencil.
- The player who chose the verse collects the slips and lays them on the table for all to see.
- Each player chooses the book he believes to be the correct one.
- Give a point to the player that picks the right answer.

• The player with the most points wins the game.
• Let each player choose a verse and write the book on a slip of paper.

914. BOW AND ARROW
C 45 MIN. 5

• Find straight twigs for arrows.
• Carve the end of the twig into a dull point.
• Find a curved twig for the bow.
• Tie together rubber bands for the string of the bow and tie around each end of the curved twig.
• Have fun playing Indians or shooting at a target.

915. TO-THE-TOP-OF-EVEREST GAME
$ 45 MIN. 3

• Draw a mountain on a 6" x 9" piece of brown construction paper.
• Cut out the mountain.
• Trace the top of the mountain onto a sheet of white paper.
• Make the bottom of the white paper look like snow at the top of a mountain.
• Cut out the snow and glue to the mountain.
• Write "Mt. Everest" on the mountain.
• Cut three 3" x 12" strips of poster board.
• Using a ruler, make a mark every inch on each strip.
• Draw a line across each strip at each inch mark.
• Starting at the bottom of one strip, number the boxes 1–12.
• Starting at the bottom of the second strip, number the boxes 14–25.
• Starting at the bottom of the third strip, number the boxes 27–38.
• Number 13 will be the space between strip one and two, and number 26 will be the space between strip two and three.
• Give each player a different marker.
• Arrange the strips and the mountain on the table so the

mountain is above number 38. Make sure to leave a space for numbers 13 and 26.
- Each player starts by rolling a die and moving his marker the number of dots.
- If a player lands on a space that has an opponent's marker, that opponent must move his marker back according to the number on the die.
- If a player rolls a 2 he must move his marker back 2 spaces.
- If a player lands on 13 or 26 he can advance 5 spaces.
- The first player to land on the mountain is the winner. He must have the exact number. For example, if his marker is on 35, he must roll 3 to win.

916. KEEP AWAY
C 45 MIN. 1

- Pick 2 or 3 players to be inside the circle.
- The rest of the players form the circle.
- The players on the circle throw a ball back and forth from one side of the circle to the other while the players in the middle try to catch it.
- If a player in the middle catches the ball, the player who threw it changes places with him.

917. AROUND-THE-WORLD BASKETBALL
C 45 MIN. 1

- Decide on 5 spots to shoot from starting at the left of the hoop and continuing on a semi-circle ending on the right side of the hoop.
- Each player takes a shot from the left side of the hoop.
- If a player misses, he can call "chance" and take another shot. Or he can wait for his next turn.
- If a player makes the shot, he advances to the second shooting spot. A player can continue shooting until he misses.
- If a player misses the chance shot he returns to the first spot.
- The first player to make a basket from all 5 spots wins!

918. BIBLE FREEZE TAG
C 45 MIN. 1

- Choose a person to be *It*.
- *It* tries to tag another person. If the other person calls out the name of a character or a book of the Bible before he is tagged, he will not be frozen.
- Other players can unfreeze a player by touching him.
- If a player is frozen three times, he becomes *It*.

919. RUBBER BAND LAUNCH
C 45 MIN. 4

Be careful not to hit anyone with a launched object.

- Tie rubber bands together to make a long string.
- Tie each end to a tree or to the legs of a swing set.
- Pull the big band back and place a small ball, toy, or acorn in the band.
- Launch the object.
- Take turns to see who can launch his object the farthest.
- Set up a target and try to hit it with the launched object.

920. ALPHABET MATH
C 45 MIN. 2

- Divide a word into syllables.
- Assign a point value to each letter of the alphabet. For example, A=1, B=2, and C=3.
- Put a greater-than or less-than symbol between the syllables. For example, Bi=11, ble=19, Bi<ble.

921. "WHERE IN THE WORLD?" GAME
C 45 MIN. 1

- Choose one person to start.
- This person thinks of a location in the world. For example, Jerusalem.
- The other players try to guess the location by asking 30 questions that can be answered with a yes or no. A good question would be to ask if the location is on a certain continent.
- The player who guesses the location is the winner and gets to pick a new location.

922. CONTINUE THE STORY
C 45 MIN. 1

- Sit everyone in a circle.
- Have one person start a story. For example, "One day in July, I stepped out my front door and the world had changed. . . ."
- Let the first person talk for a while, then have the next person continue the story.
- The last person in the circle finishes the story with, "and they all lived happily ever after."

923. BIBLE ALPHABET GAME
C 45 MIN. 2

- Pretend you are living in Bible times.
- A player starts the game by answering the question, "Where am I?" with an answer that begins with the letter A.
- Then he answers "Who am I" and "What am I" with the letter A. For example, Assyria, Abraham, and angel.
- The answers do not have to be related, but should be mentioned in the Bible.
- Use a Bible concordance or dictionary to help answer the questions.
- The next player uses the letter B and so on until the whole alphabet has been used.

924. GRAPH MULTIPLICATION GAME
C 45 MIN. 1

- Each player places 5 markers, such as dried beans, at opposite ends of a sheet of graph paper.
- The markers may be placed anywhere in the first row. Each player needs a different type of marker.
- The object of the game is to get each marker to the opposite side without getting captured.
- Place a set of dominoes face down on the table and mix them up.
- To play, the first player draws a domino and then multiplies the dots.
- The player then moves a bean the same number of squares on the graph paper.
- Moves can be made vertically, horizontally, or diagonally, but not backward.
- If a player draws a double domino, a piece that has the same number of dots on each side, he gets to draw a bonus domino. He can then move a second marker or multiply all the dots together and move one marker.
- A player can capture another player's markers by landing on the same square. That marker goes back to the starting square.
- When a player has moved all his markers to the opposite side, he is the winner.

925. BIBLE SCAVENGER HUNT
C 45 MIN. 3

- Make a list of questions that have answers in the Bible. For example, "What is the longest chapter of the Bible?" "Who was the tallest person mentioned in the Bible?" "How many times is Isaiah quoted in the New Testament?"
- Research the answers by using a Bible, a Bible dictionary, and Bible trivia books.
- Write the questions and answers in your journal or notebook.

926. SECRET CODE
C 1 HOUR 2

- Cut out 2 large circles from construction paper, one smaller than the other.
- Write numbers around the edge of the larger circle and the alphabet along the edge of the smaller circle.
- Try to space the letters and numbers the same distance apart.
- Stick a small paper fastener through the center of the circles.
- While holding the outside number wheel with one hand, turn the smaller letter wheel with the other hand. Start your secret code by lining up the letter A with a number. For example, A could be lined up with the number 8, which means that B would be lined up with the number 9, and so on.
- Make a wheel for your friend
- Make up your own secret message, then send it to a friend by leaving it at a pre-arranged spot, like under a doormat or rock, or in the hole of a tree. Mark on the message the number for the letter A.
- For example, "John, meet me after lunch at the big oak tree. Jason."

927. HEROES-OF-THE-FAITH CROSSWORD
C 1 HOUR 3

- Read Hebrews 11 and make a list of all the people mentioned by name. There are 17 heroes included!
- Write a short description of each person.
- Write out the names in crossword puzzle form.
- Draw the puzzle without the names.
- Write the descriptive clues under Down and Across, referring to the practice puzzle.
- Number the descriptions and the appropriate squares on the puzzle.
- Make up an answer key for yourself.
- Give to your friends.

928. TRAVEL IN THE HOLY LAND
$ 1 HOUR 3

- Purchase a map of the Middle East.
- Draw lines from city to city with a ruler.
- Place small dots along the lines, spacing them evenly. Towns already have a dot printed on the map.
- Let each player choose a starting city or home base.
- To travel along the dots, roll a die and move your marker the appropriate number of dots.
- The first player to travel to at least 3 cities in each country and then return to his starting city wins!

929. ART BINGO
C 1 HOUR 4

Check out books from the library to become familiar with the works of the artists on the list.

- Make a list of 25 famous artists. This could include Da Vinci, Remington, Rembrandt, Van Gogh, Cassatt, Manet, Picasso, and Monet.
- Do not use Homer on the list.
- Cut eight 7" x 9" sheets of white paper.
- Divide each paper into 30 squares, 6 rows down and 5 columns across.
- Write the artist's name "Homer" in the top row, one letter in each square.
- Write one name of an artist in each of the remaining squares. Write "Free Space" in the middle square.
- Fill out every card. Try to make each card different by placing the names in different squares. Make sure each card has all 25 names.
- Write each name on 5 slips of paper along with a letter from Homer. There will be 125 slips.
- To play, have one person draw a slip and call out the letter and the name of the artist.
- Players place a marker like a bean or button on the correct square.
- The first player to get 5 in a row says "Bingo" or "Homer" and is the winner.

930. BIBLE CHARACTERS GO-FISH GAME
C 1 HOUR 1

- Make a list of 14 categories from the Bible. For example, "Men of the Old Testament," "Gospels," "Minor Prophets," "Women of the New Testament."
- For each category, make 4 index cards. Write one example of the category on a card. For example, for "Men of the Old Testament," there could be a card for Moses, Adam, David, and Amos.
- Pass out 6 cards to each player.
- To play, one player asks an opponent if she has a card that matches a category in his hand. If the opponent has a card in that category she must give it to the other player.
- The player continues to ask for matches until the opponent does not have one that is asked for. He then draws a card from the pile. If the card is the one asked for, the player can ask another player for a card. If the drawn card is different than the asked-for card, the player keeps the card and his turn is over.
- The player with the most matches or sets of categories wins.

931. MANCALA GAME
$ 1 HOUR 4

- Cut off each end of an egg carton and staple 2 egg cups to each end of another egg carton.
- Paint the inside lid and egg cups with acrylic or tempera paint.
- Let dry.
- Paint the outside.
- Let dry.
- Place 4 buttons, beans, or pebbles in each egg cup, leaving 2 cups on each end empty.
- A player sits on each side. The 6 cups nearest a player belong to him, as well as the 2 holding cups to his right.
- One player begins the game by taking the 4 markers from any one of the 6 cups on his side and placing them one by one in the next 4 cups or the next 3 cups and his holding cup.
- Play is clockwise around the carton.

- After he has deposited his 4 markers, he can pick up the markers in the last cup and continue playing until he places a marker in an empty cup. At this point it is the other player's turn.
- The player does not place markers in the opponent's holding cup.
- If a player ends by placing his marker in his holding cup he can then choose another cup of markers on his side to distribute. Some cups will end up with more or less than 4 markers.
- The game is over when one player has no more markers on his side. The opponent takes the markers left on his side and puts them in his holding cup.
- The player who ends up with the most markers in his holding cups (the 2 end cups to his right) is the winner.

932. LIP-SYNCHING CONTEST
C 1 HOUR 5

- Set a day, time, and theme for the contest. A theme could be Christian artists.
- Invite your friends to be in the contest. Ask them to practice along with a favorite singer and to come in costume.
- Make a list of things to be judged, like costumes, how well the song is lip-synched, and the motions of the singer.
- Have two people be the judges at the contest.
- Give the winner a homemade trophy.

933. MEXICAN DOMINOES
C 1 HOUR 2

- Four players will be needed for this game.
- Place the dominoes face down and mix them up.
- Each player draws 7 dominoes and sets them up in front of himself so the other players cannot see the dots.
- The player with the double 6's goes first by laying his domino in the center of the table.
- The next player lays down a domino with 6 dots so they are touching. Play continues by laying a domino on your leg

that matches the last dot of the leg.
- Each player can only play on his leg unless someone passes, then he can play on the other person's leg.
- Another leg can be played on as long as that person passes.
- The first person to lay down all his dominoes wins that round.
- Add up the dots of all the dominoes left for each person and write down the score.
- Continue playing each round with the double 5's, then 4's, etc., down to the double blank. There will be 7 rounds.
- The person or team to have the lowest score wins.

934. WILDERNESS WANDERINGS GAME
$ 1 HOUR 2

- Cut thirty 3" x 3" squares of poster board or lightweight cardboard.
- Write "START," and draw a picture of an Egyptian pyramid on one card.
- Write "FINISH" and "PROMISED LAND" on one card.
- Write rewards and penalties on the remaining cards. For example: Take another turn, Move ahead 1, or 2, spaces, Safe, Go back 2, or 3, spaces, Go back to START, Lose a turn.
- Make equal numbers of reward and penalty cards.
- Write some of the things that happened to the Israelites on their journey. For example: Took the bones of Joseph—move ahead 2 spaces. Followed the cloud—move ahead 1 space. Chased down by the Egyptians, the Israelites afraid—move back 2 spaces. Grumbling—go back to START. Tabernacle built—move ahead 3 spaces.
- Read through the headings in Exodus, Numbers, and Deuteronomy to find out other things that happened in their journey to the Promised Land and write them on a card.
- Lay out the cards in a path on a table.
- To play the game, roll one die; the player with the highest number goes first.
- With every roll move the number of spaces and do what the card you land on says to do.
- The player who gets to the Promised Land first wins!

935. BURIED TREASURE
$ 1 HOUR 2

This project is great fun, not only for birthdays,
but anytime a gift is given.

- Place small wrapped presents in a metal lunch pail or oatmeal box.
- Bury the pail in the backyard or in a friend's backyard.
- Make a treasure map from the side of a brown bag.
- Write clues on the map.
- Crumple up the map, then smooth it out to make the map look old.
- Give the map to the person the treasure is for.
- Follow the clues and dig up the buried treasure!

936. MATH COMPUTATION GAME
$ 1 HOUR 2

- Cut a 1" x 1" square of lightweight cardboard.
- On half a sheet of poster board, make a trail of squares for a game path by tracing the square pattern. The squares could be traced with different colored markers. Make at least 42 squares.
- On the first square, write "START."
- On the last square, write "FINISH." Write a number on each square using 0–42.
- To play, place a marker on the START square and roll 3 dice.
- Add, multiply, subtract, or divide the numbers on the dice. Two different calculations should be made. For example, if a player rolls 1, 5, 2, he could calculate 1 + 5 - 2 = 4, or, 5 x 2 - 1 = 9.
- The player will move his marker the number of spaces of the highest answer.
- The first player to have an answer that lands him exactly on the FINISH square wins.

937. ALPHABET BLOCK SCRABBLE
$$$ 1 HOUR 3

- Place an alphabet sticker on blank matchboxes. You will need this number of boxes: A-9, B-2, C-2, D-4, E-12, F-2, G-3, H-2, I-9, J-1, K-1, L-4, M-2, N-6, O-8, P-2, Q-1, R-6, S-4, T-6, U-4, V-2, W-2, X-1, Y-2, Z-1. Blank-2.
- Write a point value on each block. Give the A, E, I, L, N, O, R, S, T, and U a point value of 1. Give the B, C, M, and P a point value of 3. Give the D and G a point value of 2. Give F, H, V, W, and Y a point value of 4. Give the K a point value of 5. Give J and X, a point value of 8. Give the Q and Z a point value of 10. Give the blanks a value of 0.
- Place all the blocks in a large paper bag or a box with a hole cut in the lid large enough for the blocks to be removed.
- Play on the floor or on a large table.
- Have each player choose a block. The player who chooses a letter closest to the end of the alphabet or a blank plays first.
- Assign one player to be scorekeeper.
- Each player chooses 7 blocks without looking in the bag.
- The first player will try to form a word from 2 or more blocks, placing them in the middle of the floor or table vertically or horizontally.
- The player then adds up his score and the scorekeeper writes it down.
- Blank blocks can be used as any letter.
- The player to the left of the first player then tries to form a word using the letters on the table and his own letters.
- Letters touching each other must form a word or words.
- After all the players have played one round, the player beginning the second round may choose enough blocks from the bag to total 7.
- Two-syllable words receive double points.
- Three-syllable words receive triple points.
- A player receives 40 points if every one of his 7 blocks is used to form a word during a turn.
- A player may use a turn to exchange all or some of his blocks.
- Any word may be challenged. If the word is unacceptable the player must form a new word.
- A player who forms 2 or more words counts the point value of each word formed.

- The game ends when one player has used all his letters and there are no more letters in the bag.
- If a player has blocks left, the total point value is subtracted from his score.
- The player with the most points wins.
- If a player uses 2 vowel blocks, he doubles the point value of each block.

938. BIBLE BINGO
C 1 HOUR 2

- Using a ruler, draw 5 rows of 5 squares each on a 9" x 12" sheet of paper.
- Write a capital letter from the word "BIBLE" above each column.
- Write, "Free Space" in the middle square.
- Choose a Bible category to fill in the remaining squares. For example, "Characters from the New Testament," "Books of the Bible," or "Books of the Bible That Are a Person's Name."
- Make enough different Bingo cards for the number of players.
- Be sure to use the same words, but write them in different squares and rows.
- Write a slip of paper for each square and row of every card. For example, "B-John."
- Place the slips in a box or bag.
- Decorate each card with pictures from old Sunday school papers glued around the grid.
- To begin play, have one player pull out a slip and call out the letter and the word. Lay the slips out on the table.
- Players mark the square with a marker, such as a dried bean.
- The first player to cover 5 squares in a row calls out, "Bible Bingo!" and is the winner.

939. HERSHEY'S KISS PIÑATA
$$ 2 HOURS 4

- Blow up and tie a medium-sized balloon.
- Tape a toilet paper roll to the top.

- Tape the balloon to a piece of thin cardboard a little bigger than the balloon.
- Fill in between the balloon and the cardboard by taping on wads of crumpled newspaper.
- Try to form the basic shape of a Hershey's Kiss.
- Cover with 3 layers of newspaper strips dipped in a mixture of wallpaper paste and water.
- Do not cover over a small section of the side; this will be where the piñata will be filled with candy.
- Cover with a layer of plain newsprint.
- Let dry overnight.
- Pop and remove the balloon pieces.
- Fill with wrapped candy.
- Cover the opening with layers of newspaper dipped in the paste mixture.
- Cover the opening with a layer of newsprint.
- Tape 2 ends of a length of string to the top and secure with newspaper and paste. This will be the hanger.
- Wrap the Hershey's Kiss piñata in foil.
- Hang, and have fun breaking it open!

Activities for Older Children

EDUCATIONAL PROJECTS

940. QUESTION DIARY
C 30 MIN. 1

- In a notebook, write down questions you might have. For example, What makes leaves turn colors in the fall?
- Find out the answers by looking in books and encyclopedias, and by asking people you know.
- Record your findings in your notebook diary.

941. "ALL ABOUT" BOOK
C 45 MIN. 2

- Read about your favorite Bible character.
- Write facts about the character in a notebook.
- Write how the character obeyed God, who his parents were, what they did for a living, etc.

942. MY DISCOVERY TRIP
C 45 MIN. 1

- Pretend that you were on the *Santa Maria* with Columbus.
- Write a story about the trip across the Atlantic Ocean and the people and places you discovered.

943. SKELETON
C 45 MIN. 1

- Form a skeleton by gluing different pasta shapes and cotton swabs to a 6" x 9" sheet of black construction paper.

944. FANTASTIC FUN FACTS
C 45 MIN. 2

- Fold a 9" x 12" sheet of construction paper in half.
- Decorate the front for a birthday, anniversary, wedding, or get-well card.
- On the inside of the card, write different facts about the year the person was born, or about the present year. Use an almanac to find out who won the World Series, who was president, what was invented, etc.
- Ask people what they remember about that year, and write it in the card.
- Give the card to the special person.

945. LIBERTY BELL
$ 45 MIN. 1

- Draw a simple outline of the Liberty Bell on a 9" x 12" piece of cardboard.

- Cut 2" x 2" squares of gray or silver tissue paper.
- Spread a layer of glue over a small section of the bell.
- Place the eraser end of a pencil in the center of a piece of tissue paper and twist the tissue around the pencil.
- Place the tissue-covered pencil in the glue and lift the pencil out of the tissue.
- Cover the pencil again with tissue and repeat.
- Place the tissue pieces close together so no cardboard is showing.
- Fill in the entire bell.
- Fill in the background with tissue stripes of red, white, and blue.

946. AUSTRALIA CONTINENT MAP
C 1 HOUR 1

You can tailor this project to any continent to reinforce a geography lesson or celebrate a homeland.

- On a 9" x 12" piece of white construction paper, draw the continent of Australia.
- Fill in and label the countries, major cities, bodies of water, rivers, mountains, and any other important features of Australia.
- Color the map with crayons or colored pencils.

947. AROUND-THE-WORLD SHUFFLEBOARD
$ 1 HOUR 2

This game is a great way to learn world geography.

- Buy a map of the world.
- Circle the major cities, countries, rivers, mountains, oceans, etc.
- Circle the places your friends and relatives live.
- Assign each circle a point value. Such as 5 points for a major city or 10 points for a continent.
- To play, place the map on the floor, stand behind a designated line, and aim for the circles by pushing small jar lids or

checker pieces with a broom or hockey stick.
- Decide how many turns each player gets and total the points after all the turns have been played.
- The player with the most points wins.

948. FLOWER POCKET
C 1 HOUR 2

- Cut a paper plate in half.
- Glue pictures of flowers on the back of the half plate and to the front of a whole paper plate.
- Lay the half plate, flowers up, on the whole paper plate and staple around the edge to form a pocket.
- Write down the flowers that are found growing in your neighborhood. Use a field guide to identify any flowers you don't recognize.
- Draw and color the flowers on white paper.
- Label each flower.
- Trim around each flower.
- Mount the flowers on construction paper.
- Trim the mounted flower so there is about ½" border.
- Place the flowers in the pocket, or take pictures of the flowers, then trim and mount them.
- Hang the pocket on the refrigerator or bedroom wall.
- Add to your collection whenever you see a flower that you don't already have.

949. BIBLE CHAPTER CHART
C 1 HOUR 1

- Write the books of the Old Testament along the bottom of a piece of graph paper.
- Write the numbers 1–150 (or as many as the paper will allow) up the left side of the paper.
- Look up how many chapters each book has, and place a dot at the intersecting line. For example, the book of Genesis has 50 chapters.
- Use a ruler to connect the dots with straight lines.
- Which book has the most chapters and which has the least?

950. WEATHER CHART
$ 1 HOUR 3

- Place a small plate, upside down, on a piece of white poster board and trace around it.
- Cut out the circle.
- Make a second circle.
- Write "TODAY'S WEATHER" in bubble-style letters on yellow construction paper.
- Cut out the letters.
- Arrange the letters, down the side or across the top, on a sheet of blue poster board and glue them down.
- Make a dot in the center of one cardboard circle.
- Divide the circle into 5 equal triangle-shaped areas by drawing lines from the dot to the edge of the circle.
- Draw a picture in each area to correspond with a sunny, cloudy, rainy, stormy, or snowy day.
- Label each triangle.
- Poke a small hole in the center of the circle.
- Make a dot in the center of the second circle and poke a hole.
- Around the outside edge of the second circle write degrees of temperature, from -10° up to 110°.
- Draw 2 large arrows on yellow construction paper. Cut out.
- Arrange the circles on the blue poster board.
- With a pencil, mark a dot on the blue board by putting it through the hole in each circle.
- Poke a hole through the 2 dots on the poster board.
- Attach both circles to the board with paper fasteners.
- Glue an arrow above each circle and hang the chart.
- Turn each circle so the arrow is pointing to the right type of day and temperature.

951. TWELVE TRIBES OF ISRAEL
C 1 HOUR 4

- With markers, draw and color a symbol for each tribe on a 3" x 4" piece of Styrofoam tray.

  Mandrake plant—Reuben
  Gate of Shechem—Simeon
  High priest and breastplate—Levi
  Female deer (doe)—Naphtali

  Wolf—Benjamin
  Donkey—Issachar
  Serpent—Dan
  Ship—Zebulun

Fruit—Ephraim   Tent—Gad
Ring—Judah   Olive tree—Asher
• Mount by gluing on a long piece of cardboard.

952. SEED MAP
$ 1 HOUR 1

• Write the name of a country or state at the top of a 9" x 12" sheet of paper.
• Draw the outline of the country or state, like Israel, under the name.
• Cut a 9" x 12" sheet of heavy cardboard.
• Glue the map to the cardboard.
• Spread a layer of glue on a section of the map.
• Lay seed, popcorn, or rice in the glue.
• Cover the whole map.
• For more detail add different colored seeds for mountains, lakes, or rivers.
• Cover the name with glue and seeds.
• Cover the area outside the map with glue and seeds.

953. SOUTH AMERICA MAP
C 2 HOURS 3

• Cut a sheet of butcher paper a little smaller than the size of a piece of poster board, or tape together sheets of newspaper.
• Draw the outline of South America.
• Cut out.
• Place the pattern on a piece of poster board and trace around it with a pencil.
• Draw in the countries.
• Label each country, capital, major rivers, and mountains.
• Write in block letters SOUTH AMERICA down the side or across the bottom in pencil.
• Trace over all pencil lines and words with a dark marker.
• Color each country a different color.
• Study each country, and draw or cut out pictures from magazines and glue them to that country. For example, Colombia is known for coffee. Cut out a picture of coffee and glue it to the country.

ACTIVITIES FOR
OLDER CHILDREN
FOOD PROJECTS

954. BIBLE TIME DINNER
C 30 MIN. 2

- In Bible reference books find a list of things people ate during the time of Jesus.
- Pretend you are Martha, Mary, or Lazarus preparing for Jesus' coming to dinner. Write out a menu of what you will serve.
- To make a menu card to remember your special meal, refer to Project #267.

955. APPLE TURNOVERS
$ 30 MIN. 5

• Peel and core an apple.
• Chop the apple into small chunks.
• In a bowl, mix the apple with 2 tablespoons brown sugar, 1 tablespoon white sugar, and ¼ teaspoon of cinnamon.
• Slice a croissant almost in half.
• Fill with the apple mixture.
• Place on a cookie sheet and bake at 350° for 15–20 minutes.
• For frosting, mix one-half of a box powdered sugar, 1 tablespoon of soft butter or margarine, ½ teaspoon vanilla, and a little milk.
• Drizzle frosting over the turnover, and enjoy!

956. MOLDED JELL-O
$ 30 MIN. 3

• Mix up a batch of Jell-O according to the instructions on the box.
• Pour the Jell-O into different kinds of molds, such as small candy molds or the plastic liners of boxed chocolates (or anything plastic that would be a different shape).
• Place in the refrigerator to set.
• Run hot water over the back of the mold to loosen, and place the Jell-O on a serving dish.

957. MINIATURE CAKES
$ 1 HOUR 4

• Make a batch of cupcakes.
• Remove the paper cup holder.
• Cut off the top of each cupcake to make a flat top.
• Cut each cupcake in half.
• Spread a little strawberry or seedless raspberry jam on the top of the bottom half.
• Top with the other half.
• Frost the top and sides of the cupcake.
• Let each guest decorate his miniature cake with M & M's, tube frosting, sprinkles, etc.
• Enjoy!

ACTIVITIES FOR OLDER CHILDREN

HOLIDAY PROJECTS

VALENTINE'S DAY

958. VALENTINE'S THIMBLE
$ 30 MIN. 1

- Fill a thimble with small hearts punched with a heart punch or cut from construction paper or gift wrap.
- Write a few verses of God's love on very small pieces of paper. Verses could include, 1 John 4:16, John 15:13, Romans 8:38–39, and Romans 5:8.
- Fold up the verses and place in the thimble.

- Write a special message to the person you're giving the thimble to on another small piece of paper. For example, "You are my best friend," or "I love you!"
- Cut a 5" x 5" piece of white tissue paper and a 6" x 6" piece of red tissue paper.
- Place the white tissue on top of the red tissue.
- Place the filled thimble in the middle.
- Bring up the edges of the tissue and tie with a ribbon.
- Give to your friend.

959. TISSUE PAPER HEARTS
C 1 HOUR 1

- Fold 2 sheets of 6" x 9" red construction paper in half.
- Place one sheet inside the other.
- Draw a half a heart, starting and ending on the fold.
- Cut out the hearts at the same time.
- Keeping the hearts folded together, draw a small heart starting and ending on the fold.
- Cut out the heart.
- Glue a piece of pink tissue to the front of one heart.
- Glue the second heart on top of the tissue-covered heart.
- Cut a lot of 2" x 2" squares of red and pink tissue paper.
- Place a strip of glue along the outside edge of the heart.
- Put the eraser end of a pencil in the center of a square of tissue and twist the tissue around the pencil.
- Place the tissue-covered eraser in the glue and lift out the pencil.
- Continue placing tissue, close together, all the way around the heart.

960. VALENTINE'S DAY BUCKET
$ 1 HOUR 2

- Wrap the handle of a metal bucket and the area that attaches to the bucket with newspaper and masking tape.
- Paint the outside of the bucket with 2 to 3 coats of white acrylic paint.
- Decorate around the top of the bucket with a red and white

checked border. With a pencil, mark the squares around the top. Since the white is already painted, paint every other square with red acrylic.
- Draw different-sized hearts on the side of the bucket with a pencil.
- Paint each heart with acrylic paint.
- With the handle end of the brush, scatter dots around the hearts.
- Let dry.
- Seal with a clear spray sealer.

EASTER

961. EASTER BANNER
$ 30 MIN. 1

- On a 12" x 18" piece of black construction paper, write the phrase "He Is Risen" with white chalk in bubble or block lettering.
- Shade in the words with yellow chalk.
- Fill in the background with different chalk-colored crosses.
- Spray the banner with hair spray to "set" the chalk.

962. WAX RESIST EGGS
$ 45 MIN. 3

- Poke a small hole in each end of an egg.
- Blow out the inside of the egg.
- Rinse and let dry.
- Draw crosses and write words about Jesus, with a white crayon, on the egg. For example, "Lamb of God," "He Is Risen," "Coming Again," and "He Died for Me."
- Dip the egg in the dye from an Easter egg decorating kit.
- Display in a clear bowl at Easter time.

963. EASTER EGGS
C 45 MIN. 1

- Poke a small hole in each end of 6 eggs.
- Blow out the inside of the eggs.
- Rinse and dry the eggs.
- Color each egg to represent the story of Easter: purple for Jesus the King; red for Jesus' blood; brown for the cross; green for the garden; black for sin; and yellow for the resurrection.
- Store in an egg carton.

964. PIERCED EASTER CARD
C 1 HOUR 3

- Practice the following technique by first tracing a few stencil letters onto several types of paper—watercolor, card stock, computer paper, and so on. (Thin paper will rip when the holes are pierced.)
- Place the paper on top of an old magazine.
- With a push pin, pierce holes evenly along the lines of letters. Do not punch the holes too close together.
- Decide which paper works the best.
- To make the card, cut a piece of paper twice the width and a little shorter than the length of an envelope.
- Fold the paper in half.
- On the front of the card lightly stencil the words, "He was pierced for me."
- Shade in the letters with watercolors.
- Let dry.
- Open the card and pierce holes evenly along the lines of the letters with a push pin.
- Write the message "Happy Easter" on the inside of the card, or repeat the process like the front of the card.
- Send to a friend, relative, or Sunday school teacher.

965. DECOUPAGE EGGS
C 1 HOUR 2

- Poke a small hole in each end of an egg.
- Blow out the inside of the egg.
- Rinse with water and let dry.
- Cut out small pictures and words from pretty gift wrap or magazines.
- Thin some glue with a little water.
- Coat a section of the egg with glue.
- Lay a picture or word in the glue. Use words that signify Easter. For example, Jesus, died, cross, and rose again.
- Smooth out the picture.
- Spread more glue on top of the picture.
- Cover the entire egg like a collage.
- Display in a basket or egg cup.

966. EASTER HYMN
C 1 HOUR 1

- Draw a border of crosses, hearts, and lambs around the edge of a 9" x 12" sheet of construction paper with crayons, markers, and colored pencils.
- Write a verse and chorus of "The Old Rugged Cross" in the center of the paper in bold lettering.
- Draw and color pictures for some of the words, like hill, cross, blood, lamb, and trophies.
- Hang the picture.

967. EASTER EGG SCENE
C 1 HOUR 2

- Draw a large egg on a 9" x 12" sheet of white paper.
- Holding a second sheet of white paper behind the drawn egg, cut out the egg.
- Lay one egg on several layers of newspaper.
- Place a small amount of light blue tempera or acrylic paint on a paper plate.

- Wad up a sheet of plastic wrap and dip it in the paint.
- Print over the entire egg by pressing the paint-loaded plastic onto the paper.
- Let dry.
- Repeat with yellow paint.
- In the center of the second egg, draw and color a crucifixion and resurrection scene.
- Add details, such as small pieces of fabric.
- Cut a horizontal and vertical slit in the center of the printed egg by folding in half and cutting a slit. Do not fold enough to make a crease.
- Glue around the edge of the colored scene.
- Place the printed egg on top.
- Fold back the flaps on the printed egg and glue them down so the scene is showing.

968. EASTER BOX
$ 2 HOURS 3

- Find a small box with a lid.
- Cut a sheet of bark a little smaller than the lid of the box.
- Draw a cross on the bark with a pencil.
- Cut out the cross.
- Glue the cross to the lid.
- Spread some glue on the remaining lid space.
- Cut a length of yarn and lay it in the glue up against the cross.
- Lay the yarn around the cross, pushing it in place with a Popsicle stick.
- Cover the entire lid using different colors of yarn.
- Put the lid on the box and trace a line on the box to show how far down the lid goes.
- Spread glue on one side of the box and cover with yarn.
- Cover the entire outside of the box, being careful not to glue yarn above the line where the lid sits.
- Write verses about Jesus' death and resurrection on small strips of paper.
- Fill the box with candy and the verse strips.
- Give to a friend or teacher on Easter Sunday, or pass it around at the Easter meal and let everyone have a piece of candy and read a verse.

969. THE DOZEN DISCIPLES
C 2 HOURS 1

- Poke a small hole in each end of 12 eggs.
- Blow out the inside of the eggs.
- Rinse and dry the eggs.
- Use paint, fabric, yarn, ribbon, and markers to decorate each egg to represent the 12 disciples.
- On each egg, write a name: Peter, James, John, Matthew, Simon, Judas, Philip, Thomas, Bartholomew, Judas Iscariot, James, Andrew.
- Store in an egg carton.

970. EASTER MOBILE
$ 2 HOURS 3

- Cut different colors of tissue paper into long strips about 1" wide.
- Wrap the tissue around a hanger, securing the ends with glue.
- Cut Styrofoam trays into different Easter shapes, such as a cross, a nail, a tomb and stone, and Jesus.
- Paint each shape with glue.
- Cover them with small pieces of tissue paper, overlapping each piece, adding more glue as needed. Use red or brown for the cross, black for the nail, etc.
- Coat with a thin layer of glue.
- Let dry.
- Punch a hole in each shape.
- Attach to the hanger with different lengths of ribbon or yarn.
- Hang at Easter.

MOTHER'S DAY, FATHER'S DAY

971. "WORLD'S GREATEST DAD" TROPHY
C 1 HOUR 1

- Sand the edges of a small wooden block.
- Paint the block Dad's favorite color.

- On the front of the block, write with a marker "World's Greatest Dad."
- Decorate a large spool to look like Dad. If he wears flannel shirts, cover the bottom half of the spool with flannel.
- Draw facial features on the top half of the spool.
- For hair, use yarn or cotton.
- Cover the bottom of the spool with glue and place on the wooden block.
- Add any other details that remind you of Dad. For example, a construction-paper golf club, fishing pole, or garden tools.
- Present to Dad on Father's Day.

972. "WORLD'S GREATEST MOM" TROPHY
C 1 HOUR 1

- Put some sand in a tall, empty dish soap bottle.
- Wad a small sheet of newspaper into a ball and tape with masking tape. This will be the head of the trophy.
- Attach the head to the top of a dish soap bottle with tape. The bottle spout will be the neck.
- Cover the bottle and head with several layers of newspaper strips dipped in a mixture of wallpaper paste and water.
- Let dry.
- Paint the form with acrylic paint to look like Mom. Add pants or a dress, some buttons, and maybe a necklace by painting these features on the bottle.
- On a strip of paper about 1" wide and several inches long, write, "World's Greatest Mom," and glue it to the bottle on a diagonal from the shoulder to the hip, like a sash.
- Present the trophy to Mom on Mother's Day.

4TH OF JULY

973. STARS AND STRIPES BANNER
C 1 HOUR 3

- Draw a wavy line at the top and bottom of a 12" x 18" piece of blue construction paper.

- Cut on the lines.
- Place the wavy paper on a second 12" x 18" sheet of blue construction paper.
- Trace and cut on the lines.
- Tape the wavy papers together to create one long sheet.
- Draw two lines about 1" apart at the top, in the middle, and at the bottom of the wavy paper. Follow the wavy edge of the banner.
- Trace the lines with black crayon or marker.
- Draw a musical staff at the beginning of the first set of lines and trace in black.
- Write the words of the song "America, the Beautiful" between each set of lines in capital letters.
- Cut out red and white stars from construction paper.
- Glue the stars to the banner.
- Put dots and dashes of glue all over the banner.
- Sprinkle glitter in the glue.
- Let dry and tap off the excess glitter.
- Hang the banner.

974. MELTED WAX FOURTH OF JULY POSTER
$ 1 HOUR 5

- Cut a piece of red poster board in half the long way.
- On a piece of scrap paper the size of the poster, write the words, "LET FREEDOM RING" in large block or bubble-style letters. The words do not have to be straight; they can be drawn on an angle.
- The letters O, R, and D need to have the inside circle connected to the outside edge of the letter.
- Turn the paper over and shade over the letters with a pencil.
- Lay the paper pattern, pencil side down, on the poster board.
- Trace over the letters with a pencil. This will transfer the words to the poster board.
- Cut out the letters, being careful to leave the inside circle of the O, R, and D.
- Cut 2 large pieces of wax paper.
- Lay a sheet of wax paper on a layer of newspaper.
- Sharpen white, red, and blue crayons over the paper.
- Top with the second sheet of wax paper, then a sheet of newspaper.

- Iron until the crayon shavings are melted.
- Trim off a piece of the melted crayon wax paper and glue it to the back of the poster board so it shows through the openings of the O, R, and D.
- Trace around the letters with a marker.
- Hang the words in a window or on a sliding glass door.

COLUMBUS DAY

975. COLUMBUS DAY PICTURE
C 1 HOUR 1

- Think about a scene from the time of Columbus.
- Cut pictures from old catalogs, magazines, or newspapers that could be included in the picture. For example, a ship with sails, an ocean, clouds, and a king or queen.
- Arrange the pictures on a 12" x 18" sheet of construction paper.
- Glue down the pictures.
- Draw and color in other details. For example, Columbus on the ship and Indians on the shore of the discovered land.

THANKSGIVING

976. THANKSGIVING BLESSING BOX
C 45 MIN. 1

- Cover a shoe box and lid with pictures of your favorite things cut from catalogs or old magazines. Pictures could include favorite foods, toys, people, or animals.
- Draw the letters from the title, Thanksgiving Blessing Box, onto orange construction paper.
- Glue the letters on the lid.

- Throughout the year, write things you are thankful for on slips of paper and place in the box.
- During the Thanksgiving season read a few of the slips at dinner time.

CHRISTMAS

977. LOLLIPOP CHRISTMAS ORNAMENTS
$ 30 MIN. 2

You get to eat the leftovers on this one!

- Buy several Tootsie-Roll lollipops.
- With a red or green marker, draw a stripe around the lollipop stick, turning as you go.
- Cut a 3" x 3" square of Christmas fabric with pinking shears.
- Make a loop hanger by double-threading a sewing needle. Bring the needle up through the back and center of the square of material. Put the needle back through the material leaving a small loop of thread on the front. Secure the thread on the back of the fabric.
- Wrap the sucker with the fabric making sure the loop is on the top of the sucker.
- Tie with a red or green ribbon.
- Hang on the Christmas tree.

978. CHRISTMAS STAR STRING DESIGN
C 45 MIN. 4

Magi from the east came to Jerusalem, and asked,
"Where is the one who has been born king of the Jews?
We saw his star in the east and have come
to worship Him." Matthew 2:1–2 NIV.

- Fold a 9" x 12" sheet of paper in half.
- Starting near the top of the fold draw half of a three-point star, ending at the bottom on the fold.

- Cut out the half star.
- Open the paper—you'll have a four-pointed star.
- Place the star in the center of a 10" x 13" piece of tissue paper and trace.
- Place the tissue paper on a 9" x 12" piece of black construction paper. Fold the tissue over the edge of the black paper and tape on the back.
- Mark a dot on each point of the star.
- Label the top point of the star A1.
- Label the bottom point of the star B1.
- Mark more dots evenly between the dots on the points, making sure that each line between the points has the same number of dots.
- Starting down the left side of the star, mark the second dot A2.
- Continue labeling down the left side, ending with the bottom dot already marked B1.
- Starting up the right side of the star from dot B1, mark the second dot B2.
- Continue labeling up the right side ending at the top of the star, already labeled A1.
- Thread a needle with gold or yellow thread. Knot the end of the thread.
- Bring the needle up from the back through dot A1.
- Take the needle down through the dot labeled B1. Then come up through B2 and down through A2, up through A3 and down through B3, up through B4 and down through A4, etc.
- Continue sewing until all dots have been sewn through.
- If you run out of thread, tape the end on the back and start a new piece of thread, from the back, in the next hole.
- Outline the star by sewing from point to point.
- Very carefully tear away the tissue paper.
- Hang the design in a window.

979. CHRISTMAS VOTIVE CANDLES
$ 1 HOUR 1

Candles are wonderful at Christmas.
Arrange them as a centerpiece, along a walkway, or on the mantel.

- Paint a clean terra-cotta flower pot with gold or silver. Use acrylic paint.

- Cut out pictures from old Christmas cards.
- Glue pictures to the painted pot. Apply pressure until the picture adheres to the pot.
- Seal with a clear spray sealer.
- Cut a circle from paper or felt, and glue it to the bottom of the pot.
- Place a candle inside the pot.

980. CHRISTMAS BELLS
C 1 HOUR 2

- Draw a bell on a 4" x 6" sheet of yellow construction paper.
- Place a second sheet of yellow paper behind the drawn bell and cut out 2 bells at one time.
- Cut a small circle of black and glue it to the back and bottom of one bell for the clapper so it is below the edge of the bell.
- Draw a curved line from the bottom left to the bottom right of the second bell to form the back edge of the bell.
- Cut a black circle with a stem for the clapper and glue it on the second bell so the stem touches the drawn line.
- Draw a curved ribbon on a 1" x 4" piece of red construction paper. Draw a W at one ribbon end and cut out the V center.
- Draw and cut out a red bow.
- Glue the first bell on a diagonal in the lower right corner of a 9" x 12" sheet of green construction paper.
- Arrange the second bell on an opposite diagonal to the right and overlapping the first bell.
- Arrange the red ribbon under the clapper at the bottom of the second bell.
- Glue down the bell and ribbon.
- Glue the bow to the top of the second bell.
- Cut another red ribbon and glue to the bottom of the first bell.
- Lay the picture on a sheet of newspaper.
- Trace the bells, ribbons, and bow with a strip of glue.
- Sprinkle on glitter.
- Let dry.
- Gently knock off the excess glitter onto the newspaper.

981. TISSUE PAPER WREATH
$ 1 HOUR 2

- Cut a wreath from medium-weight cardboard.
- Cut green tissue paper into 2" x 2" squares.
- Spread a little glue on the wreath.
- Glue tissue onto the wreath by placing a piece of tissue over the end of a pencil eraser.
- Twist the tissue around the pencil.
- Place the tissue-covered eraser into the glue and pull the pencil out.
- Continue covering the wreath, placing the tissue close together so no cardboard is showing.
- Twist a pipe cleaner into a bow and glue it to the top of the wreath.
- Hang.

982. 3-D EGG ORNAMENT
C 1 HOUR 1

- Poke a small hole in each end of an egg.
- Blow out the egg.
- Rinse and dry the egg.
- Glue each end of a short ribbon to the top of the egg for a hanger.
- Poke a small hole in the side of the egg and gently enlarge it with your fingers. Make the hole big enough to fit a picture inside the egg.
- Cut out tiny pictures from old Christmas cards. For example, a Nativity scene, birds, or a word like NOEL.
- Glue the pictures to a thin piece of cardboard.
- Cut out the picture on the cardboard.
- Paint the inside of the egg with watercolor, acrylic, or tempera paint.
- Glue little bits of shredded paper or raffia inside the egg.
- Glue the cardboard-backed picture in the egg so it stands up.
- Put a strip of glue around the opening to the scene.
- Sprinkle glitter onto the glue.
- Gently shake off excess glitter.
- Hang on the Christmas tree.

983. STOCKING ENVELOPE
C 1 HOUR 2

- Draw a stocking on a 9" x 12" sheet of red construction paper.
- Cut out the stocking.
- Trace the stocking and cut out a second one.
- Cut out a cuff from white construction paper.
- Glue the cuff to the top of one stocking.
- Paper-clip the stockings together with the white cuff on top.
- Punch holes, with a hole punch, all the way around the edge of the stocking, except across the top.
- Cut an 18" length of white yarn.
- Wrap Scotch tape around one end of the yarn to keep it from unraveling.
- Knot the other end of the yarn. Make the knot big enough so it won't slip through the hole.
- Bring the yarn up through the top right hole then up through the second hole.
- Continue threading the yarn around the stocking, always coming up from the bottom.
- Make a knot at the end and cut off any excess yarn.
- Decorate the front of the stocking by cutting out designs from Christmas wrapping paper and gluing them to the stocking.
- Write a name on the white cuff.
- Put a flat present like a gift certificate inside the stocking.

984. WREATH SCULPTURE
$ 1 HOUR 3

- Form 3-D Christmas ornaments from gold and silver foil wadded-up into different shapes such as stars, bells, or candy canes.
- Foil could also be formed around a cardboard shape.
- Attach ornaments on a grapevine wreath with thin wire or large paper clips.
- Add a bow.
- Hang the wreath.

985. CORN HUSK-COVERED ORNAMENTS
$$ 1 HOUR 3

• Draw a shape like a camel, wise man, or stable on a 4" x 5"
   piece of heavy cardboard.
• Cut the shape out with scissors or an X-Acto knife.
• Soak 2 or 3 corn husks in water for 5–10 minutes to soften.
• Dry the husks with a towel.
• Place the husks between paper towels and iron.
• Glue the cardboard shape to a flattened corn husk.
• Trim the husk leaving about ⅓" border.
• Fold the husk over to the back of the shape and glue down.
• Put a small circle of glue on the back of the shape, at the top.
• For a hanger, cut a small piece of ribbon or gold trim and
   place both ends in the glue.
• Let dry.
• Cut a corn husk a little smaller than the shape.
• Glue it to the back for a finished look.
• Decorate the shape with light washes of watercolor.

986. CHRISTMAS GLOBE
C 1 HOUR 4

• Cut a 4" x 4" square of white scrap paper.
• Cut off the corners to make a circle.
• Trace the circle onto 20 old Christmas cards.
• Draw a triangle in the middle of the circle pattern from one
   edge of the circle to the other.
• Cut out the triangle.
• Lightly trace the triangle onto each Christmas card circle.
• Fold the edges of each circle up to the triangle lines.
• Glue the folded parts of a circle to another circle to form a
   globe.
• Paper clips will help hold the circles together while the glue
   dries.
• Hole-punch one edge and tie a length of yarn through the
   hole.
• Hang the globe.

987. SALT DOUGH CHRISTMAS ORNAMENT
$ 1½ HOURS 3

- Make a batch of salt dough using the recipe in Project #483.
- Form the dough into different Christmas shapes, such as stars, baby Jesus, wise men, Mary, Joseph, or bells. Tools for making pieces could include a garlic press and cookie cutter.
- Ornaments should be about 3"–4" in size.
- Place ornaments on cookie sheet.
- Unfold a large paper clip and push one end through the top of each ornament.
- This will be the hanger.
- Bake at 325° for 30–40 minutes.
- Check the dough ornaments periodically while in oven. If some areas seem to be browning faster than other areas, cover with foil. If a puffy area forms on the dough while baking, prick it with a pin. Baking times will vary depending on the size of the piece.
- Let cool.
- Paint with acrylic paints.
- Spray with a clear sealer.
- Pieces could also be decorated with glitter, yarn, or scrap material.

988. STAR SPANGLED VOTIVE CANDLE
$ 1½ HOURS 1

- Several candles could be made for a table centerpiece or to place on the patio or front walkway.
- Place a votive candle inside a small flower pot to check for size.
- Paint the pot with 2 to 3 coats of red, white, or blue acrylic paint for a Fourth of July theme.
- Punch out stars from colored paper with a hole punch. Make stars a different color than the pot.
- Glue the stars around the top of the pot and on the sides, spacing them evenly.
- With markers, draw wavy lines between each star.
- Draw small dots along the lines and around the stars.
- Glue small buttons, sequins, or wooden stars on top of the paper stars.

• Seal with a clear spray sealer.
• Cut a small circle of felt, and glue it to the bottom of the pot.
• Cut a small cardboard circle, and place in the pot.
• Place a candle in the pot.

989. CLOTHESPIN CHRISTMAS DOLLS
$ 1 HOUR 3

• On the flat side of a clothespin, draw baby Jesus, Mary,
    Joseph, an angel, Magi, lambs, or a star.
• Color in with marker.
• Seal by brushing on Mod Podge or glue thinned with water.
• Hang on a garland or ribbon, or stand on a shelf.

990. GOLD NUGGET GARLAND
$$ 2 HOURS 5

• Buy unshelled walnuts, almonds, hazelnuts, etc.
• Using a $\frac{1}{8}$" drill, put a hole through each nut.
• Lay out the nuts on a covered surface and spray with gold
    paint several at a time. Paint in a well ventilated area or
    outside.
• String nuts on a strong thread.
• Hang on the Christmas tree, mantel, or doorway.

991. BRIGHT CANDLE GARLAND
$ 3 HOURS 4

• Make one- to two-dozen candles from Project #814.
• Attach the candles to a green Christmas garland with ribbon
    or string.
• Hang around an arch or doorway.
• Make other shapes, such as stars or bells, to attach to the
    garland.

992. ADVENT TREE
$$ 2 HOURS 2

- Decorate 24 matchboxes with paint, glitter, and sequins.
- Cut 24 small strips of paper, and write a verse or something to do with the Christmas story on each one. For example, Isaiah 9:6.
- Put a verse and a treat like a candy, small eraser, or rubber stamp in each box.
- If there is more than one child in the family, put enough treats for each child or use more matchboxes.
- Number the boxes 1–24.
- Hang on a small Christmas tree with ribbon.
- Each day during the holiday season, open one box, beginning on December 1.

ACTIVITIES FOR
OLDER CHILDREN
MISCELLANEOUS
PROJECTS

993. TWO-MINUTE SPEECH
C 15 MIN. 4

This can be a fun activity to help a child learn to "think on his feet."

• Give each player a subject to talk about for 2 minutes. For example, God's love, Paul's conversion, or what Jonah did

and felt when he was in the big fish.
- The speaker must not go off his subject matter or hesitate too long.
- One person can time the speech and give a signal to the speaker that he has 15 seconds left.
- End the speech with a summary sentence.

994. FINGERPRINT KIT
$$ 30 MIN. 2

- Gather sheets of dark colored construction paper, 2 sheets of white paper, wide adhesive tape, a pencil, a piece of sand paper, talcum powder, and a feather.
- Copy the instructions from Project #788 onto an index card.
- Place all the items in a decorated box.
- Give as a gift.

995. FALL BOWLS
$ 45 MIN. 3

- Cut off the top of a pumpkin. The cut can be straight, wavy, or a teeth-shaped cut.
- Clean out the inside.
- Fill with soup or chili.
- Place in the center of the table with leaves arranged around the bottom.
- Cut off the tops of small pumpkins and clean out the insides for individual bowls.

996. POPSICLE STICK VERSE
$ 45 MIN. 1

*Use this fun idea when trying to memorize something,
like a verse, poem, or famous speech.*

- Paint each Popsicle stick with a different color of acrylic paint.
- Count how many words are in the piece you want to memorize.

- If it is a short piece, use one stick per word. For a longer piece, write several words or a phrase on each stick.
- Write the word or phrase on each stick with a fine-tip marker.
- Place the Popsicle sticks in order.
- Take one away and try to quote the piece.
- Keep practicing and taking away sticks until you have memorized the piece.
- Use again by writing a different piece on the back of the sticks.

997. BLOW POP MATH AND WRITING
C 1 HOUR 2

- Cut two 7" x 7" pieces of construction paper.
- Draw a large circle on one piece.
- Holding the squares together, cut out the circle. You'll now have 2 circles.
- Glue a Popsicle stick to one circle so it hangs off the edge of the circle about 3".
- Glue the second circle on top.
- Cut 2 circles from 4" x 4" pink paper and glue them to the center of each side of the Blow Pop.
- Along the top curve of the pink circle, write, "Blow Pop Math," and on the opposite side, write, "Blow Pop Writing."
- On the Writing side, print words that tell about the inside of the Blow Pop: 1._____, 2._____, 3._____.
- On the same side, write three words that tell about the outside: 1._____, 2._____, 3._____.
- Write, "A Blow Pop is" 1. as _____ as _____. 2. as _____ as _____. 3. as _____ as _____. (For example, "A Blow Pop is as good as a candy bar.")
- Fill in the blanks with an answer.
- On the Math side, write, "How many licks will it take to get to the center of the Blow Pop? My estimate (or guess)_____."
- Draw a box and make a tally mark for each lick, then add them up. Write the sum on the actual licks line.
- Write, "It took me _____ minutes to eat the Blow Pop."
- Write, "The stick is _____ inches long."
- Fill in all the blanks with an answer.

998. ROOM COMPOSITION
C 1 HOUR 1

- Draw the shape of your room on 3 different sheets of paper.
- Mark where the door, windows, and closet are positioned.
- Make a list of the things that would make an ideal bedroom. For example, a desk area for a computer, a bookcase with a stereo, and a canopy bed.
- Look through catalogs and decide what kind of bedspread you would like and what colors your room would be. Does it have wallpaper?, etc.
- Arrange the room 3 different ways.

999. MISSIONARY STAMP COLLECTION
$$ ONGOING 3

- Purchase an inexpensive stamp album.
- Write letters to the missionaries your church supports, asking them to respond with a short note or postcard. They'll probably enjoy hearing from you!
- Save the stamps by soaking them in warm water to release them from the envelope, then drying them on a paper towel.
- Organize and place the stamps in the album. You can also include information you've found about the missionaries themselves or the country in which they serve.

1,000. PANORAMIC POSTER
$$ 2 HOURS 4

- Take 5–8 pictures of a sprawling scene, such as a landscape or the lights of a big city.
- Mount the camera on a tripod or hold it very still.
- Starting at the far right of the scene take one picture. Then take the next picture so it overlaps the left side of the first picture.
- Be careful to keep the camera in the same position. Do not move it up or down.
- Have the film developed.

• Line up the pictures to make one continuous scene.
• Trim the pictures so they are all the same width.
• Mount on a piece of poster board, side by side, edges touching, with rubber cement or photo mounting tape.
• Leave a 1"–2" border around the edge.

1,001. BIOGRAPHIES OF THE BIBLE
$$ 2 HOURS 3

• Make a book like Project #631.
• Take close-up pictures of people you know that have names that are mentioned in the Bible. For example, Mary, Stephen, Elizabeth, and Paul. If they wear glasses, ask the people to take them off.
• Have the film developed.
• Glue a picture to each page of the book.
• Look up the people in the Bible and write a few things about them under the pictures or on the next page of the book.

CONTRIBUTORS

LINDA ALVES
Roseville, CA
Candy Kiss Flowers

RHONDA AMORE
Antelope, CA
Christmas Bulb Necklace

STEVE ANDERSON
San Leandro, CA
Bouncing Greeting Card
Create an Invention
Describing Game
Father's Day Suncatcher
Fill-in-the-Blank Game
Moving Pictures
Number Sequence Game
Odd One Out
Paper Flower Vase
Positive and Negative Shapes
Squiggle Art
Sunbursts
"What If?" Game

TRUDI ANDERSON
San Leandro, CA
Add-On Game
Bible Association Game
Cursive Color
Flat Suzy
Home 20 Questions
Horseshoe Party Favor
Line Design

DANIEL BAKER
Roseville, CA
Christmas-Around-the-World Feast
Christmas-Around-the-World Play
Christmas-Around-the-World Poster

CAROLE A. BARBER
Dutch Flat, CA
Ants on a Log
Christmas Stained Glass Window
Stained Glass Easter Card

MICHELE CROWLEY
Evansville, IN
Cornucopia Treats
Hamburger Cookies

JIM DAVIS
Roseville, CA
Alphabet Game
Cruisin' Cardboard Car

JUDY DAVIS
Roseville, CA
Walnut Locket

ANN ECKER
Granite Bay, CA
Greeting Card Flower Pot

VIRGINIA EDWARDS
Roseville, CA
Snail's-Eye View Pictures
Theme Photos

AMY HANSON
Evansville, IN
Feed the Birds Party

SHIRLEY HEIBERT
Citrus Heights, CA
Pinecone Garland

MARYLIN KELLER
Roseville, CA
Ribbon and Felt Bookmark
Victorian Book

MELISA KELLER
Roseville, CA
Invisible Pet

MELODY KIRCHNER
Roseville, CA
Clown Face
Estimating Jar
Postcard Geography

GAIL MCKENNEY
Citrus Heights, CA
Paper Beads

BEVERLY MERRITT
Scottsdale, AZ
Homemade Cookie Cutter Cards
Homemade Tents

DR. DAVID MILLER
Salem, OR
Memorial Stones

KATHY OHLSON
Sacramento, CA
Tin-Punched Mobile

KIRSTEN O'SULLIVAN
Sacramento, CA
Cinnamon Wax Pinecone
Clay
Crystal Garden
Crazy Putty
Inside Obstacle Course
Multicolored Crayons
Mystery Writer
Zoological Scavenger Hunt

JEANIE PARSONS
Orangevale, CA
Rock Painting

MARY LOU PHIPPS
Warsaw, IN
Alphabet Card Game
Alphabet Hunt
Charades
Flag of Israel
Fruit Guessing Game
Grocery Store
Guessing Game
Guess Which One?
Roll-A-Bug Game
Star Gift Wrap
"To" and "From" Tags

JAN ROBERTS
Auburn, IN
Family Word Search

JASON SELLS
Roseville, CA
Bow and Arrow
Favorite Place Pennant
Potato Man
Template Chalk Drawing
Wilderness Wanderings Game

JULIANA SELLS
Roseville, CA
Alphabet Math
Bible Box
Creature Creation
Cross Buttons
Dried Flower Wreath
Joke Card
Paper Bag Pumpkin
Rubber Egg
Skeleton
State Float

PATRICK SELLS
Roseville, CA
Address Marker
Bible Summary Book
Bible Verse Flip Chart
Blade Whistle
Bubble-Blowing Contest
Commandment Plaque
Dandelion Chain
Dressing Contest
Family Crest
Fantastic Fun Facts
Flashlight Tag
Heavenly Signals
Name License Plate
Name of Jesus Collage
Penny Hockey
Root Beer Relay
Season Poster
Seed Map
Shampoo Bottle Doll
Signet Ring
The Dozen Disciples

DENA SHARP
Orangevale, CA
Thanksgiving Turkey

MICHELLE STIRTON
Horton, KS
Pumpkin Turkey

DOROTHY WONG
Citrus Heights, CA
Beeswax Candle
Cartoon Gift Wrap
Color of the Day
Football Sandwiches
Grocery Manger Scene
Hairstyling Day
Hand Wreath
Picture Ornament
Tissue-Covered Can

LAUREL WORTH
Citrus Heights, CA
Psalm 104 Nature Observations

MARQUITA WRIGHT
Roseville, CA
Newspaper Hat